Economic Policy
and
Performance
in the
Arab World

SEVEN DAY LOAN

This book is to be returned on
or before the date stamped below

1 2 JAN 2000

UNIVERSITY OF PLYMOUTH

PLYMOUTH LIBRARY

Tel: (01752) 232323

This book is subject to recall if required by another reader

Books may be renewed by phone

CHARGES WILL BE MADE FOR OVERDUE BOOKS

Economic Policy
and
Performance
in the
Arab World

Paul Rivlin

LYNNE
RIENNER
PUBLISHERS

BOULDER
LONDON

Published in the United States of America in 2001 by
Lynne Rienner Publishers, Inc.
1800 30th Street, Boulder, Colorado 80301
www.rienner.com

and in the United Kingdom by
Lynne Rienner Publishers, Inc.
3 Henrietta Street, Covent Garden, London WC2E 8LU

Library of Congress Cataloging-in-Publication Data
Rivlin, Paul.
   Economic policy and performance in the Arab world   /   Paul Rivlin.
      p.   cm.
   Includes bibliographical references and index.
   ISBN 1-55587-932-2 (alk. paper)
   1. Arab countries—Economic policy.   2. Arab countries—Economic conditions.
   I. Title.
   HC498.R58   2001
   338.9'00917'4927—dc21

                                                                    00-046001

British Cataloguing in Publication Data
A Cataloguing in Publication record for this book
is available from the British Library.

Printed and bound in the United States of America

      The paper used in this publication meets the requirements
⊗ of the American National Standard for Permanence of
      Paper for Printed Library Materials Z39.48-1984.

   5 4 3 2 1

Contents

Tables and Figures

Tables

vii

Figures

Acknowledgments

This book had its origins in a series of papers that I wrote at the Dayan Center for Middle East and African Studies at Tel Aviv University, published in the center's annual Middle East Contemporary Survey (MECS) and in its Data and Analysis series between 1995 and 1999. I am grateful to the center for permission to draw on that material.

I would like to thank my colleagues at the Dayan Center: Martin Kramer, director of the center, provided encouragement and assistance on many occasions; Asher Susser, former director, first suggested that papers of this kind might be molded into a book; Ami Ayalon made detailed comments on three chapters, which were invaluable in improving the text; Bruce Maddy-Weitzman edited some of the MECS chapters that I have drawn on; and Joshua Teitlebaum helped with Internet sources. I would like to take this opportunity to thank Yehudit Ronen and Aryeh Shmuelevitz for their help and kindness.

Also, I am grateful for the assistance of the center's administrative staff: Aryeh Ezra, Lydia Garai, Ilana Greenberg, Elena Lesnik, Roslyn Loon, Amira Margalit, with special thanks to Marion Glicksberg and Dorit Paret of the center's library, and Haim Gal of its archive.

I benefited, as well, from the comments of Timur Kuran of the University of Southern California and from discussions—over many years about economic issues in the Middle East—with Moshe Efrat, Walter Elkan, and John Page of the World Bank. Lowell Feld of the Energy Information Administration at the U.S. Department of Energy kindly supplied data on oil prices. Bridget Julian of Lynne Rienner Publishers has been the ideal editor. Two anonymous referees also made valuable comments. I, of course, am responsible for all errors and omissions.

Last but certainly not least, my family. I want to thank my mother,

Zena, for her encouragement and help. And I dedicate this book with love and gratitude to Rosemary, Ben, and Alexander: sine qua non, and much, much more.

—*P. R.*

Introduction

In the late 1980s and 1990s, Arab states faced enormous economic challenges. In the early 1980s, oil revenues slumped, sending a shock wave through the region. With the collapse of the Soviet Union in 1991, the ideological basis for state intervention in Arab economies was further weakened. The end of the Soviet Union represented the dissolution of the socialist ideal that had been very influential in the Arab world. Internal economic problems were becoming more severe as the protection offered by high oil revenues declined. The large industrial sectors built by the public sector were suffering from falling productivity. Output in the agricultural sector grew more slowly than did the population; as a result, food imports rose. Agriculture had been squeezed along Soviet lines to fund industrialization, but the results in both sectors were disappointing. Changes in economic policies were needed, but these came more slowly in many Arab countries than elsewhere. Furthermore, the international economic environment, which helped countries in East and Southeast Asia develop rapidly in the 1970s, had deteriorated.

The aim of this book is to examine Arab economic policy and performance in the 1990s. The problems that faced the Arab countries are placed in their international setting, both in terms of the advice that these countries received from abroad and changes in the international economic environment that affected them.

In the first chapter, the policies followed in the Arab states are placed within the context of the sharp debate about economic policy that has recently taken place among experts inside and outside international organizations, such as the International Monetary Fund (IMF) and the World Bank. This is followed, in Chapter 2, by a brief examination of demographic trends, the development of the labor force, unemployment, poverty, and environmental issues. These have been major concerns for policymakers, pushing them to make changes and, at the same time, limiting their room for maneuver.

Chapter 3 analyzes the role of natural resources and rental incomes. The region is blessed with oil, but it lacks water; and this imbalance has partly determined patterns of development. Oil has yielded huge economic rents that have delayed economic reform and disguised the need for them. How this pattern determined and influenced interest groups is then examined. Chapter 4 looks at the main problems facing the productive sectors of industry and agriculture. The 1980s were a period in which economic links between Arab countries weakened, as oil wealth declined and flows of funds from the rich to the poor fell. The movement of workers became less significant and the significance of remittances declined. Economic growth rates decelerated and national income per capita fell. This was, in large part, the background to the economic reform programs. The reforms implemented in Egypt, Jordan, Morocco, and Tunisia are then looked at in Chapter 5, with conclusions drawn from their experiences. Syria's hesitant policy of reforms is examined in Chapter 6 in order to see how an Arab country fared without IMF and World Bank pressure or support.

Chapter 7 looks at the international arena, especially the relationship between the Arab countries in the southern Mediterranean and the European Union (EU) following the Barcelona Declaration of November 1995. Insofar as the EU was the major market for many of the countries of the Mediterranean south, the relationship was a vital one. Given the recommendation that economies should open themselves up to international trade, the EU should have become even more important as a trading partner, investor, and source of finance.

The concluding chapter shows that the room for maneuver in economic policymaking in the Arab countries has narrowed, given the larger role that recent theory suggests the state should fulfill and the limited resources available. Although I have not made any compromises in terms of economic analysis, I hope that this book will also prove useful to Middle East scholars and others who are not economists. Middle East scholars would benefit from greater exposure to economic analysis of the region, while economists need to pay more attention to the complex political, social, and cultural realities of the region when constructing models and giving policy advice based on them.

CHAPTER 1

Economic Policy and Development in the Arab Middle East: The Framework for Discussion

The subject of this chapter is the recent development of economic theory and policy advice given to Arab countries. Many of these states have undergone stabilization and structural reform programs along lines set by the IMF and the World Bank in the late 1980s and early 1990s.

In the late 1980s, a major debate began about economic policy in developing countries. It reflected, among other things, changes in thinking in the World Bank, the IMF, the academic community, and elsewhere, as well as the problems faced in the developing countries themselves. This debate was sparked by a related controversy over the causes of rapid economic growth in the so-called East Asian Tigers (South Korea, Taiwan, Hong Kong, Malaysia, and Japan), which led to a much greater awareness of the importance of government in promoting economic growth. This new view contrasted sharply with the economic orthodoxy of the 1980s. At that time, the Reagan administration in the United States and the Thatcher government in the United Kingdom saw the state as the problem; the solution to economic problems lay in cutting taxation and public expenditure so as to reduce government's role.

This chapter looks at the economic policies adopted since World War II. Initially, these centered on import substitution (IS), state planning, and a central role for the public sector. Nationalization and expropriation were among the methods used to achieve economic independence. The policies followed in many Arab states mirrored those implemented elsewhere in the developing world, with a theoretical basis developed by Western economists. These moves formed part of a

3

reaction to the recession of the 1930s, when laissez-faire policies direct-
ed by the colonial powers had been dominant.

By the 1970s, the neglect of agriculture—with consequences for
food production, food imports, and the balance of payments—had
reached serious proportions. Rising debt, low nonoil exports, and the
failure of state-led industrialization programs to push Arab economies
onto a fast growth path led to a reassessment. The rise, in the 1980s, of
the so-called Washington consensus was also a reaction to the centralist
policies of the 1950s, 1960s, and early 1970s. Its role in the economic
reform process in Arab states is therefore also examined here. In many
respects, the policy recommendations of the 1980s went in the opposite
direction of those of the earlier period. Developing countries were
advised to cut government spending and budget deficits, to free interest
rates, and to reduce controls on foreign trade and payments. They were
also urged to privatize. The Washington consensus looked back to the
economics of the pre-Keynesian period in order to justify reliance on
market forces and the assertion that the market is the best guide to promote welfare and growth.

Reaction to the Washington consensus resulted from dissatisfaction
with some of its results, from new interpretations of the rapid growth
experience of countries in East and Southeast Asia, and from the development of new theories of economic growth. All of these issues are
addressed below, together with an examination of the consequences of
the crisis in that region in 1997.

Import Substitution

Following the end of World War II, many developing countries adopted
protectionist industrialization policies—tariffs on imports—designed to
encourage domestic production. There were several reasons why this
approach was favored. The first was the prevalence of nationalistic and
anticolonialist sentiment: colonial regimes had emphasized primary
production in developing countries, which meant developing agriculture
and/or the exploitation of mineral wealth rather than industry. Before
World War II, developing countries supplied the products of these sectors to the industries of the Western powers and imported manufactured
goods. As a result, there was only limited industrialization in developing countries. Egypt was a good example of this pattern, although it
moved toward IS in the 1930s as it began to attain independence.

Agreements signed with Britain and other Western states limited Egypt's ability to impose tariffs on imported manufactured goods, but when those agreements expired in the 1930s, the Egyptian government imposed tariffs and industrial development accelerated.

Reliance on exports of agricultural and other primary goods meant that developing countries were at the mercy of fluctuating international prices. In the 1930s, when the international economy went into recession, prices of primary commodities fell sharply and the incomes of primary producers collapsed. This led to mistrust of market forces, something that was also true in Western Europe. In 1945, the Labour Party was elected in the UK by an electorate that rejected the laissez-faire economic policies followed in the 1930s, and other Western European countries elected left-of-center governments. An unwillingness to rely exclusively on market forces was also one of the factors behind the creation, in 1952, of the European Coal and Steel Community, the forerunner of the European Union. Keynesian economic theory, which was largely developed in Britain in the 1930s and 1940s in opposition to orthodox economics, emphasized the central role of the state in maintaining demand and thus employment in a modern economy.[1] This message was not missed in developing countries.

The apparent economic success of the Soviet Union in the 1930s and 1940s also encouraged developing countries to adopt interventionist economic policies. There, under a system of central planning, the depression that affected the West in the 1930s was avoided. Rapid economic growth was achieved through public mobilization of resources and massive investment in industrialization, and this helped the Soviet Union to emerge victorious after the devastation of World War II.

The central economic question for Arab states and other developing countries was how a country just beginning the process of industrialization could compete in international markets, and even in unprotected domestic ones, when there were so many industrialized and thus competing countries already in existence. For many, the answer lay in import substitution, behind which there were a number of ideas. The first was that of infant industries: in their early years, they could not compete with more mature ones abroad and so needed protection. The second was concerned with agriculture: the experience of the depression of the 1930s led to a move away from reliance on agriculture. A general pessimism prevailed about the possibility of developing exports of primary commodities. Despite Malthusian predictions that population would increase faster than the supply of food, the prices of primary products were thought to be on a long-term downward trend.[2] Finally, it was believed that one of the most serious problems facing developing countries was the existence of surplus labor. These countries were poor because they saved little, and the explanation given was the low share of profits in gross domestic product (GDP). To raise profits, industrialization was needed; and for that, IS was required.[3]

In Western countries, which were supplying aid, voices were raised against IS. A comprehensive study of IS industrialization outside the Arab world was sponsored by the Organization for Economic Cooperation and Development (OECD). It drew conclusions that were relevant for Arab states: economic policies favored the towns and neglected agriculture, or even damaged it, by taxing it excessively. This led to urbanization on a scale that was undesirable because the towns could not generate the jobs, housing, and social services for the migrants. IS industrialization put pressure on the balance of payments because the demand for imported capital goods was not matched by a large increase in exports to finance it. Another major criticism was that economies "ran out of import substitution." This happens when a favored industry grows faster than the domestic demand for manufactured goods while IS is taking place, but eventually only exports offer growth in the market. If the industry is internationally uncompetitive because it lacks comparative advantage, then it is unable to grow. The domestic market is saturated with high-cost, not necessarily high-quality, goods that are produced behind protective barriers. The financing of this comes at the expense of other industries, and the net effect is a loss of welfare and slow economic growth.[4]

An alternative policy to IS is to look for sectors in which the developing country has comparative advantages and to try to create the conditions for them to grow and thus pull the whole economy forward. This was not, however, accepted in much of the developing world in the mid-twentieth century; and during the 1950s and 1960s, IS became almost a dogma.

What became known as "high development theory," formed in the 1940s and 1950s, also provided justification for government intervention. The "balanced growth" thesis put forward the view that investment is needed in infrastructure and a range of industries in order to get development started. Infrastructure projects have long gestation and payoff periods and therefore need state backing. To make them worthwhile, industrial development needs to be accelerated. This means pushing forward all sectors of the economy simultaneously.[5]

The "unbalanced growth" model, which was introduced in the late 1950s, rested on the proposition that unfulfilled needs would call forth new supply by providing incentives to produce. In the jargon of economics, the situation would be one of "disequilibrium." Industries that have strong backward linkages will prompt other industries to be set up or to expand their output by increasing demand for goods they supply: automobile manufacturing is an example. The need for government intervention is accepted in the unbalanced growth thesis as well, but here the criteria are different. Industries or sectors to be favored are those with linkages, and those linkages that operate relatively quickly are the most important.[6]

Although these two strategies employed at mid-century were in some respects opposites, they had a number of factors in common. First, they addressed the question of demand, although the realism of their policy prescriptions has since been questioned, partly because it was unclear how governments in poor countries would be able to finance the development of one or more sectors. Second, they both showed the need for government intervention by suggesting that the market would not operate on its own, although the unbalanced growth model left more room for the market, with its reliance on demand calling forth supply. These models did not suggest that industrialization should take place in a closed economy, but they did fit into the logic of state intervention and IS. High development theory implicitly anticipated the new growth theory by putting forward ideas about external economies and strategic complementarity (see below).[7]

Middle Eastern countries followed international trends in economic policymaking. Turkey increased its tariffs on imports in 1929, when the provisions of the Lausanne Treaty—which, inter alia, restricted its freedom to conduct foreign trade policy—expired.[8] The imposition of tariffs and then the introduction of a five-year plan in 1934 were factors behind a sharp increase in industrial production in the 1930s. Despite many other problems in its industrialization program, the Kemalist regime was seen in the Middle East as having established the foundations of economic independence, and it attracted the attention of Habib Bourguiba in Tunisia and Reza Shah in Iran twenty years later.[9]

Egypt began to industrialize using IS in 1930, when the trade treaties signed with European powers expired. These had limited the then semi-independent government's rights to raise tariffs to 8 percent. In 1930, the rate on merchandise imports rose to an average of 26 percent.[10] In many respects, the economic policies followed by Gamal

Abdul Nasser until the 1961 nationalizations were a continuation of those of the prewar period.

Import Substitution and Arab Socialism

Political developments in the Arab world and elsewhere after World War II favored government intervention in the economy and provided a congenial background for IS policies. Many Arab states introduced these policies in the 1950s and 1960s, including radical states following the Soviet model, as well as conservative monarchies.

In Egypt, IS started before the war as partial independence was achieved. In other parts of the Arab world, IS came later, with the attainment of independence. In the 1960s, a number of Arab countries adopted Arab socialism as a framework for their political and economic development. These states—Algeria, Egypt, Iraq, Sudan, Syria, and South Yemen (then, the People's Democratic Republic of Yemen)— were in varying degrees anti-Western and allied with the Soviet Union. It was therefore natural that they followed the Soviet Union and adopted IS policies along with central planning and the creation of a public sector. Their governments mistrusted the private sector, seeing it as exploitative and unreliable, and they were opposed to foreign investment that they saw as colonialist. Tunisia never went as far as the others, either in ideological or political terms, and the greater trust that was placed in the private sector served it well in the postsocialist phase.

It should be noted that most of the other Arab states—including the monarchies of Jordan, Morocco, and Saudi Arabia—adopted IS policies and created extensive public sectors. Most Arab states—both the republics, which went through a socialist phase, and the monarchies, which did not—live with the remains of IS policies and large public sectors to the present. In order to understand why much of the Arab world became disenchanted with the economic policies of the socialist period, an examination of the Egyptian experience is relevant.

Egypt Under Nasser

In 1952, the new regime in Egypt that took power in a military coup made it clear that the state would play a major role in the economy. It would have to build the infrastructure and mobilize capital. Industrialization would be achieved through IS, but neither the private sector nor foreign investment was to be discouraged. In agriculture, which was recognized to be the backbone of the economy, a major land reform was introduced to bring an end to the long-standing ownership patterns and also to encourage landowners to invest in industry. Funds would come from the forced sale of landholdings over the limit.

In practice, the agricultural reforms had limited effects in terms of redistribution. No significant investment in industry resulted, and political tensions between the military regime and civilian political parties increased, with negative consequences for private-sector investment. In 1953, Parliament was disbanded, the Constitution was suspended, and political parties were banned. In this environment, private industrial investment declined. In 1953 and 1954, the government took measures to encourage private-sector and foreign investment, with virtually no effect.

The nationalization of the Suez Canal was carried out in response to the Western refusal to finance the construction of the Aswan Dam, which was central to the regime's program for expanding the area under cultivation and generating hydroelectricity. This took place against the background of deteriorating relations between Egypt and the West.[11] This, in turn, led to the nationalization in 1957 of other foreign assets in Egypt, including banks, insurance companies, and foreign trade agencies. These measures provided assets for the public sector and a stream of income that could be used when and where the government wanted. At the same time, the private sector felt even more threatened by the increase in state power and the growth of the public sector.

It is instructive to note the contrast between the way in which Egyptian capitalists were treated and the way in which the Korean military treated the private sector after the 1960 coup there. The Egyptian regime saw the capitalists as hostile, even as enemies, while the Korean military regime saw them as the key to their own future. (The implications of this comparison are examined in "The Debate About the East Asian Miracle" section later in this chapter.)

In 1958–1959, the Egyptian government drew up the first five-year plan for the period 1960–1965. There was a serious imbalance between the intentions of the plan and the politicoeconomic realities then developing in Egypt. The plan stated that 55 percent of locally funded investment was to come from the private sector. This meant that private sector savings would have to increase from Egyptian pounds (£E) 87 million in fiscal year (FY) 1959/60 (i.e., 1 July–31 June) to £E 157 million in FY 1960/61 and to £E 214 million in FY 1964/65, in constant price terms.[12] The forecast for private-sector savings was unrealistic, even in more harmonious conditions than those that prevailed in Egypt in the late 1950s and early 1960s. The plan also implied a marginal savings rate for households of 16 percent, compared with an actual rate of 3 percent in FY 1959/60. There was virtually no discussion in the plan of how the savings rate was to be increased so radically.[13] The failure of the plan, in its first year, to raise the required level of investment was one of the factors that provoked the government into the nationalizations of 1961.[14]

In 1959, laws were enacted that forced joint-stock companies to invest 5 percent of their net distribution to stockholders in state banks and to limit profit distribution to 10 percent of the nominal value of company shares. This caused a collapse of share prices on the stock market.[15] In February 1960, two major Egyptian banks were nationalized. One of them, the Misr Bank, owned much of the country's textile industry. In July 1961, a year after the first five-year plan was launched, the remaining banks, insurance companies, shipping companies, and heavy and basic industries were all nationalized. Many firms were forced to sell 50 percent of their shares to the public sector, and others were forced to sell part of their shares to that sector. Public utilities, foreign trade, and the Alexandria Cotton Exchange were also nationalized.

The period 1960–1965 saw a number of accomplishments, as well as serious setbacks. The consensus in the literature is that the economy grew by an average annual rate of 5.5 percent, although this figure was partly inflated by the growth of civil service and public-sector payrolls.[16] One million jobs were created.[17] A total of £E 1.7 billion was invested, 25 to 28 percent of which went into industry. About 94 percent of planned investment was carried out, although industrial investment fell 10 percent below target, electricity fell 22 percent, and housing fell 20 percent. The Achilles' heel was the balance of payments. Imports rose much faster than had been planned and exports grew much more slowly. Instead of falling by a planned 6 percent between FY 1960/61 and FY 1964/65, imports rose by 80 percent, mainly because agricultural production failed to grow as anticipated and imports of intermediate goods for industry were much higher than expected.[18] As a result, as early as 1962, there was a balance-of-payments crisis.

The disappointing growth of exports was due to the lack of suitable products for sale abroad, the lack of marketing skills, and the lack of infrastructure to sell the goods. Behind this was the fact that the government did not give exports priority. Although the planners tried to identify lines of production in which Egypt had a comparative advantage, they did not put this at the center of their thinking.[19] Sales were made under barter agreements with East bloc countries, but these deals did not encourage the development of higher-quality and therefore more marketable goods. They were politically negotiated rather than being the result of economic forces.

There were three main problems with the policies adopted under the plan. The main principle adhered to in Egypt in the plan period was one that had been implemented there since the 1930s: import substitution. Its main weakness was that it reduced imports of one kind, only to increase those of others. The new industries that developed in the 1960s were designed to supply local markets; they lacked the economies of scale and the marketing expertise needed to export. Most significantly, they relied on imports but were unable to finance them through exports. The second problem was the reliance on private-sector investment at a time when private-sector activity was being strongly discouraged. The plan was not politically realistic because the planners were not party to presidential decisionmaking regarding such key issues as nationalization.[20] The third major problem was, ironically, one of the achievements: the employment drive that created one million jobs resulted in the public sector and the civil service becoming dumping grounds for university graduates who received guarantees of employment. This had major detrimental impacts on the efficiency of enterprises.

Egyptian planners aimed at progress on all fronts: heavy industry and an increasing supply of consumer goods; IS projects and expected increased exports; full employment and efficiency; finance for the Aswan Dam Project; and investment in the horizontal expansion of agriculture.[21] The economy, however, could not meet all these demands, and by 1964–1965, it came to a standstill.

The political leadership wanted all that the planners advocated and more: in the early 1960s, Egypt was involved in a war in Yemen that was the main factor behind a rise in the defense burden. Defense spending, as a share of gross national product (GNP), rose from 8 percent to 12 percent in the crucial years 1963 to 1965. This was precisely the period in which the trend should have been downward or at least stable. In 1965, the economy was in crisis, negotiations were going on with the IMF, and the government was considering how to raise revenues to fund the second five-year plan.

In early 1965, there was a fall in imports, as the means to finance them dried up; factories began to close, and in June of that year, the austerity measures were announced. A stabilization program was worked out between the government and the IMF, including familiar measures: devaluation, reduced public investment, price and tax increases. The president, however, rejected the proposals. Assistance was obtained from the USSR, but even Soviet leaders called for austerity measures in Egypt.[22] In April 1965, it was announced that the second five-year plan would be extended to seven years. But the first plan was abandoned before it ended, and the second was abandoned before it even started.

As a result of the condition of the economy that had been inherited in 1952, as well as the tensions that built up between the regime and the private sector, Nasser was fearful of potential threats to his regime by the early 1960s. In 1961, the union with Syria collapsed when an army-business alliance took power there. Nasser feared that the Syrian example might be taken up in Egypt. The appointment of officials in the government and in the Arab Socialist Union (ASU)—and perhaps most significantly, from an economic perspective, managers in the public sector—became a matter of political loyalty. Indeed, Nasser placed political loyalty above efficiency in his appointment of officials. No clear distinction was drawn between the political level and the bureaucratic one. In the end, his fear that managers in the public sector and the ASU would form an independent base overrode his desire for efficient production and increased output. Managers and workers were "contained" in a politicobureaucratic web that prevented any political developments and at the same time stifled their economic role.[23] Once again, the contrast with South Korea was stark.

In the domestic political arena, there were allegations of plots and rivalries in army, party, and government. US wheat supplies were suspended; the king of Saudi Arabia announced the formation of the Islamic Alliance, with the unspoken aim of opposing Nasser; and the fighting in Yemen intensified, with military, political, and economic consequences for Egypt. In this context, although the president had little time for economic details, he approved a gradual exit from what was called "Arab socialism" toward *infitah,* or economic opening.[24] In the 1970s and the 1980s, there was a trend away from central planning and import substitution as the main policy instruments. Egypt was one of the first countries to announce an *infitah.* This was a very limited liberalization of the foreign trade sector, and it did not reap many benefits for the economy, but it reflected dissatisfaction with the status quo and a willingness to experiment with new economic policies.

Disenchantment with Import Substitution
and the Rise of the Washington Consensus

By the mid-1980s, oil income in Arab states was falling, and therefore fewer funds were available to the state either as direct income or as aid from richer to poorer Arab states. Concurrently, Western countries, particularly with the election of Ronald Reagan in the United States and Margaret Thatcher in the UK, were moving in an antistate direction and were becoming strongly opposed to aid to developing countries.

Population growth meant that pressure on the state to provide goods and services to its population was rising while the means at its disposal were falling. The neglect of agriculture, the flip side of the promotion of industry, had left many developing countries importing ever-increasing shares of their food needs. This was especially true in the agriculturally poor Arab states.

Partly because of the rise in international oil prices, many developing countries began to run up large budget and balance-of-payments deficits in the late 1970s and early 1980s. This forced them to borrow abroad and led them to question existing policies. When private sources of finance were exhausted or when creditors were no longer willing to lend more, these countries were forced to apply for help from the IMF and the World Bank.

During the 1970s, the IMF, the World Bank, and the U.S. government's Agency for International Development (AID) pursued largely independent policies. The World Bank and AID provided assistance for projects designed to meet basic needs, such as improving water supply, drainage, and energy allocation. The IMF concentrated on macroeconomic policy and provided assistance to countries that followed conventional liberalization programs. By the 1980s, the three agencies began to coordinate their policies vis-à-vis Egypt in line with the aforementioned Washington Consensus,[25] which represented the view of the U.S. administration, academics, and many in the IMF and World Bank. The consensus was that government intervention had caused the debt and related crises in developing countries, hence a reduction in the role of the government was the remedy. This meant reducing the budget deficit by cutting public spending. Other controls on trade and production, including quotas and taxes on imports, should be removed, as should restrictions on interest rates. Overvalued currencies should be devalued to encourage exports and the repatriation of funds. Finally, the public sector should be shrunk through privatization. The critique of the

policies that had been followed emphasized that foreign aid was almost
entirely a waste.

The collapse of the Soviet Union in 1991 was the final nail in the
coffin for the philosophy of central planning and large-scale state intervention. As the failures of socialism in Eastern Europe and the Soviet
Union became more and more apparent, those in the West with opposite
ideological persuasions began to advocate more extreme free market
policies.[26] But, as so often happens, just as the Washington consensus
seemed to be in the ascendancy, some important changes in thinking
were beginning to occur (these changes are discussed in the next section). Specifically, Arab countries began to move away from socialist
policies in the 1970s and 1980s. There were many reasons for the move,
and they varied among countries. In Egypt, Jordan, Morocco, and
Tunisia (examined in Chapter 5), as well as in Algeria, the role of
increased external indebtedness was crucial. In Syria and in Iraq, the
regimes tried to encourage the private sector for political more than
economic reasons.[27] The existing system was not working, and financial
and economic pressures forced changes. Similar processes of disen-
chantment and disillusion were at work in other developing countries in
and outside the Middle East. These all led to moves away from centralized control and toward greater reliance on the market. As this was
going on, however, the center of gravity in economic theory was changing, something that, in due course, would have its effects on policy recommendations.

The New Growth Theory

In the late 1980s and early 1990s, dissatisfaction with orthodox economic theory increased because of its inability to explain the process of
economic growth.[28] It was also unable to explain disparities in the economic performance of different countries. According to conventional
economic theory, countries short of capital and rich in labor should
attract funds from those that have relative abundance, but in the 1980s,
exactly the opposite was happening: many developing countries exported capital to richer countries, thus exacerbating their balance-of-payments and foreign debt problems.

The development of endogenous growth theory was a response to
these issues. The new various models of this theory discarded the
assumption of diminishing marginal returns to capital investment that

was a key feature of the orthodox neoclassical model. They allowed for increasing returns and focused on the role of externalities in determining the rate of return on capital investments. The rate of economic growth in these models was determined by the savings rate and by the level of technology, and there was no automatic tendency for income levels in different countries to equalize over time. With regard to international capital flows, which were a dominant issue in the 1980s, the new theory suggested that such flows could increase income and wealth disparities among countries rather than act as an equalizing and thus stabilizing factor. High rates of return on investment offered by developing countries with low ratios of capital to labor (i.e., relatively simple technology) were eroded by low levels of complementary investment in education (i.e., training the workforce), in infrastructure, and in research and development. These investments typically yield social gains that are not necessarily reflected in personal gains.[29]

A major theoretical implication of the new growth theory was that markets do not work in the broadest sense of providing all that is needed for an economy to develop. As a result, differences in income levels among countries may remain or increase if capital flows from the poorer to the richer economies. One of the main policy implications here is that the government has a role in investing in those things that the market does not provide, most importantly, in education and the infrastructure.

There was another closely related factor that encouraged the move away from neoclassical models and their orthodox policy implications: the debate about the causes of rapid economic growth in East Asia. Greater understanding of the way in which dynamic comparative advantage was acquired and was sometimes policy driven came from studies of East Asia growth, although this had been a persistent theme in trade and development literature for decades. This included work done in the neoclassical framework by Kenneth Arrow and others and that done in the Keynesian framework by such scholars as Nicholas Kaldor.[30]

Keynesian or neo-Keynesian and other nonorthodox economists did not believe that markets solved all development problems. One reason was their belief that markets did not always exist and could not easily be created in the economic environment prevailing in developing countries. As they were outside the orthodoxy, they were largely ignored, especially when the Washington consensus was dominant.

The new growth theory in effect took account of many of the points made by the Keynesians and others, years earlier, but did so within a more orthodox framework. One of the most important weaknesses of neoclassical theory was the assumption of perfect information. Neoclassical models assumed perfect information: everyone in the economy had all the information they needed and it was of perfect quality. Without this assumption, the market model did not maximize welfare and could not be justified as efficient. In developing economies, information flows are imperfect and obtaining information can be costly, so relying on market mechanisms would not maximize welfare.

Even when governments tried to act for the market, as they did in so-called market socialist systems, problems arose. Market socialism was based on a comparison between the actual performance of market economies and the "hypothesized performance of a market socialist economy with an idealized view of government." This was politically and economically unrealistic. Market failures are pervasive and cumulative, resulting in major welfare losses.[31]

The Debate About the East Asian Miracle

The World Bank report *The East Asian Miracle,* published in 1993, analyzed the causes of rapid economic growth in eight countries: Indonesia, Japan, Hong Kong, Malaysia, the Republic of Korea, Singapore, Taiwan, and Thailand. It was commissioned after a sharp debate between the World Bank and the Japanese government about Japan's aid program to Asia. The Bank had advocated the adoption of free market policies and the opening of economies to international trade. This, it was felt, would provide the best environment for industrialization and economic growth. The role of the government was to provide the infrastructure, but it was not to intervene in the way in which markets work.

During the 1980s, Japan's economic and financial strength increased enormously as it became the principal co-financier of World Bank loans and the largest source of bilateral aid for Asia.[32] In providing loans, the Japanese encouraged recipient countries to "go beyond the conventional neo-classical tasks of providing a property-rights framework and moderating market failures. . . . It encouraged [them] to articulate national objectives and policy choices, to catalyst market agents, and to assist some industries more than others."[33] This was in stark contrast to the neoclassical, near-laissez-faire precepts of the

World Bank. The Japanese, as major contributors to the World Bank, wanted their views to be heard and recognized. In 1991, the Bank agreed to carry out a study of the determinants of East Asian growth, with finance from the government of Japan, and the report was published in 1993. The report stated that the eight countries had experienced rapid growth by getting the "basics" right—this meant high levels of private domestic investment and increases in human capital achieved by investment in education. High levels of domestic savings made investment possible. Agricultural production, while declining in its relative importance, had increased rapidly, and there had been significant improvements in productivity. Population growth rates declined, and the administrative system in those countries was more efficient than in other developing areas. Finally, the distribution of income was relatively equal, which meant that governments did not have to concern themselves with distribution issues at the start of the growth process. Macroeconomic policy provided a stable background for the private sector.[34]

This was the conventional side of the story, what amounted to the World Bank's admission that government intervention sometimes results in faster growth than would otherwise occur. The report also stated that other countries would find it hard to imitate the selective interventions made by East Asian governments because they lack the institutional mechanisms that permitted the former to establish performance criteria for interventions and to monitor performance.[35]

Most of the debate about growth in East Asia hinged on policy issues, the most controversial of which was the debate about industrial policy. In East Asia, this has been interpreted as an attempt to create competitive advantages through government intervention.[36] It involved policies designed to help industry as a whole and measures aimed to assist specific sectors. These included IS, export promotion, loans, grants, subsidized interest rates, privileged access to credit and foreign exchange, and the provision of infrastructure and services by the government, as well as other measures.

The East Asian Miracle was broadly dismissive of industrial policy. Defining it as an attempt to change industrial structure, the World Bank concluded that the structure that results from industrial policy is similar to that which would have been created by the market, more or less on its own. This suggested that governments are able to calculate which sectors, industries, or firms would succeed—in other words, to pick winners![37] The criticism that intervention results in the same structure that the market would have created on the basis of comparative costs means that industrial policy cannot win, whether it succeeds or not. If it succeeds, then it has done no better than the market, and the implication is that there is no point in intervention. If it fails, then it has done less well than the market would have done, and the economy would have been better off without it. The key assumption is that the market would have taken the economy to the same or to a better point than intervention could have done. This has been questioned in models of endogenous economic growth that emphasize, among other things, the imperfect nature of information, increasing returns to scale, and the fact that growth processes have no single explanation.[38]

Those critics of the report who believe that the government has a central role in development also point out that industrial policy should be seen in a much wider context. One of its aims is to protect the balance of payments (this was an explicit aim in Japan). In so doing, many sectors of the economy are helped, not just those that are the focus of industrial policy. Critics who believe that government intervention is damaging suggest that as it had not been effective in East Asia—where there were competent bureaucracies to implement it—then its effectiveness would be less likely in other countries lacking such administrative strengths.[39]

The publication of the report was followed by a debate, mainly among academic economists. Broadly speaking, three views emerged. The first was the orthodox neoclassical view that by getting basic conditions right, the East Asian states had permitted the market to work and relied on free trade to guide development according to the logic of comparative advantage. Domestic markets were also relatively undistorted in terms of government intervention, and this was the explanation for rapid growth. The second view held that at least in Japan, South Korea, and Taiwan, the neoclassical interpretation was factually incorrect. Governments intervened extensively and promoted specific industries. Alice Amsden, in her analysis of Korean development, stated that governments deliberately got prices wrong (i.e., not what free markets would have dictated) in order to foster development.[40] Robert Wade described the economic policies of these countries as one of "governing the market."[41] In between these extremes was the World Bank's view, as expressed in *The East Asian Miracle*. This stressed the importance of governments doing less in areas where markets work and more in areas where they do not. In the words of the report:

> Sustained economic growth results from the positive interaction of four critical aspects of economic policy: macroeconomic stability, human capital formation, openness to international trade, and an environment that encourages private investment and competition. . . . East Asian success sometimes occurred *in spite of* rather than *because of* market interventions. Korea's heavy and chemical industries and Japan's computer chip push did not live up to expectations. Even so other interventions combined with export targets apparently *were* consistent with rapid growth: quota based protection of domestic industries in Japan and Korea; targeted industrial policies including directed credit in Japan, Korea, Singapore and Taiwan, China; and so on. Furthermore the successes [of] these three north-eastern economies compares favorably with the successes of Hong Kong, Malaysia, and, more recently, Indonesia and Thailand, where policy choices have been less interventionist.[42]

The debate about East Asian growth has made it much harder to dismiss the role of the state in economic development. *The East Asian Miracle* conceded that state interventions have some positive effects, and the 1997 World Development Report went much further, especially in the sensitive area of industry policy. The debate has become less subject to major swings in the consensus and more nuanced, with a growing appreciation of the role of the state in providing social spending, social insurance, and safety nets for the poor.[43] This was reinforced by the development of the closely related new trade theory.

New Trade Theory

New theories of international trade also suggested significant revisions to conventional wisdom. Traditional trade theory was based on the idea of comparative advantage developed by David Ricardo in the early nineteenth century. Ricardo stated that countries will export goods (and services) in which they have a comparative advantage—that is, those goods that they can produce more cheaply than others. They will import goods that are relatively expensive for them to produce. This leads to specialization among countries on the basis of comparative costs, which are based on relative levels of productivity. The gains from free trade in this situation result from the fact that consumers benefit from lower costs. Exports are required to pay for the imports, and thus incentives are created for reciprocal trade. By permitting imports, the economy, or part of it, is opened up to competitive pressures that help to reduce costs. In this way, free trade can help to break up local monopolies and make the economy more efficient. If, however, local producers gain monopolies over imports, as often happens in small economies, then the beneficial effect is negated.

The new theory suggests that trade between countries that have similar structures, in terms of their resources and production techniques, cannot be explained by comparative advantage. It is better explained by increasing returns to scale. When costs fall as the scale of production rises, then it pays countries with relatively smaller markets to trade with one another. The economies involved can support plants that are big enough to achieve economies of scale rather than retain their respective smaller, higher-cost plants without trade. Firms can then appropriate the profits that arise from reducing costs. It is possible to conceive of a situation in which increasing returns or the reduction in costs that they cause spill over from one firm (or industry) to another and thus cannot be monopolized by the firm (or industry) that made the original investment. Alternatively, increasing returns may arise from the accumulation of know-how as a result of experience. In this case, the benefits may accrue nationally rather than at the level of the firm. If such circumstances occur, then the fact that an individual firm does not make higher profits on its investment may act as a disincentive to invest. In these cases, protection of the sectors concerned until they reach higher productivity levels may be desirable, and free trade is no longer the universal optimum. This, however, is a very restricted condition for protection. The theory also advocates investments in human capital and the infrastructure to move developing economies in the right direction.[44]

In the perfect competition model, subsidizing firms in order to help them become successful producers and exporters reduces national income. However, recent models of international trade, which allow for increasing returns to scale and imperfect competition, suggest that this conclusion may be incorrect. Assume that firms operate under increasing returns and that industrial production exhibits demand or technological spillovers; in other words, expansion of one particular firm leads to an increased demand faced by other firms or to a reduction in their costs. Under such circumstances, the pattern of comparative advantage can be largely arbitrary. Subsidies to those with such complementarities or technological spillovers would permanently alter the economy's comparative advantage and raise its income.[45] Another form of assistance, offered to firms in Japan, Korea, and Taiwan, was protection against imports. One of the sharpest arguments in the debate about East Asian growth was the role of trade policy. The orthodox view was that growth was made possible by free trade: by encouraging exports and permitting imports into the economy without excessive restriction. *The East Asian Miracle* confirmed that protection was part of the growth strategy of those countries, as was export promotion.[46]

The change in World Bank thinking has been evident for a number of years. Its 1997 *World Development Report,* significantly subtitled *The State in a Changing World,* showed how far this shift has gone.[47] According to the report, the state is vital for economic development in that apart from providing goods and services, it provides rules or institutions that enable the market to function. Without it, development is impossible. This is not, however, a return to the doctrines of fifty years ago, which advocated a dominant role for the state; now it is seen as an indispensable "partner, catalyst and facilitator."[48] The report also lamented the fact that when liberalization policies were introduced in developing countries in order, inter alia, to reduce government spending and the role of the state, the wrong items were cut. Developing countries have, as a result, inadequate levels of human capital and a lack of infrastructure.[49] It should also be noted that the idea that developing countries are in fact short of human capital stands in sharp contrast to the concept of a labor surplus, which had historically dominated much thinking about development economics. This change in understanding is, of course, reflected in the new growth theory.

East Asia and the Middle East

The contrast between the economic performance of East and Southeast Asia and many other developing countries, including those in the Middle East, was the source of much soul-searching. The economic performance of the Arab states deteriorated between the second half of the 1970s and the 1990s. The Asian states increased their average growth rates in the 1980s, despite the rise in international oil prices at the beginning of that decade, and experienced an acceleration in the early 1990s. In the developing countries group, which includes Asia, there was a slowdown in the decade 1976–1985, but there was a subsequent recovery that lasted until 1997. The recovery in the Arab states was much more modest.

South Korea's GDP growth rate accelerated from a very high rate in the 1960s and then slowed in the 1990s. In 1996–1997, it collapsed under the weight of a major financial crisis that affected much of East and Southeast Asia. Its population growth rate has fallen sharply since the 1960s, which has helped it to translate more of its GDP growth into GDP per capita growth.

Like other countries in the developing world, the Arab states have tried to emulate the success of the East Asian economies. This success was not merely the result of liberalizing the economies, opening them up to foreign trade, and privatizing their public sectors, which was the route recommended by the IMF and the World Bank to Middle East and other developing countries in the 1980s. Rather, the route followed in East Asia in the 1960s and 1970s was a complex mixture of public- and private-sector initiatives, which took place in a fast-growing, international economy. The Arab states faced at least as complex a task, in a much more difficult international economic environment. How could the East and Southeast Asian countries do so well without huge reserves of oil and other natural resources and those in the Middle East, some of which had oil, do much less well?

A brief comparison between Egypt and South Korea is instructive in this connection. The two countries had similar per capita income levels in 1960; both were ruled by military regimes that were determined to transform the economy. South Korea began to experience rapid economic growth; Egypt did not. (The problems that Egypt faced in the 1950s and 1960s were examined earlier.) The fast growth rate in Egypt in the 1970s was due to an increase in rental incomes rather than higher production in industry or agriculture. This was not sustainable, and growth slowed in the 1980s and early 1990s. Following the introduction of reforms in 1991, there was an improvement in the growth rate, although this occurred only from 1995 (see Chapter 5). Egypt's population growth rate remained high until the early 1990s, but is only now lower than South Korea's, for the latter experienced economic takeoff in the 1960s.

Park Chung Hee, who ruled South Korea from the military coup in 1961 until his assassination in 1979, placed the need for economic growth at the center of his policy prescription.[50] Within 100 days of assuming power, the military government announced that it would launch a five-year plan. The emphasis of policy was on large-scale enterprises and long-term planning, but this future planning would not be allowed to stifle creativity or private enterprise.

The military was able to play a dominant, almost "entrepreneurial" role in the economy because of the weakness of other social classes. Workers were small in number, and the capitalists relied on the state for finance and other forms of assistance. One month after the 1961 coup, a law against illicit wealth accumulation was passed, and a number of profiteers were arrested. They were threatened with the confiscation of their assets, but the threat was not carried out. Instead, they were allowed to play a central role in the economy in return for a promise to invest sums in industry equal to those that they were alleged to have gained through corruption under the previous regime. In this way, an alliance was formed between industrialists and the military government that was to form the backbone of the investment boom that followed.[51]

Land reform had dissolved the aristocracy, and peasants who were, or had recently become, smallholders were atomized and did not form a homogeneous social class. The military government was influenced by a powerful student movement. This had, in 1960, played a major part in the downfall of the regime of Syngman Rhee; the student movement then acted as a watchdog, helping to keep the military government honest.[52] The presence of the U.S. occupation forces also pushed the Korean military toward a policy of developmentalism, as a means of reducing reliance on U.S. aid. South Korea benefited economically from its strategic relationship with the United States. It was an ally of the United States in the struggle against communism in Asia and received large amounts of economic aid that helped maintain a healthy balance of payments. During the Vietnam War (1965–1975), the United States bought agricultural and industrial goods from South Korea for its war effort. It also used South Korea as a rest and recreation center for its troops. Moreover, South Korean companies won large construction contracts in Vietnam. This massive, localized form of demand assisted South Korea in expanding its industry and developing its economies. The same applied to Taiwan.

The United States was also willing to overlook the very restrictive trade practices that both South Korea and Taiwan had adopted because of its political alliance with them. This was a price that the United States was willing to pay for their support. Finally, international trade grew much faster in the 1960s and 1970s than in the 1980s and 1990s: countries entering international markets in the earlier period therefore had much greater room for maneuver than those that are now trying to follow suit. In the 1950s, the volume of world trade increased by an annual average of 7 percent; in the 1960s, it increased by nearly 9 percent. In the 1970s, however, it rose by only 5 percent, and in the 1980s, by 4 percent. In the period 1990–1997, the average annual rate of growth accelerated to 6.8 percent.[52] The World Bank and others called on developing countries to open their economies and devote more resources to exports. The international environment was deteriorating, and so these countries would have a harder time making the adjustments and would gain less from so doing.

Land Reform and Income Distribution

Around 1960, the Gini coefficient for land distribution in South Korea was 0.39, while in Egypt it was 0.67. The coefficient for income in South Korea was 0.34, and for Egypt, 0.42. The closer the Gini coefficient is to zero, the greater the level of equality.[53]

In Egypt, between 1952 and 1961, 14 percent of total cultivable land was redistributed, with property rights transferred to only 10 percent of the population. Each family received 1 hectare. Two-thirds of the tenants and nearly all of the landless wage earners were excluded from the reforms, although excluded tenants were given security of tenure and paid low, fixed rents in real terms until the liberalization of the 1990s. The ceiling for landownership was 42 hectares.[54]

In South Korea in the 1930s, 3 percent of all farm households owned two-thirds of the land. By the 1940s, less than 7 percent of the rural population was landless; and by the late 1940s, there were few landless wage earners. The land reforms dissolved the landed aristocracy.[55] These facts show that by 1960, some of the key initial conditions that the new growth theory put forward as preconditions for economic growth were much stronger in South Korea than in Egypt.

Economic Policies in South Korea

The conclusions that can be drawn from the experience of South Korea are of two kinds. The first relates to the policies followed, and the second concerns the reasons why those policies were followed.

1. Investments in human capital and infrastructure increased the private-sector rate of return on investment and thus promoted economic growth.
2. Economic policy was pragmatic and adaptive; it changed as circumstances changed and as the economy developed.

3. Policies were designed to complement or enhance markets rather than to replace them. They neither abandoned the market (through central planning) nor were slaves to it. The policy interventions were designed to fill gaps created by market imperfections.
4. Investment in real estate was discouraged, and so more resources were available for other sectors.
5. Exports were encouraged after IS was successfully used to create domestic competitive advantages.
6. Exports were encouraged through effective microeconomic policies and interventions and systems of cooperation rather than just through macroeconomic adjustments.[56]

Both the World Bank and its critics agree on the importance of strong, effective, and inclusive leadership by government. The state in South Korea and Taiwan, as well as elsewhere in Southeast Asia, was strong and often led by virtual dictators. It used its powers to develop the economy and had effective civil services to implement its policies. These policies were intended to yield widespread benefits, and although income distribution became less equal over time, it remained much more equitable than in many other developing countries.[57] Initial conditions were built on; they were not considered a given or immutable external factors. South Korea even subsidized school meals and uniforms. Between 1960 and 1989, the share of government spending devoted to education rose from 11 percent to 20 percent.[58] The importance of equality as a policy goal was reflected in the emphasis placed on primary education.[59] In 1960, the primary school enrollment rate was 94 percent, and the literacy rate was 71 percent. Both of these figures were significantly higher than those that were predicted on the basis of South Korea's national income level.[60]

Strong and effective government did not mean that there was no corruption or favoritism. In Korea, according to Amsden:

For all the venality . . . beginning in the 1960s, the government's favorite pets—the big business groups that came to account for so large a share of GNP—were outstanding performers. What with export targets—an objective, transparent criterion by which firm performance is easily judged—price controls, restrictions on capacity expansions, limits on market entry, prohibitions on capital flight, restraint on tax evasion, and a government control over the banking system, *the big business groups had to deliver.*[61]

Discipline in Korea and its absence elsewhere was due to differences in state power rather than to differential abilities among policymakers.[62] To this should be added the effects of the Confucian tradition,
with its emphasis on discipline, something that applied elsewhere in the
region. According to the World Bank, in each of the high-performing
Asian economies, new leaders faced an urgent need to establish their
political viability before economic takeoff. In all cases, leaders needed
to answer a basic question: Why should they, rather than others, lead
their countries? The answer was that they hoped that rapid, widely
shared improvement in economic welfare would bring legitimacy.[63]

Table 1.1   GDP, Population, and GDP Per Capita in Egypt and South
            Korea, 1960–1997 (at Current Prices)

	1960	1970	1980	1990	1993	1997
South Korea						
GDP (in billions $)	4.6	8.9	63	254	308	443
Population (in millions)	24.7	32.2	38.1	42.9	43.7	46.0
GDP/capita (in $)	185	276	1,643	5,921	7,047	9,630
Egypt						
GDP (in billions $)	3.9	6.8	10.8	38.4	41.3	75.6
Population (in millions)	25.9	33.3	42.1	52.7	56.5	62.1
GDP/capita (in $)	151	205	257	729	731	1,217

Source: IMF, *International Financial Statistics Yearbook, 1970* and *1980;* and
IMF, *International Financial Statistics, May 1999.*

The 1997–1998 Crisis in East and Southeast Asia and Its
Significance for Economic Policy in the Arab States

The sudden and severe nature of the crisis that hit countries in East and
Southeast Asia has made commentators feel that those countries no
longer provide an example for others to follow. One implication is that
their experiences before 1997 were flawed and made the crisis
inevitable. A brief examination of what happened in South Korea will
highlight the weak points of its development, but it will also be seen

that much that was done in the period up to 1997 was successful and formed the basis for a return to strong growth in 1999.

In the summer of 1997, a reassessment of Thailand's economic and financial prospects led to a run on the Thai currency, the baht. It was devalued in July, having been, like other currencies in the region, tied to the U.S. dollar. This led to a loss of confidence in the international financial community in other economies in the region, which were all reliant on imports of short-term funds to finance their balance-of-payments current accounts. The tying of currencies to the dollar, which had strengthened against the Japanese yen since mid-1995, resulted in a loss of competitiveness. Japanese firms were less willing to invest in the region, and China, with its cheap workforce, had become a formidable competitor.[64]

The crisis that rapidly spread to most of the East Asian economies in 1997 had a number of causes. Borrowing in dollars by companies and banks in the region meant that devaluation increased interest and repayment costs. Capital inflows in the early 1990s were huge; in some countries in the region, they equaled 10 percent of GDP. Domestic borrowers believed that governments and central banks would bail them out, and multinational companies believed that the U.S. government and the IMF would bail them out if they ran into difficulties; this was the problem of moral hazard. The IMF's remedy for the crisis and one of the conditions for its assistance was a sharp increase in interest rates, which, along with other measures, caused more deflation, bankruptcies, and defaults.[65] The moral hazard issue within the region was in part due to the nature of the relationship between the public and the private sector.

In South Korea, the interactions of the *chaebols* (large holding companies), which relied on borrowing much more than their foreign equivalents, the banks, and the government were central to the operation of the economy.[66] These close links resulted in the chaebols and the banks presuming implicit public guarantees of bank credit. These links were opaque, and when a financial crisis, due to the overvaluation of the exchange rate, hit the economy, there were no clear dividing lines among industry, banks, and government. The lessons lay in the fields of exchange rate policy, banking and credit policies, and also in a field that has become popular among economists and the international economic organization: governance. Other problems lay in the way in which international capital markets worked: foreign creditors dramatically changed their assessments of how other creditors would act.[67]

The chaebols were multicompany business groups. With the short-age of entrepreneurs in the 1960s, economic activity centered on the founders of the chaebols. They overcame market imperfections because they had personal connections with government officials. They were able to draw labor, capital, and technology into the productive process. By 1974, sales of the ten largest chaebols were equal to 15.1 percent of GNP; in 1984, they accounted for 67.4 percent.[68] Although their share has fallen since then, it remained very important in the 1990s.[69] Chaebols were characterized by high share of ownership by their found-ing families. This was due to the desire of owner-managers to maintain control: they relied on borrowing to finance the expansion of their busi-nesses rather than on selling shares, as is more common in the West. The high level of borrowing that resulted was a key issue in the 1997 crisis. The government encouraged businesses to expand and sent opaque messages that it would guarantee their borrowing. This enabled the chaebols to expand to a point where they were too big to be allowed to collapse. When business conditions deteriorated and the return on assets fell, profits were reduced and the ability to service loans (which were taken abroad as well as at home) declined. In 1997, seven of the top thirty chaebols collapsed, with serious effects on numerous smaller suppliers throughout the economy.[70]

What lessons could be drawn from all of this by the Arab states? First, the relationship among government, banks, and business needs to be transparent and work on the basis of rules and regulations. Second, opening the economy to short-term capital movements poses dangers: funds can move out as quickly as they move in, with implications for the exchange rate, the level of inflation, and the volume of credit avail-able in the economy.

Conclusion

As a result of changes in the theoretical underpinnings of economic pol-icy, the challenge facing the Arab states has become more complex. Embracing the market—and by implication, the international market—does not offer them a panacea: in certain circumstances, at least initial-ly, it may make them worse off. On the other hand, state domination of the economy, import substitution, and squeezing the private sector have also failed as paths to growth. A pragmatic, flexible, middle way is needed, between the market and the state.

Notes

1. Van Der Wee, *Prosperity and Upheaval,* pp. 32–36.
2. Krueger, *Political Economy,* chap. 3.
3. Lewis, "Economic Development," pp. 139–191.
4. Little, Scitovsky, and Scott, *Industry and Trade.*
5. Rosenstein-Rodan, "Problems of Industrialization."
6. Hirschman, *Strategies.*
7. Krugman, *Development,* p. 7.
8. Hansen, *Egypt and Turkey,* pp. 313–331.
9. Richards and Waterbury, *A Political Economy,* 1990, p. 187.
10. Hansen, *Egypt and Turkey,* p. 87.
11. Vatikiotis, *History of Egypt,* pp. 388–389.
12. O'Brien, *Revolution,* p. 333.
13. Mead, *Growth and Structural Change,* p. 242.
14. Richards and Waterbury, *A Political Economy,* 1990, p. 195.
15. Waterbury, *The Egypt of Nasser and Sadat,* p. 72.
16. Ibid., p. 89.
17. Richards and Waterbury, *A Political Economy,* 1990, p. 196.
18. Rivlin, *Dynamics,* chap. 3.
19. Mead, *Growth and Structural Change,* pp. 242–243.
20. O'Brien, *Revolution,* pp. 266 and 274.
21. Waterbury, *The Egypt of Nasser and Sadat,* p. 84.
22. Ibid., p. 97.
23. Ibid., pp. 75 and 122; and Migdal, *Strong Societies,* pp. 230–232.
24. Rivlin, *Dynamics,* chap. 3.
25. Sadowski, *Political Vegetables?* pp. 1–4.
26. Stiglitz, "The Role of Government," pp. 11–23.
27. Owen, *State, Power, and Politics,* pp. 139–153.
28. Todaro, *Economic Development,* p. 88.
29. Ibid., p. 89.
30. Bardhan, "The Contribution," p. 2984.
31. Stiglitz, *Whither Socialism?* p. 7.
32. Wade, "Japan."
33. Ibid., p. 7.
34. World Bank, *The East Asian Miracle,* p. 5.
35. Ibid., p. 6.
36. Singh, "How Did East Asia Grow So Fast?" p. 14.
37. Ibid.
38. Amsden, "Why Isn't the Whole World Experimenting," pp. 627–633.
39. Singh, "How Did East Asia Grow So Fast?" p. 13.
40. Amsden, *Asia's Next Giant,* pp. 191–192.
41. Wade, *Governing the Market,* pp. 24–29.
42. World Bank, *The East Asian Miracle,* pp. 85–86.
43. Rodrik, "The 'Paradoxes,'" pp. 411–442.
44. Brezis, "Trade, FTA, and Hub and Spokes."
45. Rodrik, "Trade and Industrial Policy Reform," pp. 2948–2949.

46. World Bank, *The East Asian Miracle,* pp. 295–298.

47. World Bank, *World Development Report, 1997.*

48. Ibid., p. 1.

49. Ibid., p. 24.

50. Quoted in Amsden, *Asia's Next Giant,* p. 49.

51. Amsden, *Asia's Next Giant,* p. 72.

52. Calculated from GATT, *International Trade, 1994,* and from WTO, *Annual Report, 1998,* p. 13.

52. WTO, *Annual Report, 1998,* p.

53. Rodrik, "King Kong Meets Godzilla," table 2.

54. el-Ghonemy, *Affluence and Poverty,* p. 160.

55. Amsden, *Asia's Next Giant,* pp. 28, 52, 203.

56. Stiglitz, "Some Lessons," pp. 151–177.

57. Wade, *Governing the Market,* p. 180; and World Bank, *The East Asian Miracle,* pp. 43–47.

58. World Bank, ibid., p. 31, fig. 1.3.

59. World Bank, "The Evolving Role," p. 6.

60. Rodrik, "King Kong Meets Godzilla," pp. 4–5 and tables 1 and 2.

61. Amsden, *Asia's Next Giant,* pp. 146–147; emphasis added.

62. Ibid., p. 147.

63. World Bank, *The East Asian Miracle,* p. 157.

64. OECD, *Economic Outlook,* pp. 9–11; and OECD, Survey, Korea, pp. 3–4 and 31.

65. Richards, "Global Financial Crisis," pp. 62–71.

66. Barrell and Pain, "Developments in South Asia," p. 65; and Sachs, "Fixing the IMF Remedy," pp. 16–17.

67. Radelet and Sachs, "The East Asian Crisis," pp. 1–90.

68. Amsden, *Asia's Next Giant,* p. 116.

69. OECD, Survey, Korea, pp. 90–91.

70. Ibid., pp. 29–31.

CHAPTER 2

Socioeconomic Conditions
in the 1990s

Although the resource base, income levels, and economic policies vary considerably among Arab countries, many of them share key development problems. In the 1990s, these included rapid population growth, inequality in the distribution of income and wealth, unemployment, falls in real earnings, and reliance on unstable and often external sources of income. Slow and irregular growth rates were a problem for countries with low per capita income levels and for those with rapid population growth. Some Arab countries suffered from both of these problems: they needed to "run" in terms of GDP growth in order to "stand still" in terms of income per capita. When GDP did not grow, they faced serious economic, social, and political tensions. This chapter briefly reviews some of the socioeconomic issues essential for understanding the context in which economic policy was made.

Population Growth

Table 2.1 shows that the rate of growth of the population in the Middle East and North Africa in 1980–1990 and in 1990–1997 was higher than the world average. It also shows that the slowdown in population growth in the region between the two periods was greater than that worldwide. The table details the rates of growth of population in seventeen Arab countries. These rates were slower in North Africa (including Egypt) than in western Asia throughout the period, but even some of the states with the fastest rates experienced a decline. Population growth was slower in Algeria, Morocco, and Tunisia because fertility rates

Table 2.1   **Population Growth in the Arab World, 1980–1990 to 1990–1997 (Average Annual %)**

	1980–1990	1990–1997
Algeria	2.9	2.3
Bahrain	3.4	3.2
Egypt	2.5	2.0
Iraq	2.7	3.4a
Jordan	3.7	4.8
Kuwait	4.5	4.9a
Lebanon	0.2	1.9
Libya	—	—
Morocco	2.6	1.9
Oman	3.9	5.0
Palestinian territoriesb	3.0	7.6
Qatar	4.2	2.6c
Saudi Arabia	5.2	3.4
Sudan	3.3	1.8c
Syria	3.3	2.9
Tunisia	2.5	1.8
UAE	5.7	4.9
Yemen	3.3	4.5
Middle East and North Africa	3.0	2.5
East Asia and Pacific	1.6	1.3
World	1.7	1.5

Sources: World Bank, *World Development Report, 1998–99;* Israel, Central Bureau of Statistics, *Statistical Abstract, 1981* and *1992;* and UN Office of the Special Coordinator in the Occupied Territories, *Quarterly Report, April 1997.*
   Notes: a. Figure is for 1991–1994.
   b. West Bank and Gaza.
   c. Figure is for 1990–1995.

declined more quickly than in the West Asian countries.[1] It should be noted that the figures in Table 2.1 include immigrant workers, who constituted a majority of the population in most of the Gulf Cooperation Council (GCC) states—that is, Bahrain, Kuwait, Oman, Qatar, Saudi Arabia, and the United Arab Emirates (UAE). Fertility rates among GCC nationals have since declined, but population growth in that section of the population remains much faster than that in North Africa. While the total population of the GCC states doubled between 1980 and 1996, the native or national population increased by 3.3 percent per annum.

    Although population growth in the Arab states has slowed, it remains much faster than the growth in East Asia. In the period 1980–1990, growth was 1.4 percent faster than in East Asia and the Pacific region; in 1990–1997, the differential had declined to 0.9 percent faster. As was suggested in Chapter 1, a decline in population growth rates is considered to be a condition for economic development in the new theory, and in this view, the Arab states are only now moving into a period in which this condition is being satisfied. Algeria, Iraq, Kuwait, Sudan, Yemen, and the Palestinian territories were, to varying degrees, affected by war or civil war, with effects on population through either loss of life or emigration. Jordan's and Egypt's resident populations also increased as a result of the large-scale return of emigrant workers during the Gulf War and its preceding events in 1990–1991.

Seven countries in the region, including the most populous (Egypt, Algeria, and Morocco), reduced their population growth rates, but they nevertheless suffered the effects of fast growth. The population of the Arab world increased by 87 million (56 percent) between 1980 and 1996; despite a slowdown in the rate of growth for the region, it is forecast to increase by a similar amount in absolute terms (85 million, or 35 percent) in the period 1996–2010.

Due to its size, Egypt is one of the most important examples of these effects. In the period 1980–1990, the population rose by an annual average of 2.5 percent. In the period 1990–1997, the average annual increase was 2.0 percent. Despite this slowdown, the annual increase in population between 1990 and 1995 was estimated at between 1.3 and 1.4 million.[2] Among many other effects, rapid population growth was accompanied by fast urbanization. Cairo, the largest city in the Arab world, has a population of 12–13 million, which may double by 2015. The city was originally planned for 1.5 million and is thus seriously overstretched in terms of infrastructure.[3] This growth put massive strains on its housing, education, health, transportation, and other services. Even more ominous is the fact that the expansion of the city resulted in a loss of agricultural land that has been built over and a loss of topsoil, some of which was used to make bricks. This occurred despite the construction of new cities in the desert, designed to relieve pressure on Cairo. Similar pressures, on a smaller scale, were evident in cities from Damascus to Casablanca.

By far, the fastest recorded rates of population growth in the Arab world were those in Gaza and the West Bank. Between 1995 and 1997, the average rate of growth of the population in the West Bank was 6.5 percent, and in Gaza, 6.4 percent. These rates were partly affected by the return of Palestinians living abroad, but the bulk of the increase was natural, due to an extremely high birthrate, even amid conditions of poverty, unemployment, extreme political uncertainty, and even periods of low-level military conflict.[4]

Although there are many problems with Palestinian population statistics, a number of trends are clear. Between 1967 and 1997, the natural rate of growth (births minus deaths) accelerated sharply. Until the early 1980s, this was somewhat mitigated by emigration, mainly to other Arab countries, where there were employment opportunities. As a result, the resident population measure, as shown in Table 2.1, grew by an annual average rate of 3 percent. In the mid- and late 1980s, emigration fell; and in the 1990s, it went into reverse. Consequently, from 1990, the population growth rate exceeded the rate of natural increase. The Palestinian population has increased at an astonishing rate, one of the highest in the world.

Labor Force Growth

Table 2.2 gives figures on the size and rate of growth of the labor force in fifteen Arab states, as well as East Asia and the Pacific. It shows that the rate of growth of the labor force between 1980 and 1996 was faster than that of the population and that this is likely to continue in the coming years (see Table 2.1). Between 1980 and 1996, an average of 2 million workers joined the labor force each year. The forecast for 1996–2010 suggests an annual increase of over 3 million.[5] The table also shows that in Egypt, Iraq, Lebanon, Oman, and Syria, the growth rate of the labor force accelerated (or will accelerate) between the periods 1980–1996 and 1996–2010 despite the decline in the rates of growth of population. The reason for this is that it takes eighteen to twenty-five years for reductions in population growth to be translated into reductions in labor force growth.

Despite the decline in Egypt's population growth rate in the 1990s, between 400,000 and 500,000 people entered the labor force annually. Emigration previously provided a safety valve in the Egyptian labor market, but the ability and the willingness of the oil-rich states in the Persian Gulf and Libya to absorb these migrants had declined. There were political as well as economic pressures militating against the entry of Arab immigrants. This meant that even if the flow of income from existing emigrants was maintained, emigration would no longer play as

Table 2.2   Labor Force Size and Growth in the Arab World, 1980–2010

	Labor Force Size (in Millions)			Labor Force Growth (in Annual Average %)	
	1980	1996	2010[a]	1980–1996	1996–2010[a]
Algeria	5	9	15	3.7	3.6
Egypt	14	22	32	2.4	2.5
Iraq	4	5	9	2.8	3.3
Jordan	1	1	2	4.7	2.8
Kuwait	1	1	1	2.6	1.7
Lebanon	1	1	2	2.7	2.8
Libya	1	1	2	2.6	2.4
Morocco	7	11	15	2.4	2.4
Oman	1	1	1	3.6	4.1
Saudi Arabia	3	6	10	5.0	3.2
Sudan	7	10	15	2.3	2.4
Syria	2	4	7	2.9	3.1
Tunisia	2	3	5	2.7	2.4
UAE	1	1	2	4.7	4.2
Yemen	2	5	9	4.3	1.8
Total for Arab countries	50	82	127	3.2	2.7
East Asia and Pacific	704	966	1,227	1.9	1.0

Source: World Bank, *World Development Indicators, 1998.*
Note: a. Projection statistics.

large a role in absorbing the growing supply of labor. Increasing employment required economic growth at faster rates than have been experienced in recent years. Slow economic growth resulted in rising unemployment and thus generated a growing backlog of people looking for work.

Rising Unemployment

The increase in the number of workers was not matched by an equal increase in employment. During the period of high oil revenues in the late 1970s and early 1980s, employment was generated through regional migration, the expansion of the public sector, and services. With the collapse of oil revenues and the implementation of stabilization and structural adjustment programs, employment growth slowed or became negative.[6] As a result, unemployment increased. In 1994, unemployment in the Arab world was estimated at 10 million (about 10 percent of the labor force) by a Western source.[7] The Arab Labor Organization estimated unemployment at 15 million (about 15 percent of the labor force) and stated that 2.5 million new workers are added to the labor force each year.[8] These figures should be treated with caution given the lack of comprehensive surveys, but they may understate real levels. Unemployment was high despite the fact that female participation in the formal labor force (i.e., outside the home) was one of the lowest in the world. In 1992, only 16 percent of all women were in the formal labor force, compared with an average of 35 percent for the entire world and for developing countries.[9] Most of the unemployment was among first-time job seekers.

In Egypt, guarantees of public-sector jobs, part of the Nasserist legacy, had helped to keep open unemployment under control. With the implementation of reforms, this guarantee was phased out; new graduates had to wait years for a job.[10] In Morocco, unemployment in the first quarter of 1999 equaled 13.8 percent of the labor force. In urban areas, where the unemployed concentrated in order to look for work, they accounted for 28.2 percent of the labor force; in rural areas, which they left, they accounted for only 5.6 percent. Among those aged fifteen to twenty-four, the national unemployment rate was 40.6 percent; among twenty-three- to twenty-four-year-olds specifically, it was 42.3 percent.[11] The high level of unemployment was partly due to the serious drought at the time, but it also reflected underlying weaknesses in the economy that did not generate enough jobs.

Falling Real Wages

As well as the rise in unemployment, there was a 30 percent decline in average real wages in the Arab world in the period 1985–1990. In Egypt, real wages in the public sector declined by 40 percent between 1981 and 1987. The fall was due to the decrease in the demand for labor, as described above. Reducing real wages was an alternative to reducing employment. Employment in the civil services and public sector was highly protected by legislation and by political commitments that made it difficult for governments to sack workers. These inflexible labor market arrangements had negative implications for productivity and real wages.[12]

Poverty

According to the World Bank, in 1990, there were 40 million extremely poor people in the Middle East and North Africa—Algeria, Egypt, Iran, Iraq, Jordan, Lebanon, Libya, Morocco, Oman, Saudi Arabia, Syria, Tunisia, and the Republic of Yemen—equal to 21 percent of the population in 1985. ("Extremely poor" was defined as those having annual incomes up to $275 on a 1985 purchasing power parity [PPP] basis.) The average for all developing countries was 18 percent. The poor (including the very poor) numbered 60 million, 31 percent of the total population, compared with 33 percent in all developing countries. ("Poor" was defined as those having annual incomes up to $370 on a 1985 PPP basis.)[13]

In 1990, the World Bank projected a 2.1 percent annual rate of growth in per capita GDP, provided that peace came to the region in the 1990s and that structural adjustment programs were enacted; population growth was expected to exceed 2 percent per year. With a modest improvement in income distribution and a real increase in per capita GDP of 1.6 percent per year in the period 1990–2000, in the year 2000, the poor would number 60 million, the same as in 1985. If these conditions were not fulfilled, the total would come to 85 million.[14] In 1992, the World Bank increased its estimate of the likely number of poor people in the region in the year 2000 to 89 million.[15]

These figures imply that the number of people in poverty increased by 4 percent per year between 1985 and 1990 and would increase by 2 percent per year between 1990 and 2000. Estimates for poverty in Algeria in 1995 show that 17.6 percent of the population, or 4.9 million, had an income below $2.00 a day, at 1985 prices and on a PPP basis. In Jordan (1992) the share was 23.5 percent, or 2.4 million; in Egypt (1990–1991), 51.9 percent, or about 27 million; in Morocco (1990–1991), 19.6 percent, or 4.9 million; and in Tunisia (1990), 22.7 percent, or 1.8 million.[16]

Estimates issued in 1999 show that the number of people in the Middle East and North Africa living below $1.00 a day fell from 9.3 million in 1987 to an estimated 5.5 million in 1998, or from 4.3 percent of the population to 1.8 percent. The number living below $2.00 a day fell from 65.1 million in 1987 to an estimated 62.4 million in 1998, or from 30 percent of the population to 21.9 percent.

In comparative terms, the Middle East and North Africa did well. The share of those living below $1.00 a day was lower than in any other developing or transition region. For example, in East Asia and the Pacific, excluding China, the share fell from 23.9 percent in 1987 to 11.3 percent in 1998. The share of the population living below $2.00 a day was also lower than in any developing region, while the share for the transition region of East Europe and Central Asia was slightly lower at 19.9 percent.[17]

Literacy and Education

Table 2.3 shows that very large sections of the Arab population are illiterate. Literacy rates are particularly low in Egypt, Iraq, Libya, Morocco, and Sudan. They are also low among women in Algeria, Saudi Arabia, Syria, and Tunisia. Although there have been improvements in these ratios since 1990, they remain very problematic and mean that large-scale resources need to be devoted to improving literacy rates in the future.

Table 2.3   Adult Literacy, 1995

	Male (%)	Female (%)
Algeria	74	62
Bahrain	85[a]	85[a]
Egypt	64	39
Iraq	58[a]	58[a]
Jordan	93	89
Kuwait	79[a]	79[a]
Lebanon	90	80
Libya	66	66
Morocco	57	31
Oman	n.a.	n.a.
Qatar	79[a]	79[a]
Saudi Arabia	71	50
Sudan	27	42
Syria	86	56
Tunisia	79	55
UAE	92	72
Yemen	n.a.	n.a.

Source: World Bank, *World Development Report, 1998–99.*
Notes: n.a. indicates that figures were not available.
a. Males and females.

Low literacy ratios are a result of failures of the education system. In the period covered in this book, serious inequalities in education existed between regions (especially urban versus rural) and between the sexes, with women faring much worse. The overall number of illiterate women in Arab countries rose from 37.1 million (62.0 percent of the female population aged fifteen and over) in 1985 to 41.2 million (62.9 percent) in 1995.[18] There were also differences in literacy rates among income groups. An emphasis on university education in Egypt (and elsewhere) meant that insufficient resources were available for the primary school system. Some changes in policy were made, but illiteracy among adults has continued to be neglected. With growing population, the demand for education increased, and this put pressure on the public sector at a time when the trend was to reduce spending. Investments in education did not prevent high unemployment rates, partly because the quality of education was not high enough. This was a disincentive to complete educational programs, so dropout rates rose.[19] School enrollment rates rose, but completion rates were lower, because the skills produced were often not relevant to the job market.[20] Despite the importance of science and technology, the share of Arab students studying those subjects for their first degree fell from 35 percent in 1991 to 28.7 percent in 1996.[21]

Public Spending on Education and Health

Although the Maghreb states (Algeria, Morocco, and Tunisia) have reduced their rates of population growth faster than elsewhere in the Arab world, they still face formidable socioeconomic problems. In Morocco, only 53 percent of children aged six to eleven were estimated to attend primary school in 1990. Increasing the rate to 100 percent would require providing facilities for an additional 1.9 million children, a 90 percent increase, even though the number of six- to eleven-year-olds was not expected to increase by the year 2000.[22]

The formidable range of socioeconomic problems in Arab countries has given rise to an increasing need for public spending on education and health. Tables 2.4 and 2.5 give some indications of the response of governments in the five countries for which figures are available. They show that educational spending was much more favored than health-related expenditures: since 1975, education has received a much higher share in all the countries listed, a trend that is still continuing. The

**Table 2.4   Public Spending on Education, 1975–1996
(in Percentage of the Budget)**

	1975–1979	1980–1985	1986–1989	1990–1992	1996
Egypt	9.6	9.7	12.0	12.5	12.8
Jordan	n.a.	11.7	14.1	14.0	15.5
Morocco	15.0	17.4	17.3	18.2	n.a.
Syria	7.6	6.2	9.5	8.3	9.8[a]
Tunisia	20.6	14.9	16.2	17.4	18.7

Sources: el-Ghonemy, *Affluence and Poverty;* and IMF, *Government Financial Statistics, 1990* and *1997.*
Notes: n.a. indicates that figures were not available.
a. Figure for 1995.

**Table 2.5   Public Spending on Health, 1975–1996
(in Percentage of the Budget)**

	1975–1979	1980–1985	1986–1989	1990–1992	1996
Egypt	3.0	2.5	2.5	2.6	2.4
Jordan	n.a.	3.7	4.7	5.2	7.1
Morocco	3.3	3.0	2.8	3.0	n.a.
Syria	0.9	0.9	1.4	2.3	3.4[a]
Tunisia	6.7	6.7	6.0	6.3	6.9

Sources: el-Ghonemy, *Affluence and Poverty;* and IMF, *Government Financial Statistics, 1990* and *1997.*
Notes: n.a. indicates that figures were not available.
a. Figure for 1995.

tables also show considerable differences among the countries listed: Jordan and Tunisia had the best overall records, despite the fall in the share allocated by Tunisia to education from 1975–1979 to 1980–1985, whereas the shares of spending allocated to education and health in Syria were the lowest. In Egypt, the share allocated to education rose during the period 1975–1979 to 1996 from a near-Syrian ratio to one much closer to Jordan's. The ratios allocated in each country reflect government priorities at the time: in Syria, defense spending accounted for over 20 percent of government spending throughout the period; in Tunisia, it was below 9 percent. The variation in spending percentages also reflects the stabilization programs that were being enacted, which often required governments to give priority to debt repayments and reduce social spending.[23]

Health spending, as a share of national income, in Egypt and Morocco fell despite rising needs. There were many socioeconomic effects of this, including increased use of private health services by those better-off and therefore greater inequality in the provision of services to different sections of the population. Tunisia's and Jordan's records were better, while in Syria, there was an improvement in allocation, though the level reached in 1995 was not high.

The Human Development Index

The human development index (HDI) summarizes three key variables that measure human welfare: life expectancy at birth, educational attainment, and national income per capita. Educational attainment is measured on the basis of a weighted average of adult literacy (two-thirds) and combined gross primary, secondary, and tertiary educational enrollment ratios (one-third). In 1997, the Arab states had an average HDI of 0.626, compared with a world average of 0.706. Sub-Saharan Africa had the lowest HDI, 0.463, and the industrialized group of countries had the highest, 0.919. Five Arab states recorded what the United Nations described as high HDIs: Kuwait (0.814), Bahrain (0.832), Qatar (0.814), and the UAE (0.814). Eleven countries had medium HDIs, ranging from the highest, Libya (0.756), to the lowest, Morocco (0.582). Two countries had low HDIs: Sudan (0.474) and Yemen (0.4490).[24] Table 2.6 shows how the index improved in those countries for which a complete series of figures is available.

Environmental Issues

The lack of water and limited amount of productive land pose severe environmental constraints on the Arab world. Although the HDI has improved and population growth has slowed in recent years, economic development and urbanization have had negative effects on land, water, and air. Policies designed to encourage output have affected the environment in a number of ways. Cheap agricultural inputs (water, fertilizers, pesticides) have caused salinity problems, depleted water tables, and pollution. In addition, soil erosion and desertification have resulted

Table 2.6   The Human Development Index, 1975–1997

	1975	1985	1989	1990	1997	Change 1985–1997 (%)
Egypt	0.432	0.479	0.531	0.573	0.616	42.6
Morocco	0.426	0.473	0.508	0.540	0.582	36.6
Tunisia	0.510	0.566	0.608	0.640	0.695	36.3
Saudi Arabia	0.595	0.651	0.671	0.707	0.740	24.4
UAE	0.735	0.767	0.780	0.803	0.812	10.5

Sources: UNDP, *Human Development Report, 1999,* pp. 152–153; and author's calculations.

from pasture policies. Coastlines have been damaged by uncontrolled tourism.[25]

The Arab states are characterized by energy-intensive methods of production (not only in the Persian Gulf) that cause dangerous levels of air pollution. In addition, old and high-polluting vehicles have dominated the passenger fleets outside the Gulf. As a result, in 1980, 35 million people in the Middle East and North Africa were exposed to air pollution levels above World Health Organization guidelines. In 1995, about 60 million were exposed, not only in the largest cities, but also in many medium-sized ones.

In 1994, 4 million people in the Middle East and North Africa lacked access to clean water; only 20 percent of urban water was purified, compared to an average of 70 percent in developed countries. Furthermore, 85 million lacked safe sanitation.[26] The prevalence of irrigation, which accounted for 85 percent of all water use in 1995, increased salinity.[27] Pollution affected the health and productivity of the increasing number of people living in urban areas, as well as part of the rural population. Pollution has therefore become yet one more factor in the Arab world contributing to the increased demand for health services and thus public spending.

Conclusion

The five Arab countries for which there are HDI measures over time made progress between 1975 and 1997. Measures for the region partly reflected increases in oil income in the 1990s. When compared to other developing regions, the Arab world did not do badly, but a caveat should be entered. There was evidence of a worsening of educational achievements in Egypt and possibly in other poorer countries. This was related to the pressure of population, the demand for education, and the failure of the state to meet this basic educational need, a key ingredient of economic development.

Enormous socioeconomic problems need to be tackled with the help of public spending. The pressure of population and labor force growth will continue for many years to come. The stabilization and structural adjustment policies of recent years have not yet brought about fast economic growth, but they have been the reason for fiscal cuts. As a result, unemployment has increased in most of the diversified economies in the region.

Notes

1. Courbage, "Migration International."
2. Courbage, "Fin de 'l'explosion.'"
3. Richards and Waterbury, *A Political Economy,* 1996, p. 94.
4. UN Office of the Special Coordinator in the Occupied Territories, *Quarterly Report, April 1997.*
5. Calculated from World Bank, *World Development Report, 1994,* pp. 210–211, table 25.
6. World Bank, *Will Arab Workers Prosper?* p. 5.
7. Page, "Securing the Peace Dividend."
8. *Jordan Times,* 2 April 1995.
9. World Bank, *World Development Report, 1994,* p. 219.
10. World Bank, *Will Arab Workers Prosper,* p. 3.
11. *Bulletin Statistique,* January–March 1999.
12. World Bank, *Will Arab Workers Prosper,* pp. 3, 15, 21.
13. World Bank, *World Development Report, 1990,* p. 29.
14. Ibid., pp. 142–143.
15. World Bank, *World Development Report, 1992,* p. 30.
16. World Bank, *World Development Report, 1998–99,* p. 196.
17. Ibid., p. 28.
18. UNESCO, *World Education Report, 1998,* p. 105.
19. UNESCO, *Survey of Economic and Social Developments, 1998–99,* p. 163.
20. World Bank, *Claiming the Future,* p. 28.
21. UNESCO, *World Education Report, 1999,* p. 166.
22. Fargues, "From Demographic Explosion."
23. el-Ghonemy, *Affluence and Poverty,* pp. 172–206.

24. UNESCWA, *Survey of Economic and Social Developments, 1998–99*, pp. 124–125.

25. UNDP, *Human Development Report, 1999*, pp. 152–153.

26. Larsen, "Environment and Natural Resource Management."

27. Richards and Waterbury, *A Political Economy,* 1996, p. 164.

CHAPTER 3

Natural Resources, the Role of Rents, and Interest Groups

This chapter examines the role of natural resources, rental incomes, and interest groups in the Arab economies in the 1980s and early 1990s. There were two resources in short supply, water and land suitable for agriculture, and one that was plentiful, hydrocarbons, principally oil. The high level of rents meant reliance on incomes both from natural resources and from outside the economy. Dependence on external sources of income, such as workers' remittances and loans and grants from abroad, characterized the economies of the poorer countries in the region; Egypt, Jordan, Syria, and Yemen were the most extreme examples of this tendency. In contrast, in the richer states, the oil sector yielded incomes that fluctuated widely.

The importance of rents in the Middle East derived from the fact that natural resources play a much more important role in the economy than anywhere else in the world. In general, per capita wealth is derived from three elements: human resources, produced resources (usually known as "physical capital"), and natural resources. Human resources are the most important, according to a World Bank study carried out in 1994. In North America, the richest area in the world, human resources accounted for 67 percent of total wealth that year; in North Africa, they accounted for 69 percent, but in the Middle East, they accounted for only 43 percent. Produced assets accounted for 19 percent in North America, 18 percent in North Africa, and 18 percent in the Middle East. Natural resources accounted for 5 percent in North America, 5 percent in North Africa, and 39 percent in the Middle East.[1] These figures constitute a large part of the reason why rents to owners of natural resources are such an important part of income in the Arab region. The implications are serious: if the ownership of wealth is concentrated, then so will be flows of income, and this makes an examination of the political economy essential. In addition, relying on natural resources for the generation of income means relying on depleting resources. Human resources and physical capital can be augmented and replaced; natural resources cannot.

Water

Many Arab states are seriously short of water. In 1996, the volume of available freshwater per head of the population per year in the Middle East and North Africa was 854 cubic meters (m³), compared with a global average of 7,342 m³.[2] It is by far the driest region in the world. Annual internal renewable water resources that same year equaled 228 billion m³, and 152 billion m³ were supplied by rivers flowing into the region while 32 billion m³ were lost in rivers flowing out of the region. The total net annual renewable supply therefore came to 348 billion m³. Annual water use was estimated at about 177 billion m³, or 51 percent of the supply, compared with a global use/supply ratio of only 8 percent. Renewable water resources per capita fell from 3,430 m³ in 1960 to 1,436 m³ in 1990. According to the World Bank, this rate is likely to fall to 667 m³ by the year 2025. These figures exclude water supplies from so-called fossil aquifers (natural, underground storage in strata dating from the remote past).[3] In the period 1980–1996, agriculture accounted for 84 percent of water use in the region. During that period, about 28 percent of cultivated land in the Middle East and North Africa was irrigated. Worldwide, agriculture accounted for 68 percent of water use, but, mainly because of greater rainfall, only 17 percent of cultivated land was irrigated.[4]

The use of water from underground aquifers in the Middle East cannot and will not last: there are signs of a falling water table throughout the region.[5] Although desalination supplies all domestic and industrial water needs in Kuwait and Qatar and about half of that in the rest of the Gulf Cooperation Council states, it is not suitable for agriculture because of the large quantities required. In addition, because seawater has to be desalinized at sea level but usually is used at higher locations, costly pumping is required.[6]

In 1991, almost 50 percent of the world's installed desalination capacity was in Arab countries, 56 percent of that in the GCC. In 1993,

Arab countries had a 4 billion m³ annual desalination capacity, equal to about 2.3 percent of annual water use.[7] Between 1974 and 1980, there was a large increase in GCC capacity, but in the 1980s, the increase in installed capacity proceeded much more slowly. With the increase in oil revenues in the GCC in 1990 and 1991, there was another acceleration in investment.[8]

The moves toward privatization and liberalization of the GCC economies have meant that the private sector has been invited to build electricity and desalination plants. Insofar as this investment is carried out by the private sector, it may in the future become less a function of fluctuating oil revenues, which dominate government revenues.

The minimum amount of water needed to support human life is 10 m³ a year, a reasonable supply is 40–80 m³; but 150 m³ is the norm in developed countries. The World Bank has estimated that by the year 2025, renewable water resources in Jordan, Libya, Saudi Arabia, and Yemen will barely cover human needs. This assumes that all water resources are fully mobilized, even though not all of the supplies can be mobilized at acceptable costs.[9] Two-thirds of all Arabic-speaking peoples already rely on water supplies from rivers that flow from non-Arab countries. Of this population, 25 percent live in countries with virtually no perennial surface supply from rivers or rain.

The water crisis has therefore begun to stimulate radical policy changes. In the 1995 Saudi budget, for example, a five-tier sliding scale of water charges was introduced, replacing the single rate system. Jordan has increased water prices, and the government is looking for private investors to finance the water infrastructure. Under the terms of the Israel-Jordan Peace Treaty of October 1994, Israel agreed to supply Jordan with 50 million m³ of water a year. The two countries decided to cooperate in attempts to raise funds to build dams on the Jordan River for water conservation purposes.[10]

Land

The other side of the water shortage concerns the aridity of much of the land in the region. The Arab states (including Mauritania) have a total area of 1,915 million hectares, of which only 130 million, or 6.8 percent, are cultivable. Sudan and Mauritania, the two poorest states, have 68 million hectares, or 52 percent of the total cultivable area.[11] Aridity is due to the low average amount of rain and the limited number of rivers in the region. Furthermore, rainfall is very uneven over time, with drought affecting parts of the region periodically. In this sense, the Arab states suffer from the lack of a major resource (the implications for agriculture are examined in Chapter 4). Rapid urbanization has resulted in the loss of agricultural land near cities and the conversion of topsoil into bricks, most notably in Cairo, something that Egypt, with a very unfavorable cultivable land/population ratio, can ill afford. Parts of the region are, however, blessed with hydrocarbon and other mineral wealth, a subject to which we now turn.

Sources of Rental Incomes

Rents are payments made for a wide range of items: for the use of a pipeline or canal, for natural resources in excess of their production costs, and for the income earned by a country from its export of labor. The most important feature of rental income is that it has little to do with production processes within the economies that earn it.[12]

Rental incomes have been received by governments and by individuals with varying economic consequences. When governments receive rents, they can be used to fund public spending or can go into the pockets of rulers, officials, and others favored by the regime. Most important is the fact that rents provide governments with funds apart from that received via taxes or other revenues. Oil income and foreign aid are the main forms of rents received by governments. When individuals receive rents, private spending and saving decisions are affected. The most significant type of rent received in the Arab world on an individual basis is remittances. It should also be noted that remittances add to the supply of foreign exchange available to an economy without it having to export goods or nonlabor services. This may enable it to run a trade deficit with notable consequences for the economy. These issues are explored below and in Chapter 5.

Oil, Gas, and Mineral Resources

The most important single source of income in the Arab countries is the sale of oil. This is also a critical example of rental income, because apart from extraction (which costs about $2.50 a barrel in the Arab Gulf), little needs to be done to the oil before it is sold for a considerably larger amount. The economies of the GCC and, to a lesser extent, those of Iran, Libya, and Algeria rely on income from the sale of crude oil, refined oil products, and petrochemical products produced from local oil and gas resources. The share of revenues from crude oil sales alone, therefore, understates the importance of the sector in GDP. For many years, oil revenues have been unstable in nominal and real price terms. Figure 3.1 shows how petroleum export revenues of the Arab members of the Organization of Petroleum Exporting Countries (OPEC) fluctuated between 1973 and 1999 in constant and current price terms.

Oil is a finite natural resource. In Bahrain, oil reserves have been nearly exhausted; in Dubai (the second largest of the UAE's principalities), they are declining rapidly, as is oil production. Oman is also trying to diversify its economy in view of the fact that its oil reserves are likely to be exhausted by 2010. Only Saudi Arabia, Kuwait, Iraq, and Abu Dhabi (the largest UAE principality) are in the special position of having both reserves that will last for more than eighty years and relatively small populations.

Although the OPEC basket price fell to a low of $12.28 in 1998, it still yielded an average rental income of about $10.00 a barrel in the GCC.[13] This income was not the result of a production process or value added, and it did not require a sizeable workforce to produce and deliver the product. The rental income mainly accrued to governments and without the need to industrialize or develop the economy. Arab producers have tried to add value to crude oil by refining it and using hydrocarbon resources to manufacture petrochemicals. Low prices for inputs, the financial ability to import technology, and know-how have enabled the GCC states to develop these industries.

The Development of the Oil Market and Its Impact on the GCC

The rises in oil prices in 1973–1974 and 1979 resulted in huge increases in the income and wealth of the GCC states. They used these finances to develop their economies, investing large amounts in expensive economic and social infrastructures and developing social services that were provided free or at minimal cost to their populations. The states encouraged population growth by providing social benefits to large families and by importing workers for construction and other projects. They also had, at least until the mid-1980s, surplus funds that were invested abroad and that yielded substantial incomes. These accrued to the pub-

Figure 3.1 Petroleum Export Revenues of Arab OPEC Members, 1973–1999

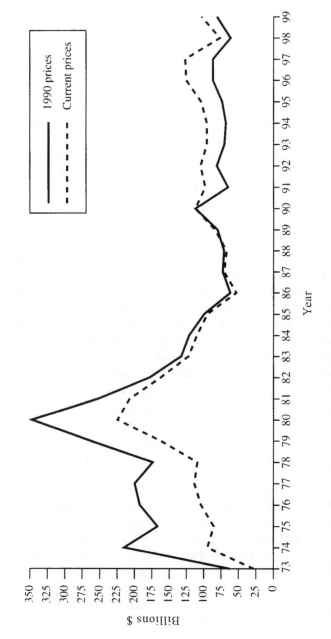

Source: U.S. Department of Energy, Energy Information Administration.

lic and private sectors, and so for many years, the GCC states were able to avoid problems in financing their state budgets and their balance of payments. But these large expenditures did sow the seeds of financial problems that were to affect the economies of the region from the late 1980s onward.

The rise in oil prices in 1973–1974 and 1979 also resulted in a series of decisions in major industrialized consuming countries to reduce their reliance on oil. They introduced energy-saving technologies in an effort to decrease the amount of energy used per unit of output; and they encouraged the use of nonoil energy sources and oil production outside of OPEC and the Gulf. These developments, along with a recession brought about by the rise in oil prices, caused demand for oil to decline. In the major industrialized countries of the OECD, demand peaked in 1978 at 40.9 million barrels per day (b/d); over the course of the following seventeen years, it failed to reach that level again, and only in 1996 did it reach 41.4 million b/d. Furthermore, the price of oil, which peaked at about $35.00 a barrel in 1981, fell to $20.60 in 1996, a fall of just over 40 percent in nominal terms and a 59 percent fall in real terms.[14] As a result, during the period 1982 to 1988, GCC oil revenues in real terms fell sharply.[15]

The events leading to the Gulf War of 1991 resulted in an increase in oil prices, and as a consequence of the international boycott of Iraqi and occupied-Kuwait's oil, a redistribution of oil revenues from Iraq and Kuwait to the other Gulf producers occurred. The major beneficiary was Saudi Arabia, the oil revenues of which rose between 1989 and 1990 by 67 percent. For the GCC as a whole, 1990 saw a rise in oil revenues of 38 percent in current dollar terms.

Following the end of the Gulf War, international oil prices declined, and although they have been volatile over short periods since then, the movements in prices were smaller then than they were in the periods 1973–1974 and 1979–1980. From October 1995 to April 1996, there was a 25 percent rise, to about $20.60 per barrel.[16] This came about as a result of increased tension between the United States and Iraq and a low level of U.S. oil stocks, coupled with strong demand in northern, industrialized economies for oil. In the first quarter of 1996, oil prices reached their highest level in five years, with the OPEC basket price reaching $19.35 in March of that year. The following month, President Bill Clinton announced that, in order to counter rising prices, 12 million barrels of oil would be released from the U.S. strategic reserves over the following six months.[17]

After a fall in the second quarter, prices continued to increase in the second half of 1996. The rise in prices caused GCC oil revenues to also rise between the years 1993–1944 and 1995–1996 by 22 percent on an annual average basis in current dollar terms. The average annual oil export revenues of the four GCC states that are in OPEC (Kuwait, Qatar, Saudi Arabia, and the UAE) rose from $34.6 billion in the period 1985–1989 to $69.5 billion in the period 1992–1996. This doubling of oil revenues reflected increased production partly made possible by the near disappearance of Iraqi oil from world markets since mid-1990 and by higher oil prices in the second period. In 1997, oil revenues in those four countries were estimated to have declined by 5 percent as a result of a 3 percent production rise and an 8 percent fall in prices.[18]

Another dramatic change in the region's economy in 1998 was the sharp fall in oil revenues that stemmed from the 50 percent fall in oil prices. World oil demand, which had increased by 2.3–2.4 percent in both 1996 and 1997, ceased to grow in 1998, mainly due to the severe economic crisis in East and Southeast Asia. The OPEC basket price that averaged $20.29 per barrel (b) in 1996 and $18.26/b in 1997 fell to $12.28/b in 1998.[19] The fall in Middle East oil revenues in 1998 occurred despite a nearly 5 percent (930,000 b/d) increase in oil production in the region, which was largely due to a near doubling of Iraqi production. Oil income in the Arab producers other than Iraq fell by 30 to 35 percent in 1998.

The main paradox of the oil market since the mid-1980s has been that production has expanded in relatively costly areas of production, such as the North Sea, and has stagnated or fallen in the area of lowest costs, namely, the Gulf, especially in the GCC states. The cost of producing a barrel of oil in the Gulf, which is between $1.00 and $2.00, is much lower than in the rest of the world. Given the huge reserves and low costs in the region, simple economic reasoning suggests that increases in international output would come from the GCC; but during the last decade of the twentieth century, they did not. Production increases have been concentrated outside the GCC, the Gulf, and much of OPEC. There have been several reasons for this.

First, Britain and Norway encouraged oil production in the North Sea through generous tax policies; as a result, output rose from 3.5 million b/d in 1988 to 5.9 million b/d in 1996. Second, there were major technological breakthroughs that reduced the cost of producing oil in non-OPEC areas. Third, international oil companies were discouraged from increasing their involvement in the GCC by the unwillingness of those states to permit foreign investment in their upstream activities, and so these companies invested elsewhere, in countries where the investment possibilities were greater. Fourth, poorer OPEC members outside the Gulf offered international oil companies better terms. Algeria and Venezuela went as far as to change their foreign investment regimes. Finally, the political climate in the Middle East, despite the defeat of Iraq in the 1991 war, was less attractive than that in other regions.

There were other changes that affected the market: in 1988, Soviet oil production fell sharply, and in 1990, the international embargo on Iraq, following its invasion of Kuwait, removed nearly 3 million b/d from international markets. The GCC states, especially Saudi Arabia, responded by increasing their production, but the Gulf nevertheless accounted for only one-third of the increase in international demand of 12.1 million b/d between 1988 and 1996.[20]

Table 3.1 shows how important oil revenues were as a share of total government revenues in 1996–1997, accounting for 77 percent in Saudi Arabia and for only 12 percent in Egypt. The other countries listed had shares between these extremes. Government oil revenues as a share of GDP, in 1998, are also given, and these figures illustrate that the role of oil was smallest in Egypt and largest in Kuwait.

Table 3.1   Arab Oil-Exporting Countries: Budgetary Impact of Oil Price Decline

	1996–97 Averages	1998	
	Oil Revenues as % of Total Government Revenues	Government Oil Revenues as % of GDP	Impact of Prices on Fiscal Receipts as % of GDP
Bahrain	61	14.6	–5.7
Egypt	12	2.4	–0.3
Kuwait	74	37.7	–8.5
Libya	57	14.8	–4.8
Oman	76	23.4	–10.0
Qatar	66	26.8	–3.2
Saudi Arabia	77	19.3	–7.9
Syria	45	10.2	–2.9
UAE	72	16.4	–5.5
Yemen	70	17.4	–8.3

Source: IMF, *World Economic Outlook, October 1998.*

Changes in Oil Prices and Revenues, 1997–1999

Between November 1997 and December 1998, the OPEC basket price fell sharply from nearly $19.00 per barrel to under $10.00 per barrel. Low oil prices from late 1997 through early 1999 were caused by several factors. In December 1997, OPEC agreed to increase its production quota by ten. Warmer-than-normal winters in 1997/1998 and 1998/1999 in the Northern Hemisphere reduced demand for energy and for oil. Increased Iraqi oil exports contributed to a glut, and oil demand was depressed due to the economic crisis in East Asia. During 1998, a number of initiatives were taken to reduce production. Significantly, they included non-OPEC producers, such as Mexico, Russia, and China. Although the reductions by some OPEC and non-OPEC states were implemented, they did not result in a fall in output; as such, prices fell. In March 1999, OPEC members pledged to cut 1.716 million barrels per day, while several non-OPEC countries agreed to total reductions of 388,000 barrels per day. Following this agreement, oil prices rose sharply.

The total OPEC quota was reduced in April 1999 by 7 percent, to 22.98 million b/d. Production of the ten OPEC states excluding Iraq fell from 25.32 million b/d in March to 23.53 million b/d in April, also a decline of 7 percent.[21] Further, smaller reductions occurred in May and June 1999. Non-OPEC producers cooperated in this effort by reducing their production; and against a background of strong international demand, oil prices rose. By the end of the year, prices were almost double the level that they had been at the beginning.[22] As a result, the OPEC basket price in the second quarter rose by 39 percent, to $15.38/b. The increase in prices continued in the third and fourth quarters, when there were increases of 30 percent and 17 percent, respectively.

World oil demand increased by 1.2 million b/d to 75.2 million b/d in 1999 (1.6 percent), compared to an increase of 600,000 b/d (0.8 percent) in 1998. Most of this was due to the recovery of the East and Southeast Asian economies after their 1997–1998 slump.[23] The stronger state of demand made it possible for reductions in output to be translated into price rises. Total output fell by 2 percent in 1999, with OPEC down by 5 percent and non-OPEC supplies by 0.2 percent. The balance was made up by a reduction in stocks, which fell by 1.2 million b/d, compared to a rise of 1.5 million b/d in 1998.

The OPEC basket price fell from an annual average of $18.68 a barrel in 1997 to $12.28 a barrel in 1998. In March 1999, in an effort to raise oil prices, OPEC and some non-OPEC countries agreed to cut oil from 1 April 1999 onward. This was successful; and, amid strong demand, prices rose. The OPEC basket price averaged $17.47 in 1999, an increase of 42 percent over 1998.

For 1999, Middle East members of OPEC earned total oil export revenues of $103.5 billion, an increase of slightly more than 34 percent over 1998. In constant 1990 prices, the rise was 32 percent. In constant prices as well, Middle East OPEC revenues peaked in 1980, at $350 billion. The worst revenue year since the early 1970s was 1986, in constant dollar terms, with revenues totaling only $62 billion as a result of the oil price collapse of 1985–1986.

The issue of oil revenues, even in constant prices, should be placed in perspective. The population of the oil-producing states has increased sharply since the oil price explosions of 1973–1974 and 1979. In 1972, the population of Middle East OPEC members totaled 68 million. In 1980, when oil prices were at their peak, the population was 90 million; and in 1986, when prices were at their lowest, it was 106 million. By 1999, the population had grown to an estimated 143 million. This meant that oil revenues per capita in those countries, after rising dramatically between 1972 and 1980, fell sharply in the early 1990s, and in 1999, despite the sharp rise in prices, they remained lower than in 1972. This discrepancy was based on the fact that the increase in the real value of oil revenues was more than balanced by the rise in population. The rise in the population, even though part of it consisted of foreign workers, resulted in increased demand for basic services. Oil revenues no longer provided a surplus that could be used on large-scale development projects, applied toward imports, or deposited in banks at home or abroad. Annual average oil revenues per capita in OPEC Middle East countries rose from $858 in 1972 to $3,874 in 1980 and fell to $567 in 1999.[24]

Oil Production in the GCC

The GCC states are, to varying degrees, oil and gas rich. These assets dominate their economies, and many of the features of their economic systems derive from the fact that they are oil rich but have relatively small populations. Accordingly, oil wealth has meant high average per capita income.

In the GCC, the state has been able to provide its citizens with Western levels of welfare and to develop the economy without the need to rely on taxation. The implicit return has been public acquiescence to the ruler's decisions with no debate. The slogan "No taxation without representation" has therefore been replaced by a GCC variant, "No taxation and no representation" or, at most, "Very little taxation and very little representation."

Historically speaking, the provision of free or heavily subsidized services by the state reduced pressures for political freedom during periods of economic growth and prosperity. The state and/or the ruler was seen by many to be successful in providing most of the population with rising standards of living. But problems arose when economic growth slowed, or even went into reverse. In economies that relied on one product, this was an ever-present danger, and the lack of democratic freedoms meant that responsibility for making cutbacks was entirely the responsibility of the ruler. He could not announce tax increases or subsidy cuts with the same ease as could the finance minister of a democratically elected government. The lack of public debate about economic and social issues in such states meant that little could be expected from the public in terms of solidarity with the ruler during hard times. The personal responsibility of the ruler and his family was reinforced by the extensive involvement of the royal family in government and in the economy. Princes were ministers, and in some of these states, they were also businessmen operating in the public and private sectors and in the large areas where the two overlap.

In the case of the GCC states in the late twentieth century, there was an additional factor at play, and that was the fact that the oil resources of those countries were considered the personal property of the ruler; this concept was not only internationally condoned, but it had its origin in international agreements. The basis for this lies in the way in which oil concessions were allocated as a result of negotiations with the ruler: the latter became the link among the international oil companies, powerful foreign governments (particularly Britain and the United States), and the domestic economy. Foreigners bought oil from the king or the emir, and he allocated oil wealth at home. None of the Gulf states have ever disclosed in any detail how much they earn from oil, because this is still considered the personal income of the ruler.[25]

In recent years, oil has accounted for between 35 and 40 percent of GDP in the GCC. It has provided up to 80 percent of government revenues and over 85 percent of exports.[26] Increases in oil revenues, such as those that occurred in 1995–1996, have had rapid effects on the economies of the regions, reducing budget deficits, easing balance-of-payments constraints, and providing a stimulus to the private sector. They have also reduced the pressure for economic reform.

Bahrain. Bahrain is by far the smallest oil producer in the GCC, and it thus has the most diversified economy. It has a small onshore oil field at Awali and shares the larger offshore Abu Saafa field with Saudi Arabia. The latter field is operated by Saudi Aramco (see "Saudi Arabia" section below), and Bahrain receives half of the oil produced there. In 1993 and 1996, Saudi Arabia gave Bahrain a greater share in the oil produced as a way of providing economic aid.[27] The Bahrain oil refinery at Sitrah imports oil from Saudi Arabia and provides much of the country's exports. Bahrain exports petroleum products rather than crude oil.

Kuwait. The Kuwaiti oil industry suffered massive damage as the result of the Iraqi invasion. The Iraqis used explosives on over 700 oil wells in Kuwait and in the neutral zone, which Kuwait shares with Saudi Arabia. About 650 wells were damaged, with oil lakes being created. Furthermore, all of the country's twenty-six oil-gathering centers were either destroyed or damaged. The initial reconstruction effort cost about $2.5 billion, permitting production to restart in June 1991. By 1993, production had returned to its prewar level.[28]

Kuwait does not have a petroleum law, and the emir is the final decisionmaker on all matters related to the oil industry. The Supreme Petroleum Council directs the Kuwait Petroleum Corporation, a state-owned holding company for all oil-related companies in Kuwait. Although plans to expand production were scaled back due to rising costs after the 1991 war, Kuwait has placed the emphasis of its future development on oil and has reduced subsidies and assistance to other sectors in order to help fund this expansion.

Oman. Oman is the only country in the GCC that is not a member of either OPEC or the Organization of Arab Petroleum Exporting Countries (OAPEC). Oil that was first discovered in 1967 has been used since 1970 to develop the economy, with an emphasis on diversification including investment in agriculture. Petroleum Development Oman is the company responsible for most of the country's oil production; the government owns 60 percent of the company, Shell owns 34 percent, and the remainder resides with other foreign companies. After declining in the 1980s, oil production increased in Oman in the 1990s as a result of the development of new fields and investment in pipelines.

Qatar. Qatar is a relatively small oil producer, and its output has been falling since 1973. Crude is produced from onshore and offshore fields, and Qatar has signed production-sharing agreements with foreign companies.

Saudi Arabia. Saudi Arabia has the world's largest proven oil reserves and is the world's largest exporter of oil. Its oil industry is state owned, and the government maintains control over all of the kingdom's mineral resources. The Saudi Arabian Oil Company, known as Saudi Aramco, is the world's largest oil company, and it holds the nation's oil and gas concessions and is responsible for 95 percent of crude oil production, from onshore and offshore fields. The Ghawar oil field, with 70–85 billion barrels, is the world's largest onshore field; the Safaniyeh field, with 19 billion barrels, is the world's largest offshore field. These two fields, together with the Abqaiq and Berri fields, account for about 90 percent of Saudi oil production.

The total value of investment plans in crude oil, natural gas, and petrochemicals was estimated in 1995 to be between $34 and $50 billion. The main purpose of these investments was to maintain Saudi Arabia's role as the world's largest crude oil exporter. The country aimed to refine half of its crude at refineries at home or in Saudi-owned refineries abroad and to transport 50 percent of its oil in its own tankers.[29]

Saudi Arabia has tried to increase its production of light oils that require less refining and are therefore easier to sell. Saudi Aramco has invested in massive storage facilities in different parts of the world so as to increase its influence in world markets. It has also invested in foreign refineries and distribution networks. This is part of a long-term strategy designed to secure Saudi oil in world markets, which has involved preventing jumps in prices and interruptions in supply. The commitment of Saudi Arabia to this policy was demonstrated before and during the Gulf War, in 1990–1991, when it increased production sharply following the international boycott of Iraq in order to maintain stability in international oil markets. It was a policy that paid off handsomely for Saudi Arabia and other GCC producers in terms of increased revenues. After the second oil price jump in 1979, Saudi oil production fell as international demand slumped. Its revenues declined accordingly, from a peak of $108 billion in 1980 to $26 billion in 1985.[30]

United Arab Emirates. The UAE oil industry is owned and controlled by the emirates rather than at the federal level. UAE-owned companies accounted for about half of production in 1992. Abu Dhabi produces about 85 percent of the UAE's oil, and its crown prince chairs the Abu Dhabi Supreme Petroleum Council that directs the state-owned Abu Dhabi National Oil Company. This company has investments in onshore and offshore fields, in gas installations, pipelines, refining, and distribution. Its main aim is to maximize oil recovery, and it has invested heavily in order to achieve this.

Gas in the GCC

Qatar, Saudi Arabia, Kuwait, and the UAE have very large reserves of natural gas and are among the largest producers in the world. According to estimates of proven reserves on 1 January 1998, Qatar had 300,000 billion cubic feet (ft^3), the third largest reserves in the world after Russia and Iran. Its reserves equaled 6 percent of the world's and 14 percent of OPEC's. The UAE has the fourth largest reserves in the world, with 205,000 billion ft^3; Saudi Arabia is next, with 190,000 billion ft^3; and Kuwait comes in eighteenth, with 52,400 billion ft^3. Oman's reserves were calculated in 1993 to be 27,450 billion ft^3 and Bahrain's, 5,100 billion ft^3.[31]

Gas resources in the Persian Gulf, as in other parts of the Middle East, have been underused. Associated gas, which is found in oil fields, has traditionally been flared, and only in recent years have attempts been made to make use of it, including reinjecting it into oil fields so as to maintain pressure. Other main uses of gas are for domestic consumption, electricity generation, and water desalination. Gas is also exported, both as liquid natural gas (LNG) via tankers and through pipelines.

The export of LNG requires large-scale investments in equipment to liquefy and compress the gas, as well as to buy tankers. This means that long-term contracts, usually for periods of twenty-five years, are necessary to make the investment worthwhile. The fact that oil has a greater thermal content and does not require such large-scale investments has discouraged the development of the gas industry. The main market for GCC gas is the Far East, especially Japan. Pipelines to

Europe and to the Indian Subcontinent have been under consideration
for years but have not so far been constructed.

Kuwait's natural gas reserves are associated with oil, and therefore
the production of gas has fluctuated with that of oil. The share of gas
that was flared declined in the 1980s and 1990s, which permitted more
to be marketed. In the late 1980s, Kuwait imported gas from Iraq to
meet growing domestic needs, but this ended with the Iraqi invasion.
Oman has been very active in developing its gas resources and has discovered large reserves of nonassociated gas. As a result of these discov-
eries, gas may overtake oil in its importance as an export fuel.[32]

Large investments have been made in LNG for domestic use and
for export to the Far East, which commenced in the year 2000. As mentioned earlier, Qatar is the gas state par excellence, with gas reserves
equivalent to 40 billion barrels of oil. About 5 percent of the reserves
are associated, and the rest are nonassociated, with the bulk in the offshore North field that borders on Iranian offshore fields. After initial
uncertainties, contracts have been signed with Japanese companies for
the development of the field and downstream (processing) plants.
Japanese companies are also buying gas and are involved in its shipping
to Japan. Between 1991 and the year 2000, about $39 billion was to be
invested in North field development projects.[33]

Saudi Arabia does not export gas, and it lacks processing capacity.
The flaring of associated gas remains relatively large: in 1993, it flared
about 35 percent of gas produced, although this has fallen since then. Gas
is supplied to domestic consumers at very low prices, and this has been a
disincentive for Saudi Aramco to increase processing capacity. The development of the gas industry in Saudi Arabia has suffered from the financial
difficulties that have faced the country during the last decade. Given the
scale of financing required, foreign investments are necessary, and the
government has not been willing to countenance them.

As for the UAE, most of its proven reserves are in Abu Dhabi, with
Sharjah and Dubai being smaller but significant producers. Flaring
accounted for about 35 percent of production in 1993, but domestic production has increased sharply since the mid-1980s, with large investments in offshore and onshore fields.

Other Arab Producers

Algeria. Despite the state of near civil war in Algeria throughout the
1990s, oil, oil products, and gas production have been unaffected. One

of the main reasons why oil has been unaffected by the civil war is that most of its installations are in the south of the country, far away from the main centers of population.

Algeria has gone further than any other country in the Middle East or North Africa in encouraging foreign investors through liberal legislation permit production sharing. The state-owned hydocarbon development company, Sonatrach, plans to increase noncondensate oil production from 850,000 b/d in early 1998 to 1.5 million b/d in the year 2004.[34]

Algeria has nearly 10 billion barrels of oil reserves and 4.5 trillion cubic meters of natural gas reserves, or 36 billion barrels of oil equivalent. In November 1996, the Maghreb-Europe Gas Pipeline, which runs from Algeria to Europe via Morocco, was completed. It was designed to transport 10 billion m^3 of gas a year to Europe. The Transmed Gas Pipeline, which runs from Algeria to Italy, has been expanded to a 25 billion m^3 per year capacity. There are plans to further expand its capacity to 75 billion m^3 early in the twenty-first century.

Egypt.   In 1997, Egypt had 3.8 billion barrels of oil reserves and 631 billion m^3 (or about 17 billion barrels of oil equivalent) of gas reserves. Oil production declined between its peak in 1993 and 1997 by 8 percent.[35] Exports of crude oil and petroleum products were worth $2.5 billion in FY 1996/97 (i.e., 1 July–31 June) and fell to $1.6 billion in FY 1997/98. In FY 1996/97, they accounted for about half of all exports of goods.[36] Egypt also earns income from Suez Canal tolls and from the use of the Suez Mediterranean Oil Pipeline. Both are used to transport Gulf oil to the West.

Iraq.   Iraq has the second largest oil reserves in the world after Saudi Arabia: 112 billion barrels, with 215 billion barrels of probable and possible reserves. That it produced 1.2 million b/d on average in 1997 and about 2 million b/d in the first eight months of 1998, compared with 3.5 million b/d in the first half of 1990, was the clearest testament to the fact that politics dominate economics in the Middle East. Iraq's oil exports are regulated by UN Resolution 986 of 1995, which was passed as a result of Iraq's invasion of Kuwait and the subsequent UN decision to detect and end Iraq's nonconventional weapons production capacity. Having removed most Iraqi oil from world markets, the amount that can be sold by other producers, particularly Saudi Arabia, has been increased and so, therefore, have their revenues. The increase in Iraqi production and exports in 1998 was one of the factors that resulted in lower international oil prices.

During the war against Iran, Iraq demonstrated parity in OPEC quotas, and at the end of the war in 1988, it was agreed that Iraq would maintain this parity. In need of funds to rebuild a war-damaged economy, however, Iraq demanded that Arab Gulf states stop producing above their OPEC quotas as well. When they didn't, in July 1990, Iraq threatened action against Kuwait and the UAE; and in August 1990, it invaded Kuwait. This led to an international boycott of Iraq, and its oil sales virtually ceased. Air attacks against it during the Gulf War of 1991 led to massive damage, including that of the oil industry. Experts estimated that production could be restarted rapidly under the right conditions but that it would take up to three years to reach an export capacity of 3.2 million b/d and that the cost would equal $6 billion. At the end of 1993, the UN proposed an emergency export quota that would permit Iraq to export $1.6 billion worth of oil a year. The first sales were made in December 1996.

Iraq has 110 trillion cubic feet of proven gas reserves and 150 trillion cubic feet of probable reserves. About 70 percent of this is associated gas, which is produced along with oil. Production in 1996 was 128 billion ft^3, compared with the peak of 700 billion ft^3 reached in 1979.

Iraq's oil fields are huge and are the cheapest in the world to exploit. It is, therefore, generally agreed that Iraq's oil production could be increased quite rapidly if international sanctions were lifted. Most of the damage caused by the Gulf War has been repaired, although some facilities operate in rotation and the quality of oil produced is lower than the Iraqi authorities desire.

At the beginning of 1998, the UN increased the amount of oil that Iraq could export. By specifying the value of oil that Iraq may export ($5.2 billion each six months), the United Nations caused unintended effects on the oil market. As oil prices fell in 1998, Iraq had to sell a larger quantity of oil in order to reach its revenue quota, and so Iraqi exports rose. The increase in the volume available, given the weak state of international demand, resulted in downward pressure on oil prices. This, in turn, made it necessary for Iraq to sell even more in order to earn its permitted amount. Saudi Arabia and other Gulf and OPEC producers have benefited from Iraq's partial absence from the international market, but because a revenue quota rather than a quantity of oil that Iraq may sell was specified, in conditions of weak demand, the market has been partly destabilized.[37]

Libya. Libya's oil industry has been run by the state-owned National Oil Corporation (NOC) since 1968. The NOC has production/exploration agreements with a number of foreign companies, the most important of which is the Italian Agip-ENI group. Libyan oil is high-quality, low-sulfur crude. Production estimated at nearly 1.5 million b/d in 1997 and 1998 is well below the peak of 3.3 million b/d reached in 1970.

In response to Libya's links with international terrorism, the United States imposed sanctions on the country in 1982, and the United Nations did the same in 1992. In 1993, the UN expanded its sanctions, and three years later, the United States also expanded those that it was applying. UN sanctions banned the sale of oil equipment for the Libyan oil and gas industries by member states and tightly restricted civil aviation. U.S. measures include provisions for sanctions on foreign companies that invest more than $40 million a year in Libya.[38]

These sanctions have prevented Libya from fully developing its oil and gas resources. Although it is able to sell oil and gas in Europe (Italy being its main customer), total production has been restricted by a lack of investment. The unwillingness of many foreign companies to invest in Libya (despite the efforts of the NOC in offering production-sharing agreements), coupled with low oil revenues due to weak prices, has limited growth. This has affected the operation of existing fields as well as prevented the exploration of new ones.

Libya probably has the largest oil reserves in Africa, but only 50 percent of its territory has been explored. The NOC planned to increase production capacity to 1.65 million b/d by the year 2000, an increase of almost 14 percent over 1998. This and other expansion plans seem technically feasible, but the finances and equipment are not available because of sanctions.

Libya also has significant proven gas reserves, estimated at 46.3 trillion ft^3 in 1997. Potential reserves (including proven reserves) may total 50–70 trillion ft^3. A contract to export large volumes of gas by underwater pipeline to Italy was signed in 1996, making Libya only the second country in the world, after Algeria, to export liquid natural gas; but due to technical factors, this development has not been fully exploited.[39]

In 1999, the United Nations cancelled its sanctions against Libya following the latter's agreement to hand over two Libyans accused of terrorism to a court in the Netherlands. Following the end of sanctions by the UN, but not by the United States, a number of international companies and foreign governments have showed interest in investing in Libya and expanding economic ties.[40]

Syria.   Oil has been the leading sector in the Syrian economy since the start of the 1990s. In 1992, the level of oil production was more than three times its 1982 level. Oil revenues, which were $336 million in 1986, rose to $2.4 billion in 1995. In that year, oil accounted for about 20 percent of GDP, for 60 percent of exports, and for a substantial part of government revenues.[41] In the late 1980s and early 1990s, revenues from oil, more than any other factor, permitted the economy to grow and gave the government unprecedented room for maneuver.

On 1 January 1997, Syria had estimated proven oil reserves of 2.5 billion barrels, which, at the rate at which it was used in 1996, would last for about a decade.[42] Approximately half of Syria's oil production is exported.[43]

Mineral Resources

There is also a rental element in revenues from sales of natural resources other than oil in the Arab world. Mineral resources play an important role in a number of Middle East countries. The most notable example is Morocco, which is one of the world's largest phosphate exporters. Morocco exports phosphates, phosphoric acid, and fertilizers derived from phosphates. World phosphate prices rose sharply in the mid-1970s, and this led to an increase in the value of exports and government revenues.[44] In 1984, phosphates, phosphoric acid, and fertilizers accounted for a peak 47 percent of total exports.[45] Output peaked in 1988, and by 1990, they accounted for 28 percent of total exports. By 1997, however, they had fallen to 19.5 percent.[46]

Jordan is also one of the world's largest phosphate exporters. In 1989, phosphates accounted for 41 percent of Jordanian exports, but by 1993, as a result of a 35 percent fall in quantity sold and increases in other exports, this had fallen to 27 percent. Output of raw phosphates fell by 35 percent over this period, while potash production, much smaller in scale, rose by 11 percent.[47] The role of mineral resources in the Jordanian economy is greater than these figures indicate because of the significance of processed derivatives, such as fertilizers. Using this wider definition, mineral resources accounted for 53 percent of exports in 1997.[48] The effects of the reductions in these revenues on the Moroccan and Jordanian economies are examined in Chapter 5.

Producers of phosphates, potash, and other minerals are subject to the same uncertainties as oil producers: prices fluctuate on international markets, and the quantities sold depend on levels of demand and changes in technology abroad. They are also, of course, affected by production outside the Middle East. International recession and changes in the patterns of demand, therefore, result in lower prices and fewer exports.

Economic Aid and Debt Write-Offs

The next form of rental income in the Arab world consists of economic aid granted by richer states in the region, by countries outside the region, and by multinational organizations to the poorer states in the region. Historically, this assistance took the form of grants and loans at subsidized rates of interest and/or preferential repayment terms. Between 1973 and 1981, 85 percent of OPEC aid was given on a bilateral basis by Kuwait, Qatar, Saudi Arabia, and the UAE almost entirely to other Arab states.[49] It was given in order to further political ends, including strengthening the recipient's economy, but in the region, economic stability was seen primarily as a political concern rather than as an end in itself. Financial aid could therefore be considered a kind of rent paid in return for political services granted to the donor; as with other forms of rent, it was not generated by production within the recipient economy.

Table 3.2 details aid provided by Middle East members of OPEC between 1973 and 1992: nearly all of this aid was provided to other countries in the region. As has been noted, the main reason for this aid was political: to support the regimes of the poorer states especially at a time when the cost of one of their major imports—oil—had increased. More specifically, it was provided at a time when the oil producers had large surpluses of foreign currency; when oil revenues declined, they became much less generous.

"Concessional aid" broadly conforms to the definition of grants and loans on beneficial terms. "Nonconcessional aid" consists of loans made at market rates of interest. Between 1973 and 1975, there was close to a sevenfold increase in total aid and close to a fivefold increase in concessional aid. By 1980, the level of aid had fallen by 12 percent, but nearly all of it was provided on a concessional basis. Between 1980 and 1989, levels of total and concessional aid both fell dramatically. This corresponded to the changing fortunes of oil-rich states in the Gulf

Table 3.2   Net Financial Flows from Middle Eastern OPEC Members to Developing Countries and Multinational Agencies, 1973–1992 (in Millions)

	Concessional	Nonconcessional	Total
1973	1.1	0.44	1.5
1975	5.2	4.4	9.6
1980	9.6	−0.73	9.5
1984	4.6	1.7	6.3
1985	3.9	−0.19	3.7
1986	4.9	−0.17	4.7
1987	2.5	−0.69	1.8
1988	1.9	−0.38	1.5
1989	1.4	0.07	1.5
1990	5.8	−0.03	5.8
1991	n.a.	n.a.	2.6
1992	n.a.	n.a.	1.1

Sources: For 1973–1990: UNCTAD, *Handbook of International Trade, 1993;* for 1991–1992: OECD Development Assistance Committee statistics, quoted in *Arab Oil and Gas,* 1 April 1994.
Note: n.a. indicates that figures were not available.

and Libya. The large increase in aid in 1990 was due to the Gulf crisis, during which Saudi Arabia, Kuwait, and the UAE transferred large sums to other states in the anti-Iraq coalition, which was financed by a large increase in oil income. During the two years after the Gulf War, aid from Arab countries (principally Saudi Arabia, Kuwait, and the UAE) declined from almost $6 billion to about $1 billion.

Table 3.3 shows the volume of aid received from all sources by the main Arab recipients between 1973 and 1986. The total amount received, in current dollar terms, changed little in that period, and its relative importance in the balance of payments and economies of the recipient states declined. Egypt was the largest recipient throughout the period, a reflection of the size of its economy, the scale of its needs, and its political importance in the Middle East. The fall in grants received by Syria in the late 1980s was due to its support for Iran in the war with Iraq. Its support for the U.S. coalition against Iraq in 1990–1991 resulted in an increase in aid received, which was true for Egypt and Morocco as well.

Increased foreign aid to Egypt came from several sources. In November 1990, the United States unconditionally wrote off $7.1 bil-

Table 3.3 Total Official Assistance from Arab Countries and Agencies and Net Workers' Remittances as a Percentage of GNP in Major Arab Recipient Countries, 1973–1986

	1973	1975	1980	1981	1982	1983	1984	1985	1986	1987	1988	1989
Arab Middle East[a]	4.2	5.1	9.0	7.4	5.5	5.1	4.1	3.1	2.9	2.3	1.8	1.6
Jordan	20.4	45.2	55.1	53.9	44.1	41.8	43.7	32.5	31.7	24.3	22.8	15.3
Lebanon	0.1	0.3	4.9	9.6	3.1	0.3	0.0	0.6	0.1	0.8	—	—
Syria	10.0	10.4	18.0	12.8	8.3	7.1	5.8	5.7	5.2	3.9	1.9	4.1
YAR[b]	3.2	44.8	39.3	27.6	23.0	24.0	19.9	17.5	12.9	15.3	5.9	—
PDRY[c]	16.1	34.2	52.0	48.4	61.1	49.4	49.7	45.4	32.3	36.9	25.9	16.8
Arab Africa[d]	5.1	10.0	6.0	5.4	4.9	5.7	5.3	4.8	3.8	4.7	5.1	9.1
Algeria	4.0	3.0	0.7	0.8	0.4	0.5	0.3	0.4	0.4	0.6	1.0	—
Egypt	8.7	26.6	12.6	9.9	10.2	13.7	13.8	10.1	8.1	11.2	14.0	15.4
Morocco	3.4	6.7	9.5	12.0	9.0	7.2	7.0	11.2	8.1	7.7	5.9	6.0
Sudan	0.9	4.6	6.5	4.9	4.0	9.1	4.1	6.7	2.9	3.0	2.8	4.5
Tunisia	3.6	4.6	4.8	5.1	5.2	4.7	4.7	3.6	4.1	5.6	5.2	4.6
Total	5.0	8.4	7.3	6.3	5.2	5.5	4.8	4.1	3.4	3.7	3.7	5.3

Source: IMF, "Financial Assistance from Arab Countries."

Notes: a. Includes Bahrain and Iraq.

b. Yemen Arab Republic.

c. People's Democratic Republic of Yemen.

d. Includes Mauritania and Somalia.

lion of debt owed by Egypt. At the same time, Kuwait, Saudi Arabia, the UAE, and Qatar wrote off $3 billion that had been lent to Egypt. These debt write-offs were political acts designed to reward Egypt for its support for Kuwait and Saudi Arabia following the Iraqi invasion of Kuwait. Additional aid to Egypt was linked to a reform package negotiated with the IMF and the World Bank. European countries and Japan also agreed, within the framework of the Paris Club (a group of official international creditors), to write off and suspend parts of Egypt's debts but only within the context of a package of economic measures agreed upon with the IMF and the World Bank. Their actions constituted a reward for changes in Egyptian economic policy and corresponded to other reform programs introduced in the region under the aegis of the IMF and the World Bank.

In the 1980s, Tunisia, Jordan, and Morocco also implemented adjustment programs involving debt reductions. These were, in part, a response to reduced inflows of foreign aid. Despite its much more socialist orientation, Algeria also introduced a stabilization and structural reform program in 1989, and the IMF and the World Bank provided support.

It should be noted that debt write-offs usually do not appear in data on aid; they are treated as a financing source in balance-of-payments data.

International Capital Flows

In recent years, there have been two important changes in the nature of global capital flows. First, the role of the private sector as a supplier of finance has increased, while that of the public sector has remained stable in absolute terms and has fallen in relative terms. Second, there has been a large increase in private-sector capital flows to developing countries, both in absolute terms and as a percentage of the recipient state's GNP. In 1993, about $155 billion in private capital was invested abroad (remittances are not considered investments and are therefore not included in these calculations). A total of $66.6 billion was directly invested in developing countries, but only $1.7 billion went to the Middle East and North Africa, while East Asia received $36 billion. The Middle East received virtually none of the $42 billion of portfolio investment in government bonds and share issues.[50]

Net transfers, including those from the public sector (which equaled

$50 billion worldwide in 1993), accounted for 0.5 percent of GNP in developing countries in 1990 and 3.0 percent in 1993. This increase was mainly due to the globalization of the world economy that involved large increases in investment in East Asia by Western companies. In the Middle East and North Africa, net transfers fell from 0.4 percent in 1990 to 0.1 percent in 1993. The absolute amount of foreign investment, measured in current dollar terms, was only about 3 percent higher in 1993 than the annual average in 1987–1989.

In 1997, however, there was a large increase in private capital flowing into the region. In 1991, private capital flows to the Middle East and North Africa came to $2 billion. In 1977, they equaled $14 billion, of which 57 percent was loans, 18 percent direct investment, 11 percent portfolio equity flows, and 14 percent bond sales. Most of the increase occurred after 1995 and was carried on into 1997, despite the slowdown in growth rates in the region due to low oil prices and poor harvests. Positive factors included the continuation of economic reforms and the increased attractiveness of the region toward the end of the year compared with countries in East and Southeast Asia.[51]

Official assistance was granted by state or multinational bodies to governments or public-sector organizations. Only a very small share of such funding went to the private sector. As a result, the flow of funds among Arab states, as well as the flow into the region from outside, was essentially political. Its effects were also political, as aid provided governments with resources for distribution on the basis of political decisions rather than economic ones.

The flow of remittances had very different characteristics. These funds were earned by individuals, mainly from employment in the private sector. They were sent home through either the banks or outside official networks to workers' families and were thus spread through wide sections of the population. Funds that were not remitted could be kept in banks abroad, and individual decisions govern their eventual use (see below).

Between 1980 and 1989, total official assistance from Arab states and Arab multinational agencies to Arab countries came to about $27 billion. Total net remittances received by Arab countries in the 1980s equaled nearly $68 billion. The total inflow from Arab aid and remittances therefore came to $95 billion, or about 5 percent of GNP.[52] These inflows of foreign currency were of particular importance in financing imports. In the 1980s, they covered 16.5 percent of the import bill of

Arab aid recipients. They also covered almost 20 percent of investment in these countries and thus had significant effects on the level of output.[53]

The overall figures mask a number of trends among countries and over time. For example, Egypt alone accounted for $32 billion, or over one-third, of the total capital inflow, almost entirely from remittances. Like other countries in the region, Egypt also received non-Arab aid that is not included in these figures.

Official aid flows declined sharply in the 1980s, and after a temporary upsurge during the Gulf crisis of 1990–1991, they declined again. The reduced availability of external funds during the 1980s forced governments in Jordan, Morocco, and Tunisia to implement structural reform programs and seek IMF and World Bank assistance.

Foreign Debt

The 1980s saw a huge increase in the foreign debt of the major Arab borrowers, as shown in Table 3.4. As grants from richer Arab states declined, they were forced to borrow more in order to finance imports and investments. In dollar terms, their foreign debt rose by 112 percent between 1980 and 1990 and by a further 6 percent by 1996. The ratio of debt to GNP rose from 53 percent in 1980 to 78.2 percent in 1990, a rise of 25.2 percent in the share of GNP.

The debt/GNP ratio fell by 11 percent between 1994 and 1996 as a result of debt write-offs, rescheduling, and economic growth (see Table 3.4). Easing the debt burden was one of the major aims of the stabilization programs of the 1980s and early 1990s (see Chapter 5). Servicing the debt consumed an increasing share of resources; the share of interest payments and principal repayments in GNP rose by 12 percent between 1980 and 1990. The debt service ratios all declined modestly between 1990 and 1996.

It should be noted that most of the borrowing carried out in the 1980s and early 1990s was done by the governments of the region or by public-sector agencies. Consequently, most of the region's debt accrued to the public sector. This began to change slowly in the period 1995–1997 as the private sector became more active.

The volume of debt and the burden of financing it (as measured by the ratio of total debt servicing to exports of goods and services) rose sharply in Egypt, Jordan, and Tunisia between 1980 and 1990. In Morocco, the debt rose in absolute terms, but the burden, which was

Table 3.4 Foreign Debt of Major Indebted Arab Countries, 1980–1996ᵃ

	1980	1990	1994	1995	1996
Total debt					
(in millions $)	58,477	123,758	127,742	134,597	131,215
Principal repayments					
(in millions)	4,308	11,899	8,018	7,061	6,412
Interest					
(in millions $)	3,670	5,301	5,268	5,630	5,750
Debt as percent of GNP	53.0	78.2	78.6	76.6	67.6
Interest payments					
As % of GNP	3.3	3.3	3.2	3.2	3.0
As % of export of					
goods and services	9.7	10.3	9.3	8.7	8.1
Interest and principal					
repayments as % of GNP	21.2	33.6	23.5	19.6	17.1

Source: World Bank, Global Finance Development, 1998, vol. 2.
Note: a. Countries included are: Algeria, Egypt, Jordan, Morocco, Oman, Syria, Tunisia, and Yemen.

already high, did not because the exports rose (see Table 5.1 in Chapter 5).

Severe fluctuations in weather conditions led to rapid changes in the volume of agricultural production, in food imports, and thus in the state of the balance of payments and the need for foreign borrowing. The effect of the debt crisis in Egypt, Jordan, Morocco, and Tunisia is examined within the context of economic reform programs in Chapter 5. The volume of debt and the burden of servicing it also rose sharply between 1980 and 1990 in Algeria, Oman, Sudan, Syria, and Yemen. The most serious burden was in Algeria, where total debt servicing accounted for 66.8 percent of exports of goods and services in 1989. Between 1990 and 1996, the burden declined in Algeria, Oman, and Yemen. In Sudan, it increased after 1990; and in Syria, it declined because debt repayments were partly suspended in 1991.[54]

Labor Migration and Remittances

The emigration of labor from poorer countries in the Middle East to oil-rich states in the Gulf, to Libya, and to Europe has not only provided an important source of foreign currency, but it has also reduced pressure on the labor market. The labor-exporting states have been able to achieve fuller employment than they would have otherwise. This has, in turn, reduced pressures for economic reforms and for development. It has also resulted in economic cooperation among countries in the region. Banking services have been provided for immigrants to enable them to remit funds home. Transport systems have been created and expanded to facilitate their movement and that of their families. This movement of labor has been one of the few elements of economic integration in the region, and a very superficial one at that.

Reduced pressure on the labor markets of poorer countries of the region has thus been achieved without additional development within their economies. It has been the result of economic development elsewhere, and consequently, the benefit that it brings—in terms of political stability as well as in direct economic gains—has a rental aspect to it. It therefore also features the instability characteristic of rental income. The presence of foreign workers is always subject to both political and economic considerations.

Labor market pressures have been particularly severe in Egypt. Between 1976 and 1986, the labor force increased by 2 percent a year, but domestic employment rose by only 1.5 percent annually. Construction accounted for 21 percent of the increase in employment and government services for 53 percent, while the agricultural labor force declined by 7 percent.[55]

A major reason for the import of labor has been the unwillingness of nationals in Saudi Arabia, Kuwait, the UAE, and Qatar to work in the private sector. As much as 90 percent of the national labor force in these countries is employed in the public sector, where, unlike the conditions in many other countries, wages are often higher than in the private sector. There are other incentives for nationals to work in the public sector: employment is often guaranteed to graduates (and university tuition is free), and early retirement ages provide public-sector workers with the opportunity to move into the private sector with the security of a state pension.[56]

The internationalization of the labor market was one of the most important aspects of economic relations among states in the region in the late twentieth century. Large numbers of workers from Egypt and Jordan worked in the Gulf and in Libya. Those from Algeria, Tunisia, and Morocco mostly worked in Europe. They sent funds home, which played an important part in funding investment and imports. These remittances, like oil, did not require economic development. With minimal levels of education, workers from the poorer countries of the region could go abroad and earn far more than they could at home. The oil-rich Gulf states have imported Arab labor mainly since the 1970s (Kuwait since the 1950s), but their needs fluctuated as a result of changes in rates of economic growth and political developments in the region. Remittances were therefore an external source of income that was inherently unstable.

Table 3.5 provides details of private unrequited transfers received by the main recipient nations, in current prices. The table shows that between 1980 and 1990, the total amount received by the eight Arab countries listed rose by 36 percent in nominal terms. From 1991 to 1992, there was a sharp increase, but since 1993, the total has fallen. This increase, like that of 1983, was mainly due to a rise in remittances received in Egypt, the largest recipient in the region. Jordan also experienced increases, 85 percent in 1992 and 24 percent in 1993, but in absolute terms, the volume was much smaller than in Egypt.

The increase in remittances received by Egypt in 1992 was due to a major liberalization of the financial system: interest rates on local currency deposits increased sharply in early 1991, the multiple exchange rate system was unified, and there was a large devaluation.[57] In 1989–1990, many Egyptians returned from Iraq, where they had been employed during the war against Iran. Estimates of the numbers who returned vary, but it is reasonable to assume that the figure was about 500,000, given that 1 million or more Egyptians had been working there.[58]

It is important to note that in Egypt, as in other labor-exporting countries in the region, remittances recorded in the balance of payments cover only part of the influx of private funds from workers abroad or from those who returned. Low levels of recorded remittances may therefore reflect either small real inflows or disincentives to remit funds or to place them in banks. Financial reforms, such as those carried out in Egypt in 1991, encouraged placement of funds in banks, allowing them to be recorded in the balance of payments.

Other countries in the region also benefited from increased remittances during the early 1990s. Following the Iraqi invasion of Kuwait, 300,000 Jordanians returned home from Kuwait, bringing funds with them.[59] Though only a onetime boost, these funds helped stimulate investment, particularly in construction. Remittances were interrupted

Table 3.5 Private Transfers by Main Recipient Countries, 1980–1996 (in Millions $)

	1980	1981	1982	1983	1984	1985	1986	1987	1988	1989	1990	1991	1992	1993	1994	1995	1996
Algeria	60	48	15	398	333	510	903	611	455	587	386	269	n.a.	n.a.	n.a.	n.a.	n.a.
Egypt	2,736	2,201	2,479	3,688	3,981	3,216	2,515	3,604	3,770	3,295	4,284	4,054	6,104	5,664	3,672	3,226	3,107
Jordan	812	1,071	1,116	1,130	1,292	1,089	1,239	948	895	627	499	448	843	1,040	1,094	1,244	1,544
Morocco	149	139	200	929	884	990	1,415	1,606	1,303	1,480	2,006	1,990	2,170	1,959	1,827	1,904	2,010
Syria	758	574	446	387	321	350	323	334	360	430	385	350	550	426	570	598	618
Tunisia	102	51	51	365	322	276	368	495	498	512	551	525	531	446	629	680	736
YAR[a]	1,295	963	1,176	1,223	1,069	826	600	751	343	278							
PDRY[a]	321	378	442	491	506	429	294	305	255	174							
ROY[a]											1,498	998	1,018	1,034	1,059	1,081	1,135
Total	6,233	5,425	5,925	8,611	8,708	7,686	7,657	8,654	7,879	7,383	9,609	8,634	11,216	10,569	8,851	8,733	9,150

Sources: IMF, *Balance of Payments Yearbook, 1987, 1990, 1994,* and *1997.*

Note: n.a. indicates that figures were not available.

a. The YAR and the PDRY formally merged in 1990, forming the Republic of Yemen (ROY).

by the Gulf crisis in 1990–1991, but the return of many Palestinians and Jordanians to Jordan as a result of the Gulf War resulted in an increase of remittances between 1991 and 1996.

As indicated in Table 3.5, the volume of remittances received in the major labor-exporting countries declined by about 10 percent between 1990 and 1995. This was true for Egypt, Jordan, and Yemen, which had exported labor to the Gulf. The recession in the Gulf following the collapse of oil revenues in the mid-1980s resulted in a secular decline in the demand for labor, and there was also a move toward replacing Arab workers with South and Southeast Asians. In Europe, recession and increasingly tight controls on immigration were factors that helped to reduce the volume of remittances to Morocco.

Syria also experienced an increase in workers' remittances of about 60 percent between 1990 and 1963. This occurred despite the fact that the balance-of-payments entries for workers' remittances "may be underestimated because [they] are believed to be a principal source of foreign exchange entering the unregulated foreign exchange market."[60] Syria experienced an increase as the foreign exchange and investment laws provided more incentives for émigrés to remit funds home.

Remittances played an important role in the economies of the region. In Egypt, they accounted for 1.3 percent of GNP in 1973, 12.6 percent in 1980, and 14.5 percent in 1992.[61] In 1989, remittances equaled 57 percent of Egypt's imports.[62] In Jordan, remittances equaled 12.6 percent of GNP in 1991, 19 percent in 1992, and nearly 22 percent in 1993.[63] In the 1990s, the amount of remittances as share of GNP rose in Egypt and Morocco but fell in Tunisia.

Implications of Rental Incomes for the GCC

Due to the age structure of the indigenous populations in the region and the low female participation rate in the workforce, the overall labor force participation rate (for indigenous males and females) was very low in the final decades of the twentieth century. In 1995, it was estimated at 32 percent in Bahrain, 24 percent in Kuwait, 30 percent in Saudi Arabia, and 20 percent in the UAE.[64] In 1975, 1.13 million nonnationals worked in the GCC countries; by 1980, as a result of the oil boom, this number had risen to almost 3 million. By 1985, there were 4.4 million, and in 1990, 5.2 million. In 1994, total employment in GCC countries came to more than 9.4 million, of which about 2.4 million were GCC nationals and more than 7 million were expatriates. Thus, over the period 1990-1994, the annual growth of total employment in the GCC countries averaged about 2.5 percent for both GCC nationals and expatriates.

In the period 1980–1990, total employment in the GCC increased at a substantially higher annual rate, more than 7.5 percent, or three times higher than in the period 1990–1994. The low rate of the employment growth in this earlier period was mainly the result of the massive expulsion of expatriate workers following the Gulf crisis and, to a lesser extent, the decline in investment. The development of employment in the GCC countries over the 1980–1990 decade was characterized by a declining share of GCC nationals in total employment: from 35 percent in 1980 to 25 percent in 1990. The share of expatriate workers increased from 65 percent in 1980 to 75 percent in 1990, or from about 3 million to more than 7 million workers, respectively. On average, GCC citizens constituted only 20 percent of the increase in employment over the period 1980–1990; expatriates accounted for 80 percent.

The number of non-nationals did not fall when oil revenues declined and the economies of the region ceased to grow. Immigrants adapted to changes in the economy, and employers were reluctant to do without them. Despite the increasing burden of remittances, the cost of providing services to non-nationals also rose as more of them brought their families to the region. Immigrants from non-GCC Arab states brought their families with the intention of staying in the region for long periods or permanently; non-Arab immigrants did not. Migrants from South and Southeast Asia were mobilized by agencies for specific projects. Pakistan and the Philippines trained some labor for the Gulf. Most of these immigrants earned less than Arab workers because they had low skill levels or worked in lower-status jobs. Between 1994 and 1996, the population of the GCC rose by almost 7 percent. The indigenous population rose by 5.4 percent, but the immigrant population rose by 10 percent, or almost 900,000. In 1994, the immigrant population accounted for 36 percent of the total population, and in 1996, for 37 percent. This was despite the efforts made to reduce its growth.

The substitution of nationals for non-nationals has involved replacing non-GCC Arabs because the latter occupied public-sector posts favored by locals. Workers from Southeast Asia tended to work more in production, construction, and maintenance.[65] GCC governments emphasized the importance of replacing foreign workers with nationals. This was a response to the challenge of population growth that resulted in large annual increases in the labor force. If successful, it would reduce the burden of remittances sent home by foreign workers (see below). Saudi Arabia's sixth development plan for the period 1995–2000 stated that 320,000 expatriate workers would be replaced with Saudi nationals by the year 2000.[66] Attempts have been made elsewhere, especially in Bahrain and Oman, to indigenize the workforce, but only with limited success, given the lack of skills among the national populations and their unwillingness to do more menial work.

The UAE has introduced regulations requiring that the expatriate has attained a certain minimum salary before he can bring in his family. Health charges for expatriates have also been increased. Kuwait charges high visa fees to help cover the cost of services used by expatriates. The draft of the five-year plan issued in 1995 sought to reduce the recruitment of foreign labor.[67]

The growing proportion of foreign workers in GCC employment since 1980 has had an increasingly negative impact on the balance of payments. During the period 1990–1995, total expatriates' remittances averaged $21 billion a year, twice as high as in the period 1980–1989. They also absorbed an increasing share of GCC export earnings: during 1980–1989, they accounted for 13 percent of total GCC exports, while in 1990–1996, they accounted for 26 percent.[68]

Summary of Rental Incomes

Rental incomes have played a major role in the pattern of economic development in the Arab world. In the GCC, Libya, Algeria, and Iraq until 1991, income from the sale of oil and gas provided billions of dollars that were used for massive economic development programs; in the case of Iraq, this money was directly used for war. The boom that this created resulted in the import of workers from elsewhere in the Arab world and made possible flows of aid from richer to poorer Arab states. This helped to create elements of a regional economy: the oil- and gas-rich states provided capital; the poorer states, labor. In the 1980s, both the rich and the poor states remained very dependent on outside help. The rich imported skilled as well as unskilled labor and still remain reliant on them today, even though revenues have fallen sharply. The poorer states felt the effects of the fall in oil revenues indirectly in the 1980s, when the aid they received from the oil-rich states declined. They could no longer borrow from international banks and were forced to reform their economies (see Chapter 5).

Rental incomes have also helped to produce a rental mentality: in the Persian Gulf and in Libya, the economies have relied on enormous oil and gas resources; in the diversified economies of Egypt, Syria, and Jordan, natural resources remittances and political rents (derived from each country's geopolitical situation) have been vital. In Algeria and Morocco, remittances as well as income from gas have played an important role. Tunisia has been exceptional: it has been less reliant on rents and more reliant on industry. As a result, its economic growth rates have been faster and more stable than those of most other Arab countries.

Interest Groups

As Arab states began the process of economic liberalization, they were constrained by various interest groups. The first was the state itself, defined as the central government and all the bodies that it directly controls. These include local government, public-sector companies and other bodies supplying services, and the military. When proposals for economic liberalization were put forward, a major consideration was whether the state would lose power to the private sector. Insofar as this was usually the case, it reduced the willingness of governments to decentralize power. This section examines the political economy of these relationships mainly with reference to Egypt, the most populous and, in many respects, powerful Arab state.

The State

In the Arab world, the state has traditionally been much stronger than the society at large and has been basically autonomous. Limits on the development of private property under the Ottoman Empire meant that the private sector was much weaker vis-à-vis the state than in Europe.[69] One quantitative measure of this was the expansion of the Egyptian bureaucracy after independence: it expanded from 350,000 people in 1952 to 4 million in 1992. In the period of economic liberalization, 1980–1992, the bureaucracy grew by 240 percent. Despite the size of the government, the political elite supporting the leadership was often a very small group, one insulated from criticism by the centralized and undemocratic nature of the regime.[70]

Although the state suffered revenue losses from the failures of the public sector, the role of rents reinforced its importance. In all Arab states, revenues from the sale of oil went to the state (in the GCC, they are virtually the private property of the ruler). In addition, countries such as Egypt, Jordan, and Syria were able, with varying degrees of success, to extract strategic rents from powers outside the region. During the period of superpower rivalry that preceded the Arab-Israel peace process, these countries gained backing from the United States or the Soviet Union. Since the demise of the Soviet Union, Egypt, Jordan, and the Palestinian territories have received aid in order to reinforce the peace process.

The Military

Arab countries are notable for the central role of the state in political and economic life. In the not-so-distant past, the military, which was often synonymous with the state, was powerful, if not dominant, in nearly every Arab country. Indeed, many of the regimes that now rule came to power in coups d'état staged by the army. In recent years, however, a separation of government and the military has developed. The latter was rewarded for its loyalty by being supplied with foreign arms, with jobs, with access to economic benefits in the civilian sector (and in Syria, with control over trade with Lebanon), and with political functions (for example, Egypt's late president Anwar Sadat appointed an air force general, Hosni Mubarak, as his vice president).

Considering this history, it is not surprising that the military receives a large budget in Arab states. It plays a key role in maintaining political order, not only in terms of the use of force, but also by keeping 4.5 million people off the Arab unemployment register.[71]

Labor

When economic policy changes, different sections of the population stand to gain or to lose. The IS phase, for instance, was one in which urban workers gained employment and higher incomes. The rural sector paid through deliveries of agricultural products to the government at low prices. These were then sold to urban workers at subsidized prices. When the economy was liberalized, urban employment ceased to grow (at least in the public sector), and the rural sector was encouraged with higher prices. In Egypt, the liberalization of agriculture led to a growing differentiation between the poor and the middle classes.

Urban workers were the main ideological focus for many of the regimes that adopted Arab socialism. As in the Soviet Union, they saw industrialization as the way out of poverty, and urban, industrial workers were the means. Public-sector employment (in and outside industry) grew rapidly during the socialist phase of development. When economic liberalization was implemented, the urban working class, employed in the public sector, suffered falls in real wages and employment losses. Those working outside the public sector, in small workshops manufacturing basic goods, faced increased competition from cheap imported goods.

The Middle Class

Entrepreneurial classes have traditionally been weak, something that dates back to the period of Ottoman rule and even earlier, when private property rights were restricted.[72] The most notable exceptions were Lebanon, where the private sector has played a central role since its creation; Egypt in the 1930s, where Taalat Harb played an important part in developing the private sector; and Fez, Morocco, where for many years a group of prominent families have had a major economic role in the national economy. The latter can be called an old elite because of their long-standing connections to the court. Through these connections, they were able to gain monopolies over the import and export of certain goods. They also won public procurement contracts on the same basis. In the late 1980s, however, a new group rose to prominence, taking advantage of the liberalization of the economy. This group pushed for the end of the traditional privileges that had been granted to the "Fez elite"; they also demanded reform of business practices and called for Morocco to adopt international standards in taxation and regulation.

Another partial exception was in Syria, where, in 1961, a group of conservative business leaders, together with members of the armed forces, staged a military coup that brought an end to Syria's membership, with Egypt, in the United Arab Republic. The coup also resulted in the denationalization of a number of companies and raised the ceiling on landownership. But in 1963, the Baath staged a coup, and the nationalization program was renewed.[73]

The growth of a capitalist class (often referred to as the "new middle class") in the last quarter of the twentieth century was largely a function of government initiative. As state-owned sectors of the economy buckled under the strains of overemployment and low productivity, governments had to find other ways to generate revenues. In most Arab states, they turned to the private sector and encouraged it to expand. This included permission to operate with or within sectors run by the state. In a situation in which resources are scarce and the government plays a central role in controlling the economy, rent-seeking becomes an important activity. According to economist David Ricardo, rent was paid for the use of the "original and indestructible powers of the soil,"[74] conforming to the sense of the word "rent" that has been used throughout this chapter. Anne Krueger later adapted the Ricardian definition to cover legal and illegal competitive seeking of returns from commodities in short or fixed supply.[75]

Rent-seeking inside an economy was, therefore, the search for privilege in domestic markets. Such privilege was usually made available by the state to those that it favored through the issuance of licenses to produce, import, or sell. For when competition is limited by the state, those who sell or supply make monopoly profits. And when there are restrictions or shortages that are under state control or influence, individuals or groups will act to obtain privileges. If they are significant politically and/or economically (the two usually run together), then they can be called "interest groups," "lobbies," or "vested interests." Another term, used in a mixed economy, is "crony capitalism."

Yahya Sadowski has analyzed the role of interest groups in the liberalization of Egyptian agriculture in the 1980s. He showed how a relationship developed between businesspeople in agriculture and bureaucrats in government. Both sides felt that the other was indispensable. Businesspeople gained influence through political parties and lobbies to such an extent that they could not be ignored.[76] The rise of the middle class was thus a result of changes in state policy, most notably, the shift away from public-sector domination of the economy toward a liberalized system. Both Marxists and liberals have claimed that these new forces have captured the state. An alternative view holds that these new forces were created by economic policy change.[77]

Relations such as those described above are implicit. The negotiations take place behind closed doors. They are not documented or recorded and are not subject to public scrutiny.

Foreign Interests

In recent decades, the most important force pushing for economic liberalization in the Arab world has been the international community, led by the World Bank and the International Monetary Fund. Their role in the Arab world increased when economic crises hit parts of the region in the 1970s and 1980s (see Chapter 5). Their power lay in the fact that they controlled the purse strings, and they usually laid down strict conditions in exchange for aid. The U.S. government and, more recently, the European Union have played a similar role on a bilateral basis.

With the exception of foreign donors, no interest group has been able to stop the state from adopting its chosen path. It should be noted that in Egypt, strategic rents eased the conditions imposed by the IMF: the United States intervened to soften IMF decisions regarding conditions for aid. In Syria, foreign loans were not taken, but even there, the direction has been one of liberalization even if the speed has been slow.

Conclusion

Nazih Ayubi has called the Arab state "fierce" rather than strong.[78] It is stronger than other groups in the society, but its attempts to mobilize the society around development objectives have been weak. Because of its undemocratic nature, it has relied on force to obtain resources (nationalization, expropriation) instead of on taxation, which requires a greater degree of representation. The prevalence of external rents (oil, emigrant remittances, and strategic rents) has helped to sustain the lack of accountability of the state. Forces pushing for reform have therefore been relatively weak, and the state, while not short of power, has been unable to yield it as a galvanizing force in the development process.

Notes

1. World Bank, *Expanding the Measure of Wealth,* p. 25.
2. World Bank, *World Development Report, 1998–99.*
3. World Bank, *A Strategy for Managing Water,* p. 1.
4. World Bank, *World Development Report, 1998–99.*
5. Kolars and Mitchell, *The Euphrates River,* pp. 283–284.
6. Rogers and Lydon, eds., *Water in the Arab World,* p. 300.
7. *Middle East Economic Digest* (hereafter *MEED*), 5 February 1995.
8. Rogers and Lydon, eds., *Water in the Arab World,* p. 300.
9. World Bank, *A Strategy for Managing Water,* p. 3.
10. Susser, "Jordan," p. 413.
11. Calculated from el-Ghonemy, *Affluence and Poverty,* p. 66, and from World Bank, *World Development Report, 1995.*

12. Mahdary, "Patterns and Problems," pp. 428–429.

13. *Middle East Economic Survey* (hereafter *MEES*), 8 February 1999.

14. Calculated from OAPEC, *Secretary General's Report,* p. 40.

15. OPEC, *Annual Statistical Bulletin, 1995.*

16. IMF, *World Economic Outlook, October 1996,* p. 135.

17. *The Middle East and North Africa, 1997,* p. 115.

18. Author's calculations based on *MEES,* 19 January 1998 and 9 February 1998.

19. *MEES,* 11 January 1999.

20. Mohamedi, "Oil, Gas, and the Future."

21. *MEES,* 20 December 1999.

22. *MEES,* 13 December 1999.

23. IEA, *Monthly Oil Market Report.*

24. Author's calculation based on U.S. Department of Energy, Energy Information Agency data, and on UN, *Demographic Yearbook,* various annual editions.

25. Rivlin, "The Economics of Monarchy."

26. UNESCWA, *Survey of Economic and Social Developments,* 1996–97, p. 123.

27. *The Middle East and North Africa, 1997,* pp. 322–323.

28. IEA, *Middle East Oil and Gas,* p. 154.

29. Ibid., p. 204.

30. OPEC, *Statistical Bulletin, 1996.*

31. *Oil and Gas Journal,* 29 December 1997.

32. IEA, *Natural Gas Security Study,* p. 543.

33. Ibid., p. 546.

34. Enav, "Non-OPEC Oil."

35. British Petroleum, *BP Statistical Review;* and IEA, *North Africa Oil and Gas.*

36. Calculated from IMF, *International Financial Statistics,* 1998.

37. U.S. Department of Energy, Energy Information Agency, Iraq Internet note, 1998.

38. Ibid., Libya Internet note, 1998.

39. Ibid.

40. EIU, *Country Report* (hereafter *CR*): *Libya, 2000,* no. 1, p. 5.

41. EIU, *Country Profile* (hereafter *CP*): *Syria, 1997–98,* p. 23.

42. British Petroleum, *BP Statistical Review.*

43. EIU, *CP: Syria, 1997–98,* p. 23.

44. Richards and Waterbury, *A Political Economy,* 1990, p. 210.

45. Ibid.

46. EIU, *CP: Morocco, 1999–2000,* p. 52.

47. EIU, *CP: Jordan, 1995–96,* pp. 23 and 33.

48. Central Bank of Jordan, *Monthly Bulletin of Statistics,* p. 11.

49. Mattione, *OPEC's Investments,* pp. 142–145.

50. World Bank, *World Debt Tables, 1994–95,* vol. 1, pp. 97 and 159.

51. World Bank, *Global Finance Development, 1998,* pp. 130–131 and 168–169.

52. Calculated from van den Boogaerde, "Financial Assistance," p. 87.

53. Ibid., p. 86.

54. World Bank, *Global Finance Development, 1998.*

55. Handousa and Potter, eds., *Employment*, p. 5.

56. Sassanpour et al., "Labor Market Challenges," p. 31.

57. EIU, *CR: Egypt, 1991*, no. 1, pp. 10–13.

58. Ayalon, "Egypt," p. 318; and Ayalon, ed., *Middle East Contemporary Survey*, p. 344.

59. Maciejewski and Mansur, eds., *Jordan*, p. 15.

60. IMF, *Balance of Payments Yearbook, 1994*, p. 686.

61. IMF, *International Financial Statistics, December 1994;* 1992 calculation based on GDP for FY 1991/92 (i.e., 1 July 1991–30 June 1992).

62. van den Boogaerde, "Financial Assistance," p. 88.

63. IMF, *International Financial Statistics, December 1994.*

64. NCB, *NCB Economist*, vol. 5, no. 4 (June–July 1995).

65. UNESCWA, *Survey of Economic and Social Developments, 1992*, p. 120.

66. *UNESCWA, Survey of Economic and Social Developments, 1996–97,* p. 137.

67. IEA, *Middle East Oil and Gas*, pp. 95–96.

68. Based on IMF, *Balance of Payments Yearbook, 1997*, and on author's estimates.

69. Ayubi, *Overstating the Arab State*, pp. 68–70; and Rivlin, "The Middle East and Europe."

70. Weiss and Wurzel, *Economics and Politics*, pp. 139 and 190–191.

71. Brookes, *Political-Military Relations*, p. 42.

72. Richards and Waterbury, *A Political Economy, 1990*, p. 402.

73. Ibid.; and Denoeux, "The Politics of Morocco's Flight," p. 6.

74. Ricardo, *Principles.*

75. Krueger, *Political Economy*, pp. 291–303.

76. Sadowski, *Political Vegetables?* p. 139.

77. Richards and Waterbury, *A Political Economy, 1996*, p. 34.

78. Ayubi, *Overstating the Arab State*, pp. 447–458.

CHAPTER 4

The Productive Sectors: Agriculture and Industry

Agriculture

Agriculture accounted for about 35 percent of employment and about 14 percent of output in the Middle East and North Africa in 1993 and has changed little since then. Despite this, the Arab world cannot feed itself, and a very large volume of food imports has been a feature of the economy for many years. Agricultural development is a prerequisite for industrial development: there are backward and forward linkages from agriculture to industry. The problems that have been faced in the rural sector have, therefore, had a negative effect on industry.[1]

In the time period covered in this book, the agricultural sector faced three main challenges. The first was the increase in demand due to rapid population growth. In order to maintain current, and not always adequate, levels of food self-sufficiency, as well as to prevent imports from increasing, output needed to rise in line with population growth and increasing per capita demand. Second, agriculture had to cope with the serious water crisis. Third, it had to face a range of policy-related problems concerning price controls, inputs, and landholding systems.

Labor moved from the countryside to the cities, and the latter consumed more imported food, often with subsidies on basic commodities. Austerity programs affected the agricultural sector, given the greater political sensitivity of changes in urban living standards. Governments tended to back larger, more successful farmers and provide irrigation systems, frequently at the expense of smaller, poorer farmers.

Between 1979 and 1997, agricultural production in the Middle East and North Africa rose by nearly 60 percent. This enabled the region to increase food production at the same rate as that of the population. Between 1980 and 1996, the volume of imports of food and animals also rose by 54 percent, but lower prices on international markets held down their cost. The net effect was a rise in the value of imports of 35 percent, to $20.6 billion. Exports increased in volume terms by nearly 100 percent, but as prices jumped sharply, the value of agricultural exports increased by 235 percent. Despite that, the food deficit rose from $12.5 billion in 1980 to $13.9 billion in 1996; in quantity terms, the import surplus rose from 34.5 million tons to 50.3 million tons.[2] Given the increase in population, that in the value of imports was moderate; the quantity increase reflected improved nutrition and more liberal import regimes, as well as weaknesses in agriculture.

In the nonoil Arab states, food accounted for about 50 percent of export revenues in the early 1970s. This fell to an average of about 30 percent in the 1980s and, in 1991, reached a low of 20 percent. By 1995, however, this amount had risen back to about 28 percent.[3] Imports of cereals as a share of consumption in the Middle East and North Africa rose from 15 percent in 1970–1975 to 33 percent in 1980–1985 and fell slightly to 30 percent in 1990–1996. In recent years, Egypt, Algeria, and Yemen imported 55 percent, 70 percent, and 85 percent, respectively, of their wheat flour needs.[4]

The main foodstuff, and single most important product, in the region is wheat. Imports of wheat by Arab countries increased from an average of 8 million tons in 1981–1982 to a peak of 12.2 million tons in 1989; there was a fairly steady decline to 8.6 million tons in 1996.[5] Wheat is largely produced in temperate regions with cooler climates and more plentiful rainfall than that found in the Arab countries. International trade theory advocates international specialization, and it is therefore efficient for the Arab countries to import cereals. The problem of self-sufficiency arises when the quantity and/or the cost of imports of a particular crop increase sharply. The cost of wheat imports, which averaged $1.8 billion in 1981–1982, peaked at $2.2 billion in 1984. Between 1993 and 1996, the quantity of wheat imported rose by only 3.6 percent, but the cost rose by 73 percent because of a rapid increase in international prices.[6]

A number of countries invested heavily in wheat production, particularly Saudi Arabia, which considered wheat to be a strategic commodity. In so doing, they rejected the economic orthodoxy based on the idea of comparative advantage.[7] Wheat production in Saudi Arabia amounted to about 266,000 tons in 1980. By 1985, the kingdom produced over

2 million tons, more than the domestic demand. Since 1987, Saudi Arabia has exported wheat, becoming the world's sixth largest wheat exporter, as output has exceeded both domestic demand and even storage capacity. In 1986, Saudi Arabia exported 588,000 tons of wheat worth $64 million. In 1991, it exported 2 million tons worth $275 million.[8] In 1995, output peaked at 5 million tons, but it fell to 2.4 million tons by 1997 as a result of changes in government policies designed to reduce subsidies and cut water consumption.[9]

The wheat production program, like other programs to develop food production, has been enormously expensive. Wheat is grown in the Ḥā'il and other areas northwest of Riyadh, using an irrigation system that draws water from underground aquifers. Farmers received subsidized loans, subsidized inputs, and free land, and they benefited from a protected market. They received relatively high prices for their products. In 1991, the government paid $2.2 billion to Saudi farmers for wheat. Procurement prices in that year were about four times the international level. This meant that instead of importing wheat at a price of $100 to $125 per ton, the government paid local farmers between $400 and $533 a ton.[10] The costs of this and other support programs in agriculture became a growing burden on the state budget.

Another problem caused by the wheat production program was the depletion of water resources. In 1987, agriculture accounted for 10 percent of Saudi Arabian water consumption. Wheat accounted for 5.3 billion cubic meters, and total agricultural use came to 14 billion cubic meters. With very little rainfall and little desalination for agriculture, the water came from underground aquifers. According to the Food and Agriculture Organization (FAO), these may be exhausted in thirty to forty years if they continue to be used at current rates.[11] As discussed in more detail below, Saudi Arabia began to change its agricultural policies in 1994, partly in response to the water shortage. In 1994, the Saudi Arabian government ceased to buy wheat from six major domestic producers. This had major effects on the agricultural sector and on the demand for water.

In Egypt, Morocco, and Tunisia, the population increased by over 2 percent a year from the 1950s until the 1980s. Between 1950 and 1980, the Egyptian and Moroccan populations doubled and the Tunisian population rose by 80 percent. None of these countries had new cropland on which to produce more foodstuffs, and urbanization reduced the amount of land available for agriculture. From the 1950s, the governments of these countries discouraged domestic food produc-

tion by controlling producer prices at relatively low levels so as to subsidize urban consumption. As a result, by 1980, Morocco and Tunisia
had lost the self-sufficiency in cereal production that they had in
1950.[12] Although cereal production rose in Morocco and Tunisia in the
1960s and 1970s, it did not do so fast enough to meet the needs of
expanding populations, and per capita output fell. More grains were
used as animal feed in the three countries, but the consumption of meat
was restricted to better-off sections of the population. The prices of
cereals on international markets increased sharply in 1974, and by the
early 1980s, Morocco was importing two-thirds of its cereal needs and
Tunisia, one-half.

In 1982–1983, wheat and flour subsidies cost the Egyptian government £E 758 million (approximately $1.1 billion), equal to nearly 8 per-
cent of total government revenues. The cost of wheat and flour imports
came to $834 million, equal to 15 percent of the government's total for-
eign currency earnings.[13] In 1987, Egypt imported 9 million tons of
wheat and was the fourth largest importer in the world. Population
growth, urbanization, and low producer prices with compulsory deliveries to the state of many products were the main factors behind the agricultural crisis in Egypt.

Reforms began in all three countries before the IMF- and World
Bank–backed programs did. They centered on increasing producer
prices so as to improve the incentives to farmers. Compulsory deliveries
to the state were phased out, and farmers were given much more freedom to choose what to produce in response to market forces. These
improvements were most dramatic in Morocco, where they were even
accompanied by import duties to prevent the entry of cheaper foreign
grains. There were riots related to increasing food prices in Morocco in
1981 and 1984 and in Tunisia in 1984. Egypt accelerated its agricultural
reform program in the early 1990s.

Agricultural development in Egypt is somewhat more representa-
tive of the Middle East as a whole, if only because few countries have
had the resources that Saudi Arabia has invested. In 1991, agriculture
accounted for nearly one-fifth of Egyptian GDP and exports and about
one-half of employment. The Nile Delta and valley are extremely fertile
and productive areas: three crops a year are the norm. Furthermore,
there are few water shortage problems like those that plague most of the
region. The sector has, in recent years, also benefited from extensive
economic liberalization. This resulted in reduced government interference in agriculture, which had squeezed resources out of the sector
mainly through the payment of low prices for compulsory deliveries of

basic goods to the state trading monopolies. These policies resulted in falling per capita agricultural production and rising imports until the mid-1980s.

At the end of the 1980s, Egypt removed most crop area allotments and delivery quotas at fixed procurement prices. Producer prices for most crops were liberalized and soon moved much closer to international levels. Fertilizer and pesticide subsidies were reduced, and the government encouraged the development of private-sector input and output marketing. Publicly owned land was sold. Finally, import controls were eased, and agricultural imports and exports were traded through the liberalized foreign exchange market. However, serious problems remain. Agriculture still receives free irrigation water, while urban demand for water is increasing. Moreover, the moves toward more economic rents for agricultural land have resulted in the displacement of some farmers and associated social problems.

Between 1991 and 1996, agricultural output in Egypt rose by an annual average of 2.7 percent, compared to a population growth rate of 2 percent. Food production per capita rose faster, by about 2 percent a year, with wheat output rising by 35 percent. Egypt's self-sufficiency in wheat rose from 28 percent in the mid-1980s to 45 percent in 1996, and there have since been large increases in the supply of fruit and vegetables, which have also contributed toward more stable and even lower prices.[14] Reforms of agricultural policy have been at the center of the economic changes implemented in many Arab countries in recent years. These changes have played an important part in stabilizing their economies, but much remains to be done. The fact that the Middle East is chronically short of water suggests that it should not rely on agriculture as a main source of income or exports. This implies that other sectors need to be developed that will, inter alia, supply the exports to fund food and other imports. In terms of stages of development, the sector that usually develops after agriculture is industry, specifically manufacturing. This is also the only sector in the region with the potential for large-scale employment.

Despite the fact that Morocco is one of the most industrialized Arab states, agriculture has played a crucial role there, and fluctuations in agricultural production have had major effects on the economy as a whole. In 1996, as a result of good rainfall levels, agricultural production increased by 78 percent. Other sectors of the economy grew very modestly, and GDP rose by 12 percent in real terms. In 1997, however, agricultural production fell by 26 percent. Despite the fact that mining output rose by 14 percent, that output in the energy and water sectors

rose by 10 percent, and that all other sectors experienced growth, GDP
fell by 2 percent. Fluctuations in agricultural production also affected
employment, given that the sector accounted for about 40 percent of
employment.[15] When the harvest failed, many workers left for the
towns and swelled the ranks of the unemployed (see Chapter 5).

Industry

Industrialization has long been considered the route to economic development, according to a wide range of experts, as well as on the basis of
the experience of developed countries, although there are differences of
opinion as to how it should be achieved.[16] Manufacturing is considered
even more critical for development than the industrial sector as a whole,
which also includes extractive industries, such as mining and oil. These
do not necessarily require significant quantities of labor; the product
can be extracted from the ground and exported without further processing. Manufacturing requires a mixture of labor, capital, and management expertise. It offers an opportunity to introduce modern technology
and economies of scale and to complement agricultural production.[17] It
does not guarantee development, but it nevertheless fulfills an important condition.

Manufacturing in the Arab states has been dominated by large-
scale, capital-intensive plants. Chemicals, nonmetallic mineral products, and basic metals accounted for about two-thirds of total manufacturing valued added (MVA) in the early 1990s.[18] Value added is a
measure of the difference between volume of inputs and volume of outputs; it indicates what is contributed to the value of a product by the
economy concerned. Since the 1970s, manufacturing in West Asia and
North Africa has grown faster than agriculture, services, or GDP.
Growth was dominated by the oil industry, which underwent a huge
expansion in the 1970s and early 1980s. Petroleum refining was the
largest single industry in the region accounting for 12 percent of MVA
in 1994, whereas high-tech industries accounted for only 8.2 percent of
MVA that same year. The share of manufacturing investment that went
to high technology in Egypt, Morocco, and Tunisia was between 4 and
6 percent in the 1990s, compared to 10 percent in Turkey and Iran and
even higher percentages in other developing countries.[19] This reflected
the lack of manpower, the low state of technology, and the low levels of
foreign investment in the region, among other factors.

Industrial development during the 1960s in Algeria, Egypt, Iraq, Syria, and Tunisia was strongly influenced by the Soviet model. This affected the planning system and resulted in an emphasis on heavy industry, large plants, and Soviet technology. The Arab regimes of the 1950s and 1960s rejected Western (previously colonialist) reliance on free markets in order to push forward structural change and industrialization. By the 1970s, they were all reconsidering their economic ideologies and are now at various stages of liberalization.

The period 1975–1985 was one of rapid growth in manufacturing output in many Arab countries, largely due to investments made possible by huge oil income earned in the region. The period from 1985 to 1990 was one of much lower oil income and of industrial consolidation. These factors do not account for all of the slowdown: the Iran-Iraq War resulted in a decline in production and value added. Many countries fared better in the second period, notably Syria and Tunisia. The reasons for the generally poor performance are analyzed below.

Between 1980 and 1996, value added in manufacturing as a share of GDP in Egypt rose from 12 percent to 25 percent; in Jordan it increased from 13 percent to 16 percent; and in Tunisia, from 12 percent to 18 percent. In Algeria, it remained constant at 9 percent, as it did in Morocco, at 17 percent.[20] The large increase in the share in Egypt was almost entirely due to petroleum refining, which developed rapidly from 1988 onward.[21]

The development of the manufacturing industry in the Arab world has been hindered by the way in which the public sector was run prior to reforms and by the environment in which the private sector existed. In many Arab countries, the public sector was run along politicobureaucratic lines: managers were appointed on the basis of their political loyalty to the relevant minister, and the system of decisionmaking was bureaucratic as opposed to being based on market considerations. (The adverse effects of this in Egypt were reviewed in Chapter 1.) The private sector was allowed to function in areas not reserved for the public sector. During the period of Arab socialism, the private sector was often subject to political hostility, and the legacy of this in terms of restrictive legislation and overregulation continues. The effects of uncertainty on private investment and thus on the private sector have been emphasized by the World Bank, and its recommendations have been implemented, at least in part, in Arab countries.

Arab countries with large populations, such as Egypt, Morocco, and Algeria, have to industrialize in order to provide employment. Egypt and Morocco have experienced growth in industrial production, but much needs to be done in terms of legal reform, environmental protection, manpower training, and export marketing. Countries with smaller populations, such as Syria and Jordan, face similar challenges, although on a smaller scale.[22] Tunisia is in the lead in terms of industrial development, but its internal market is limited and its export markets are problematic (see Chapter 6).

The GCC

In the Gulf Cooperation Council states, oil-related industries dominate; in Egypt, Iraq, Jordan, Lebanon, Syria, Morocco, and Tunisia, there is a more diversified pattern, with food, chemicals, and textiles being relatively more important. Industrial strategies in the GCC differ from those of the diversified economies in two important ways. First, they are designed to operate within very different resource bases. The second difference is ideological: GCC states have always been conservative, using state investments, although not in a socialist context. The state traditionally played a leading role because the domestic private sector was too small and too weak to act as an intermediary with multinational companies, which were the only ones that could provide the technology and know-how to develop capital-intensive and large-scale oil refineries and petrochemical plants, as well as aluminum smelters and other energy-intensive industries. Close links developed between the public and private sectors in GCC states as private-sector involvement was encouraged in small-scale industries and as shares in public-sector corporations were sold.

Most GCC states, like Iraq, have huge oil and gas resources. They developed their economies on the basis of the comparative advantages offered by these resources. The GCC states also have relatively small populations, and so employment generation was not a major objective when they began industrialization. The attempt to diversify by adding value to natural resources—refining oil and producing petrochemicals—has been welcomed by a number of experts, even though it has been far from successful.[23] As mentioned earlier, petrochemicals face problems in terms of selling abroad, as markets in Europe, North America, and, to a lesser extent, the Far East are locally supplied. There has also been a lack of coordination among GCC members in supplying the regional market.[24]

The structure of industry in the GCC is dominated by the production of oil. This has given the region a comparative advantage in petro-leum products and some advantages in other industries, such as alu-minum, which are heavy energy consumers. The oil and gas industry is examined in Chapter 5.

Given the region's huge petroleum resources, refining oil and pro-ducing petrochemicals offer the opportunity to add value and partially diversify the economy. Oil can be supplied to refineries at low cost because upstream costs in the GCC are the lowest in the world and because governments own and control the oil industry and can therefore direct oil where they want it. Saudi Arabia's petrochemical exports increased from $60 million in the early 1980s to over $2 billion in the early 1990s. The expansion of the industry in Saudi Arabia, Oman, and Qatar took place as a result of high petrochemical product prices in the early 1980s. Large investments were made at that time; the industry is very capital-intensive, and as a result, there are large economies of scale. In the early 1990s, due to an excess capacity, prices declined and the industry went into recession.

The petrochemical industry relies on two factors for its success: access to raw materials and access to markets. The most profitable loca-tions were traditionally those that combined both of those factors: the southern states of the United States offer the best example. Western Europe was a market-based location relying on imported raw materials, and the Gulf was a raw material supply-based location.

The GCC now faces tariffs on its exports of petrochemicals to the European Union and to other countries in the OECD, but these are being reduced under the multilateral World Trade Organization (WTO) agreements. The effect of the tariffs, along with high domestic taxes on oil products in the OECD, is of concern to the GCC states because it means that their main exports are at a disadvantage on international markets. The fact that most petroleum exporters were not members of the General Agreement on Tariffs and Trade (GATT) when the Uruguay Round agreements were signed meant that no major provisions were made to improve trade conditions for hydrocarbons.

Notes

1. Derosa, *Agricultural Trade and Rural Development,* p. 31.
2. Calculated from FAO, FAOSTAT database.
3. Alonso-Gamo, Annalisa, and Paris, "Globalization," pp. 22–23.
4. FAO, *Towards a Strategic Framework.*

5. Calculated from FAO, FOASTAT database.

6. Ibid.

7. Askari, *Saudi Arabia's Economy,* pp. 94–99.

8. UNCTAD, *Commodity Yearbook, 1993,* p. 125.

9. FAO, *State of Food and Agriculture, 1997,* p. 3, and calculations from the FAO's FAOSTAT database.

10. FAO, *State of Food and Agriculture, 1992,* p. 100.

11. Ibid., p. 99.

12. Swearingen, "Agricultural Reform," pp. 68–71.

13. Calculated from Sadowski, *Political Vegetables?* pp. 18–19.

14. FAO, *State of Food and Agriculture, 1997,* pp. 4–8.

15. EIU, *CP: Morocco, 1999–2000,* p. 27.

16. Chenery, *Structural Change,* p. 70; World Bank, *World Development Report, 1987;* and Handousa and Potter, eds., *Employment,* pp. 15–20 and 95–124.

17. Issawi, *An Economic History,* p. 169.

18. UNESCWA, *Survey of Economic and Social Developments, 1993,* pp. 122–123.

19. UNIDO, *Industrial Development Global Report, 1997,* pp. 30–32.

20. World Bank, *World Development Report, 1998–99.*

21. UNIDO, *Egypt,* p. 36.

22. Richards and Waterbury, *A Political Economy,* 1996, pp. 62–75.

23. Katouzian, "Oil and Economic Development," p. 53.

24. UNESCWA, *Survey of Economic and Social Developments, 1987,* pp. 109–110.

CHAPTER 5

Stabilization and Structural Adjustment in Egypt, Jordan, Morocco, and Tunisia

This chapter analyzes the reasons why Egypt, Jordan, Morocco, and Tunisia introduced stabilization and structural reform programs, including privatization, in the 1980s and early 1990s. It then examines what the changes were and their effectiveness.

During the 1960s and 1970s, Egypt, Jordan, Morocco, and Tunisia followed a policy of import substitution to industrialize. Imports were restricted in order to protect local producers, and the government set up public-sector firms to push forward industrialization. The state allocated credit and land, licensed private-sector activities, took control of foreign trade, and nationalized many sectors of the economy. Much of this activity was financed by external grants and loans, by workers' remittances, and by revenues from exports of oil and minerals. All of these sources of income were unstable and depended on economic and political conditions abroad.

The rise in oil prices in 1973–1974 and 1979 resulted in a huge accumulation of wealth in the Arab oil-producing countries. Those countries, in turn, provided financial aid to poorer Arab states and began to import workers from them. The latter remitted part of their earnings home, and in this way, inter-Arab labor and capital markets developed. This became the mechanism by which changes in oil wealth affected nonoil producers and relatively small-scale oil producers in the Arab world, both positively and negatively. Although rising oil prices meant that the Arab oil economies boomed, they hurt the poorer oil-importing Arab states. The net effect depended on whether the value of the aid received and the increase in remittances outweighed the cost of increase in oil prices.

Following the 1973–1974 oil price rise, the Arab states experienced an economic boom. Egypt, Jordan, Morocco, and Tunisia, not major oil producers, benefited from increased Arab aid, and Egypt and Jordan began to export workers to the Gulf. This resulted in a rise in remittances that helped to boost their economies. Although they were small producers by international standards, Egypt and Tunisia had significant oil resources, and oil sales constituted a large share of their exports. Morocco was a major producer of phosphates, the price of which quintupled after 1973. These countries, like others in the region, were able to increase investment and thus boost their rate of growth. They were also able to attract foreign capital because the rise in the oil price pushed the developed economies in the Organization for Economic Cooperation and Development into recession. Banks in the OECD region were flooded with petro-dollars, mainly from the Gulf, but the local demands for funds were limited. Western banks, therefore, were keen to lend to Middle East countries, which were growing relatively rapidly. The four countries thus benefited from an increase in incomes that was largely unconnected with developments in their domestic economies and that depended on changes in international markets.

During the 1980s, much of this pattern was reversed; 1979–1982 was a period of recession for nonoil-producing states. Oil prices tumbled after 1981, and the volume of funds sent to Western banks by Gulf oil producers declined sharply.[1] Real interest rates in the OECD rose, borrowing became more expensive, and Western bankers were less keen to lend to Middle Eastern countries after the oil price decline because their economies looked less attractive.[2] Aid from the rich to the poor in the Arab world fell, as did oil income in Egypt and Tunisia. By 1976, Moroccan phosphate prices had fallen back to their 1973 level, and so Morocco too suffered from a fall in rental incomes.

As a result of these changes in the international environment and the dependence of their economies on sources of income that were largely externally determined, the economies of Egypt, Jordan, Morocco, and Tunisia began to experience difficulties. These became so severe that during the 1980s, the four countries applied to the International Monetary Fund and the International Bank for Reconstruction and Development (IBRD; World Bank) for assistance. In 1983, Morocco began to implement economic reforms in cooperation with the IMF and the World Bank. Tunisia followed in 1986. In 1987, Egypt reached an agreement with the IMF that it did not implement, but in 1991, under different circumstances, it reached agreement and carried out radical changes. Jordan began to implement major reforms in 1989.

Following the collapse of oil prices in the early 1980s, aid extended by oil-rich Arab states to poorer ones declined. From 1973 to 1981, these inflows, together with remittances of workers, had exceeded the value of exported goods and services in the poorer Arab states (they reached 26.6 percent of GNP in Egypt in 1975).[3] In Morocco, official assistance from Arab countries and agencies fell as a share of GNP, from a peak of 12 percent in 1981 to a low of 6 percent in 1989. In Tunisia, it fell from a peak of 5.1 percent in 1981 to 3.6 percent in 1985. In Egypt, the peak in the 1980s was in 1984, at 13.8 percent, with a low of 8.1 percent in 1986. Most dramatic was the fall in Jordan, from 55.1 percent in 1986 to 15.3 percent in 1989.[4]

During the early 1980s, lower export prices and higher import prices caused a deterioration of the Arab terms of trade. As a result of this and of the reduction in aid and in incoming remittances, between 1980 and 1985, the total foreign debt of Egypt, Jordan, Morocco, and Tunisia rose from $34 billion to $67 billion. In 1989, it reached a high of $82 billion (see Table 5.1). Furthermore, the rates of interest paid on foreign borrowing rose in real terms, and the burden of financing foreign debt also rose. The burden of servicing the foreign debt rose as well. In 1980, it accounted for 13.4 percent of exports in Egypt, 11.2 percent in Jordan, 33.4 percent in Morocco, and 14.8 percent in Tunisia. In 1989, it reached 32 percent in Egypt, 19.7 percent in Jordan, 32.3 percent in Morocco, and 22.5 percent in Tunisia.

The decline in aid flows affected the whole economy and specifically government budgets. With increased deficits, one of the easiest items of spending to cut was investment, and as public investment was a large share of total investment, the latter fell, with serious consequences for economic growth. In the mid-1980s in Morocco and Tunisia and in the early 1990s in Egypt, following the introduction of economic reforms that, at least initially, meant an element of austerity, per capita income declined. The ability of the three economies to generate employment also fell. Hidden and then open unemployment became an increasingly serious problem.

Table 5.1 Foreign Debt: Egypt, Jordan, Morocco, and Tunisia, 1980–1996

	1980	1985	1989	1990	1994	1995	1996
Egypt							
Total debt (in millions $)	19,131	41,836	45,484	32,924	32,426	33,174	31,407
Short term as % of total debt	21.1	14.9	17.3	13.5	6.0	7.1	7.5
Total debt service paid[a] (in millions $)	1,235	3,014	2,907	3,074	2,264	2,413	2,309
Total debt as % of GNP	89.2	133.2	117.2	78.5	62.8	56.6	46.3
Total debt service as % of exports	13.4	27.6	32.0	26.6	14.8	13.1	11.6
Jordan							
Total debt (in millions $)	1,971	4,153	7,157	8,177	7,708	8,111	8,118
Short term as % of total debt	24.6	16.7	11.2	12.7	8.8	9.7	7.4
Total debt service paid[a] (in millions $)	210	558	594	625	564	614	656
Total debt as % of GNP	48.4	133.9	188.6	223.5	133.0	125.3	114.3
Total debt service as % of exports	11.2	18.0	19.7	20.3	13.6	12.7	12.3
Morocco							
Total debt (in millions $)	9,247	16,527	21,865	23,675	22,665	23,006	21,767
Short term as percent of total debt	8.0	7.4	1.3	1.8	2.1	2.2	2.7
Total debt service paid[a] (in millions $)	1,413	1,373	2,053	1,809	3,406	3,639	3,174
Total debt as % of GNP	50.7	136.5	100.8	95.3	74.2	72.8	61.1
Total debt service as % of exports	33.4	33.3	32.3	21.7	35.5	33.0	27.7
Tunisia							
Total debt (in millions $)	3,527	4,880	6,974	7,691	9,254	9,846	9,887
Short term as % of total debt	3.9	3.7	5.4	8.2	9.0	6.4	7.8
Total debt service paid[a] (in millions $)	545	746	1,101	1,432	1,423	753	692
Total debt as % of GNP	41.7	61.6	72.5	64.7	63.4	57.5	53.6
Total debt service as % of exports	14.8	25.0	22.5	24.5	19.2	17.0	16.5

Source: World Bank, *World Debt Tables, 1991–92;* and World Bank, *Global Finance Development, 1998.*
Note: a. Includes principal and interest.

Stabilization, Structural Reform, and Privatization: Definitions

The aim of stabilization programs advocated by the IMF and the World Bank is to reduce large budget deficits and the expansion of inflationary credit used to finance them. Emphasis is usually placed on cutting public spending, so stabilization programs reduce both total demand and that of the public sector. Other measures used in stabilization programs are increases in interest rates (to reduce domestic demand for credit and to encourage inflows from abroad) and restrictions on domestic credit and money creation. The IMF also encourages member states seeking its assistance to follow policies designed to raise interest rates to real levels (i.e., above the rate of inflation) in order to encourage savings and reverse capital flight. All these measures are also designed to strengthen the balance of payments. The IMF and the World Bank also place emphasis on the liberalization of foreign trade and the need to devalue overvalued exchange rates so as to encourage exports and discourage imports.

Structural adjustment usually refers to changes in relative prices and in institutions. These include changes in exchange rates and interest rates, and thus they overlap with stabilization measures. Structural adjustment is a longer-term policy than stabilization and is designed to increase the efficiency of the economy so that it can attain sustained growth with less government prompting than in the past. It includes tax reforms; reforms in the ownership, control, and operation of the financial sector; deregulation of the economy designed to encourage private-sector activity; and privatization.[5]

The IMF and the World Bank have several goals when they are called upon to assist in stabilizing an economy and then to help in structural adjustment. They aim to tackle large budget deficits, multiple exchange rate systems, negative real interest rates, balance-of-payments deficits, biases against agriculture, bloated and mismanaged public sectors, regulated credit markets, excessive bureaucracy, a lack of transparency in sales, and bias against the private sector and foreign investment.[6] Institutional changes advocated by the World Bank in connection with structural adjustment programs are centered on privatization, which is defined as the sale of assets by the public sector to the private sector or their transfer from the former to the latter. According to conventional economic theory and empirical evidence, private ownership is the most efficient system of ownership.[7] Privatization has therefore traditionally been advocated as a way of increasing the efficiency of an economy as a whole. There are, however, some limiting conditions on this statement, as well as serious controversies about the process.

The first is that where competitive markets do not exist, privatization is likely to create more problems than it solves. Privatization does not, by itself, bring about efficiency improvements unless it takes place in a competitive context. Furthermore, there is a danger that privatization can take the place of the much more complex and lengthy task of creating competitive markets. This involves a series of policy, legal, and institutional changes, with the correct sequencing and timing.[8]

Another problematic issue concerns the privatization of public utilities, such as telecommunications, gas, water, and electricity companies. In developed economies, organization and control of these companies are complicated endeavors, and under private ownership, they may become so acute that public ownership is preferable. This is because, under conditions of large economies of scale, high barriers to entry, or externalities, private ownership performs badly. These conditions of natural monopoly or restricted competition due to natural conditions create incentives and opportunities to exploit consumers. This reduces efficiency and thus makes the benefit of privatization questionable.[9] Publicly owned companies do not necessarily operate for the benefit of the public. Their managers may be political appointees rather than those appointed on the basis of merit. In the United States, publicly owned nuclear power stations have endangered public health, as they did in the Soviet Union and elsewhere in communist Eastern Europe. On the other hand, the massive growth in China's Guodang province between 1979 and 1992 was based on the activity of public-sector firms. In developing countries, where the government's ability to monitor and control the private sector is limited, the losses from privatizing natural monopolies may be greater.

Given all these potential dangers of privatization, Joseph Stiglitz has nevertheless identified a number of advantages of the process. When a company is privately owned, it is harder, although not impossible, for the government to subsidize it. It is also harder for the government to limit competition in the market in which the company operates. Privately owned companies will not be tied into public-sector job security or pay schemes that often provide tenure even when it is inappropriate and limits pay when incentives are needed. Private ownership without subsidies provides the competitive framework within which successful firms survive and unsuccessful ones do not.[10] The conclusion is that privatization will yield benefits for the economy as a whole only if it results in an increase in efficiency. And this will occur only under competitive conditions.

Egypt

The Egyptian economy grew impressively in the 1970s and early 1980s. This was due to increases in foreign exchange income from oil, the Suez Canal, tourism revenues, and workers' remittances. These sources of income, which were equal to 6 percent of GDP in 1974, rose to 40 percent in 1984. The increase in foreign earnings led to a real appreciation of the exchange rate, which in turn encouraged the development of noninternationally traded sectors of the economy, such as housing, infrastructure, and other services, at the expense of nonoil tradables, such as textiles, agricultural goods, and other industrial products. The rapid growth of the economy permitted income to grow and enabled the government to spend money on the badly neglected infrastructure. This effort included improvements in nutrition, life expectancy, educational enrollment, electrification, housing, and other services, all of which contributed to an increase in welfare.

The weakness in this pattern of development was that income inequality increased, as did reliance on imports rather than on domestic production. Furthermore, it was based on unstable sources of income that were largely determined by conditions abroad. The state benefited from the boom in that much of the income from foreign sources went to the treasury, and the state therefore became a major supporter of investment and welfare. This could not, however, be sustained when incomes fell in the 1980s; as a result, large budget deficits developed.

By 1975, Egypt had begun discussions with the IMF, for the first time since 1962. A letter of intent was signed in 1976, but reductions in food subsidies, which were part of the agreement with the Fund, resulted in major riots in January 1977. These riots have affected Egyptian policymaking ever since: they made the government unwilling to take steps that would reduce the living standards of the poor, especially in urban areas; and they made it impossible for the government to implement the reforms contained in the agreement.

In 1978, Egypt reached an Extended Fund Facility (EFF) agreement with the IMF for a three-year period. This enabled Egypt to obtain an additional $650 million from the Gulf Organization for the

Development of Egypt. As a result of the September 1978 Camp David agreement with Israel, the Gulf states stopped all concessional loans to Egypt. Western donors took their place. With increasing oil revenues, Suez Canal tolls, tourism receipts, and workers' remittances, Egypt did not need to implement IMF-based measures that called for budget cuts, austerity, and structural reforms. At the same time, it lagged behind on interest payments on foreign debt. In January 1981, Egypt's non-Arab creditors agreed to provide an additional $3 billion in concessional loans and grants.

In 1981, Egypt's foreign debt equaled about $30 billion, and its servicing cost $2.9 billion a year, $1.3 billion in repayments of principal and $1.6 billion in interest. Debt servicing consumed 28 percent of total foreign exchange earnings. During the period 1980–1984, Egypt's oil revenues fell by 36 percent and its other main foreign currency earnings were stagnant. Between the years 1981 and 1982 and in 1985–1986, the total value of exports of goods and services declined by 11 percent. In June 1986, the foreign debt equaled $46.3 billion. Although debt servicing increased more slowly in the first half of the 1980s than in the 1970s, military debt rose rapidly after the 1979 peace treaty with Israel. The debt service ratio in 1989 reached 32 percent when total debt equaled 117 percent of GNP (see Table 5.1).

In 1986, Egypt's oil revenues fell sharply, and workers' remittances plus Suez Canal tolls declined. Arrears on foreign debt had been accumulating since at least 1979, and by FY 1985/86, they had reached $2 billion.[11] In the same fiscal year, the balance-of-payments deficit equaled 15 percent of GDP. The economy had failed to adjust to the fall in international oil prices and the rising interest rates that led to huge increases in the balance-of-payments and fiscal deficits and to an unsustainable increase in foreign debt. The inability to service the foreign debt led to a reduction in capital inflows and the accumulation of foreign debt arrears.[12]

At the end of 1986, in response to the increasing foreign debt burden, accelerating inflation, large balance-of-payments and budget deficits, and slow economic growth, the government prepared an economic reform package. The main aims were to reduce the budget deficit, eliminate many price distortions by bringing energy and electricity prices closer to international levels, and increase the role of the private sector. A number of changes were introduced, but they were too late and too small to have an impact on accelerating inflation and the deteriorating balance of payments.

1987: A False Start in the Reform Process

In the spring of 1987, Egypt began consultations with the IMF on a standby credit, but by November of that year, the Fund cancelled the agreements signed because of Egypt's failure to comply with the conditions imposed by them. The IMF proposed that the Egyptian pound be devalued and that the multiple exchange rate system be replaced by a unified one. Interest rates were to be increased, something that was partly carried out. The budget deficit was to be reduced by increasing consumption duties, reforming income and sales tax, and converting firm-specific import duties and licenses to ad valorem duties. The IMF urged that subsidies on wheat, wheat flour, tea, and edible oil be reduced, but the government refused on the grounds that they formed a large part of the consumption basket of the poor. Product prices for cotton, sugar, and part of the rice crop, which were under government control, were increased in order to improve the incentive to produce, but the consumer price of these commodities was not altered. Under the standby agreement, the government agreed to increase petroleum prices so that they would gradually reach world levels.[13]

The failure to implement reforms in 1987 meant that many problems had accumulated and become more serious. The current account of the balance of payments, after improving in 1987, deteriorated sharply in 1988 and 1989. Debt servicing increased, both in terms of the amount paid and in terms of its ratio to exports. The volume of debt rose in 1988, and the share of short-term borrowing in total debt increased in the period 1987–1989 (see Table 5.1). Economic growth decelerated, and the budget deficit remained large. Foreign funding became less available and increasingly expensive, and as a result, the budget deficit was financed more and more by borrowing from the banks, which resulted in inflationary pressures. Inflation averaged 20 percent a year in the late 1980s (see Figure 5.1), and interest rates were negative in real terms. This discouraged savings and widened the gap between investment and domestic savings. The overvalued exchange rate encouraged imports and discouraged exports, thus widening the trade gap.[14]

At the microeconomic level, prices were highly distorted in that they were far from levels that market forces would have dictated. One example was the price paid to farmers for cotton, which was about half the international price. This provided farmers with little incentive to produce, and that was one of the reasons that the cotton export index

**Figure 5.1   Inflation: Egypt, Jordan, Morocco, and Tunisia, 1980—1997
(per Consumer Price Index, annual increase in %)**

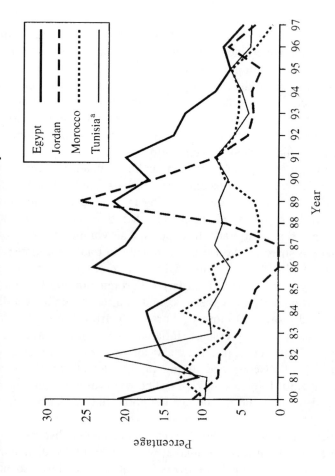

Sources: IMF, *International Financial Statistics Yearbook, 1997*; and IMF, *International Financial Statistics, August 1998.*
Note: a. Tunisia, 1980–1984: producer prices of home goods.

(1990 = 100) fell from a peak of 883 in 1966 to 420 in 1976 and to 48 in 1992.[15] Another example was the very low price of energy on domestic markets, which encouraged consumption and reduced oil exports.[16] These microeconomic distortions had negative macroeconomic effects on the growth of the economy and on the balance of payments.

The Reforms of 1991

The Gulf War of 1991 provided the Egyptian government with the opportunity to introduce radical reforms and the international community with reasons to reduce Egypt's debt burden. The government could sell the reforms at home as being a necessary part of Egypt's international commitments, and foreign creditors could reward Egypt for its participation in supporting the U.S.-led coalition against Iraq.

In May 1991, Egypt and the IMF agreed on a $372 million standby loan. This involved the government increasing energy prices, reducing subsidies (both explicit and implicit ones), unifying the exchange rate, increasing interest rates, liberalizing foreign trade, controlling the growth of credit, reforming the tax system, and reducing government spending and the budget deficit. The Paris Club agreed to a program of debt write-offs linked to progress in the implementation of the IMF package. Its members—the United States, the United Kingdom, Japan, Germany, France, Sweden, Switzerland, Belgium, Luxembourg, Australia, Netherlands, Austria, Spain, and Italy—agreed to write off $10.1 billion of Egyptian debt by mid-1994. This equaled 50 percent of the amount owed to those countries. The World Bank agreed to lend Egypt $300 million, and the African Development Bank, $250 million. A $400 million social fund was also assembled with foreign assistance. Its main aim was to help cover the social costs of structural change, especially compensating workers laid off as a result of privatization.

The Paris Club agreements stipulated that 15 percent of the debt would be written off by July 1991, another 15 percent by January 1993, and the final 20 percent by July 1994. There was also to be a reduction in interest payments on outstanding debt, together with a three- to four-year grace period. Finally, the remaining debt was to be rescheduled over a twenty-five-year period. The implementation of the write-offs would depend on how the reform program was carried out, and an IMF seal of approval would be required at each stage. In the spring of 1991, during the Gulf War, the United States wrote off nearly $7 billion of military debt, which had been costing Egypt about $700 million a year to service. The Gulf Arab states wrote off about $6 billion, none of which was being serviced.

The main feature of the 1991 stabilization program was a large reduction in the budget deficit (see Figure 5.2). This was done by cutting public-sector investment, increasing energy prices, and introducing a general sales tax and improved tax collection. The reduction in the deficit permitted a deceleration in monetary expansion, which in turn helped to reduce inflationary pressures. In the monetary sphere, nominal ceilings on interest rates were abolished, as were administrative controls on the allocation of credit. Treasury bill sales were introduced to control the amount of liquidity in the economy, and foreign exchange controls were eased with the movement to a unified exchange rate and then the creation of a unified exchange rate. This permitted greater mobility of capital in and out of the economy.

The reduction in inflation was a considerable achievement given the increases in government-administered prices that occurred between 1991 and 1993. The government also removed a significant number of commodities from price control, and the prices of other goods produced by monopolies were increased to levels closer to those of their international counterparts. In the field of foreign trade, a reduction in the dispersion of import tariffs was implemented. Almost all export quotas were abolished, as were many nontariff bureaucratic obstacles to trade. A securities market law was introduced to improve the functioning of the stock exchange. The public sector was restructured: seventeen diversified holding companies were set up, each with financial autonomy. The government ceased to provide investment funding and public credit guarantees. The aim of this reform was to prepare companies for privatization. Finally, the government took steps to improve the environment for private-sector business. Numerous controls and licensing requirements were either abolished or simplified, although many others remained in force, especially at the local level.

The 1991 package was very successful financially. The budget deficit was sharply reduced from 20 percent of GDP in FY 1991/92 to 1.6 percent in FY 1995/96. Excluding interest payments, the change was even more dramatic: from a deficit of 12.8 percent in FY 1991 to a surplus of 8.4 percent in FY 1995.[17] Interest payments on domestic debt rose as treasury bills were sold to cover much of the budget deficit. In order to stabilize the economy and attract funds from abroad, as well as to encourage saving, interest rates were sharply increased in 1991. This meant high interest payments on the treasury bills issued: in 1994, they

Figure 5.2   Fiscal Balance: Egypt, Jordan, Morocco, and Tunisia, 1980–1995 (Total Government Expenditure Minus Revenue as % of GDP)

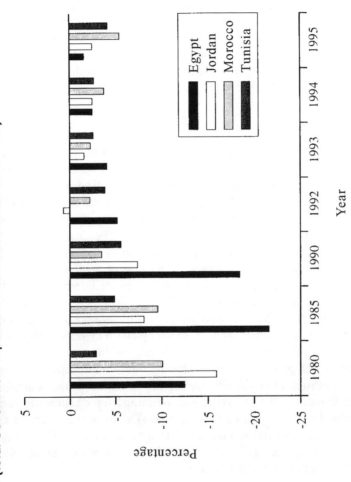

Sources: World Bank, *Trends in Developing Countries, 1995* and *1996*; World Bank, *World Development Report 1985, 1987,* and *1994*; Nsouli et al., *Resilience and Growth*; Maciejewski and Mansour, eds., *Jordan*; and IMF, *Government Financial Statistics, 1999.*

reached the equivalent of 11.3 percent of GDP. By 1995, they had fallen to 7 percent as a result of lower domestic interest rates and debt stocks that, in turn, were made possible by the decline in the budget deficit.[18]

At the same time, inflation decelerated and there was a major improvement in the balance of payments. The current account moved from a deficit of $1.3 billion in 1989 to a surplus of $1.9 billion in 1991. This was the result of the slowdown in the economy due to the Gulf crisis and the deflationary impact of the 1991 measures, which reduced demand for imports. There was also an increase in remittances as a result of higher interest rates on Egyptian pound deposits and the easing of exchange rate controls. Finally, the Paris Club agreements reduced the debt-servicing burden; the amount due in 1991 was $7.9 billion, while that in 1992 was $3.9 billion.

The Economy Since the Reforms

The World Bank has stated that the slow growth in Egypt in the early 1990s can be explained by the impact of fiscal austerity and by the monetary squeeze that was part of the 1991 stabilization program. The reduction in public expenditure, especially public investment, was supposed to make room for more private-sector investment and exports. This did not take place on a large enough scale because reforms of the tax system, public enterprises, and regulation of the private sector did not take place at the required pace.[19] One cost of the fiscal changes and financial deepening was an increase in the cost of interest payments on the domestic debt as a share of GDP to 11.3 percent in FY 1994/95. This resulted from the increased use of government bonds to finance the budget deficit and higher rates of interest paid on them. The payment of higher rates of interest was made possible by the ending of nominal ceilings on interest rates and the phasing out of administrative controls on the allocation of credit. The ending of foreign exchange controls and the unification of the exchange rate permitted freer capital movement and helped to attract funds from abroad. The most important of these sources were workers' remittances. As a result of the inflow, Egypt's foreign exchange reserves rose from $2.7 billion at the end of 1990 to $16.7 billion at the end of June 1996.[20]

Inflation was reduced from an annual average of over 17 percent in the period 1991–1993 to an annual average of 6.6 percent in the period 1994–1997.[21] This fall in inflation and the stable, nominal exchange rate that followed the 25 percent depreciation of June 1990–March 1991 resulted in a massive move from dollar denominated to domestic currency assets. The latter became more attractive since they paid relatively high interest rates, there was no perceived risk of devaluation, and the funds could be freely transferred out of Egypt. This movement of funds into domestic currency resulted in an appreciation of the real exchange rate by a cumulative 35 percent between February 1991 and June 1994. Consequently, imports became relatively cheaper, exports more expensive, and the economy lost competitiveness. This resulted in a worsening of the trade balance.

As service incomes rose, the current was much healthier in the 1990s than it had been in the 1980s. Between 1991 and 1996, exports of goods rose by only 15 percent in current dollar terms. There was a large improvement in nonoil exports from the manufacturing sector, but total exports continued to be dominated by traditional products: cotton goods and oil. Imports of goods rose by 25 percent, and as a result, the trade deficit increased. Exports of services, including tourism, rose by 27 percent between 1991 and 1995. Inflows of interest, profits, and dividends rose from 1991 to 1995. Current transfers (official assistance and workers' remittances) increased from 1991 to 1993 and then declined. The net effect of these trends was a current account surplus averaging $2.2 billion between 1991 and 1993 and an average deficit of $300 million in 1994 and 1997. The other major change in the balance of payments was in the capital account. As a result of the debt rescheduling agreements referred to above, the capital account moved from a deficit of $4.7 billion in 1991 to a surplus of about $2 billion in 1997.

Between 1991 and 1996, the economy benefited from the improvement in the fiscal balance and the balance of payments. Having taken painful steps in fiscal and budgetary policy, the government hesitated to deepen the process of structural change. The privatization process, which was at the heart of the reform program advocated by the World Bank, hardly progressed, and other institutional and legal changes were enacted very slowly. As such, in 1996, the public sector still produced nearly half of GDP and two-thirds of nonagricultural GDP, and in industry and mining petroleum, the public sector's share exceeded 60 percent.[22]

In January 1996, the new cabinet, led by Prime Minister Kamal al-Ganzoury, made privatization an economic priority. It published a list of 120 companies worth $4.1 billion, accounting for 45 percent of public enterprises, to be privatized. Port services and electricity distribution were included in the privatization program from 1997 onward. The inclusion of these infrastructure services was an indication of the seriousness of the program. Forty companies, mainly industrial in nature, were to sell the majority of their shares to the public. A total of sixteen companies were to sell 40 percent of their shares, and fourteen were to be offered for total sale. In addition, thirty-seven hotels were to be sold.[23] The aim was to sell $7.96 billion in assets in 1996, $5.9 billion from assets of 314 companies affiliated with 17 public-sector holding companies. The balance was to come from sales of joint-venture banks.[24]

Other measures announced in early 1996 included a reduction in import duties on capital goods and liberalization of the regulations affecting tourism and investment. Desert land was to be made available to industry without cost. Reforms in the housing market were also proposed: as a result of pro-tenant laws, which froze rents at low levels, an estimated 1–2 million housing units were vacant in early 1996. Investors refused to build housing for rent because of the lack of incentives. An easing of rent controls was announced, but the private sector's response was predicted to be cautious and slow.[25]

In October 1996, the IMF approved a two-year $400 million standby credit for Egypt. This replaced the three-year EFF agreement that had been signed in 1993. The IMF decision paved the way for the third and final stage of the 1991 Paris Club debt relief and rescheduling agreement to be implemented. In July 1991, 15 percent of Egypt's official and government-guaranteed debt to members of the Paris Club was written off. In March 1993, following the successful implementation of the next phase of the 1991 package, a further 15 percent was written off. The final phase was originally scheduled for 1 July 1994 and was linked to conditions set out in the 1993 EFF agreement. This provided for a 30 percent cut in interest payments on nonconcessional aid, with the remaining 50 percent of debt to be rescheduled over twenty-five years. This was implemented in October 1996 and was estimated to be worth $290 million in reduced debt servicing. The undiscounted value of the debt relief was worth $5.4 billion.[26] Between 1989 and 1994, Egypt's foreign debt declined by 29 percent, and its share of GNP fell from 117.2 percent to 62.8 percent; debt service as a share of exports fell from 32.0 percent to 14.8 percent (see Table 5.1).

The 1996 EFF was approved after Egypt agreed to a series of economic measures. These included a further reduction in the budget deficit to 1.1 percent of GDP in FY 1996/97. Additional tax reforms were to be introduced, including a new value added tax to replace the sales tax by 1 July 1997. Measures were to be taken to simplify the income tax system and to reduce civil service costs and employment levels. The implicit energy subsidy for petroleum was to be eliminated by July 1999, and gas and electricity prices were to be increased to their long-run marginal levels. Foreign trade was to be further liberalized, with the maximum tariff rate reduced to 40 percent and nontariff restrictions on imports and exports eliminated. The investment incentives system was to be reformed, and steps were to be taken to strengthen banking regulations.[27] The privatization of enterprises was planned to yield between 5 and 6 percent of GDP in fiscal years 1996/97 and 1997/98. As well as selling joint-venture banks to the private sector, a public-sector insurance company was to be sold in 1997, and two remaining joint-venture insurance companies were to be sold by June 1997.

Between 1993 and 1997, the growth rate of GDP increased every year, from 2.9 percent to 5.9 percent.[28] This five-year period of accelerating growth was unique in Egypt's postrevolutionary history because it was achieved against a background of low fiscal deficits and stability in the balance of payments. The latter was achieved despite a deterioration in the current account, largely due to an increase in imports resulting from trade liberalization. The foreign exchange reserves increased and inflation was reduced to 4.6 percent in 1997. At the same time, the banking system was strengthened and international recognition of Egypt's improved economic position led to a rise in portfolio investment from abroad.

The 1996 policy changes convinced markets that the government was serious about structural reform; most importantly, it accelerated the privatization program, liberalized the foreign trade system, and reformed the investment laws. The steps taken until then had concentrated on stabilization and had, inter alia, deflationary effects. The 1996 announcements also drew attention to the achievements of the stabilization measures of FY 1990/91 that provided a sound financial basis for structural changes. These steps were reinforced by the IMF's approval of a two-year standby credit of nearly $400 million on which Egypt did not need to draw.

Evaluation

The reforms of 1991 and 1996 were comprehensive, and the government implemented the packages of measures agreed upon with the IMF and the World Bank with a determination not seen before. In 1991, Egypt received considerable foreign aid, mainly in the form of debt write-offs, but the key difference from previous reform attempts was the government's willingness to reduce living standards and contemplate growing unemployment, which the initial stages of the stabilization program caused. This was the first time since the riots of 1977 that it had gone so far.

Egypt has a long way to go in terms of restructuring the public sector, reforming its bureaucracy, and improving the welfare of much of the population. Reasons for optimism, however, include the fact that the economy has, at last, started to grow at rates that allow for rises in living standards and increased employment. This has been achieved without reliance on unsustainable factors, which had boosted growth in the past. Unlike the 1970s and 1980s, recent budget deficits have been low and the balance of payments and foreign debt servicing have not been problematic. Most importantly, investment, industry, and agricultural production have grown.

Yet the dangers are socioeconomic: despite recent emphasis on health, education, and welfare, these systems remain inadequate. Another danger is that a surge in capital flows from abroad could pose threats in terms of financial management, as it has in East and Southeast Asia.[29] Net portfolio investment from abroad, which can be liquidated quickly, rose from $258 million in FY 1995/96 to $1.43 billion in FY 1996/97. Direct foreign investment, which is a longer-term flow, rose much more modestly, from $627 million to $770 million during the same period.[30]

Egypt's experience is, along with that of Tunisia, the most important example of the successes of economic liberalization in the Arab world. Its economic growth rate accelerated for five consecutive years despite weaknesses in traditional sources of income such as oil, Suez Canal tolls, and tourism.

Jordan

Jordan has a small economy, with a GDP of about $6 billion and a population of about 4.7 million. It has no oil, and its mineral resources—phosphates and potash—account for over half of its exports.[31] Managing the economy, like managing Jordan's foreign policy, has been a matter of tightrope walking. Yet the two are linked, because the country's crucial geopolitical situation has enabled it to extract a form of rent from the international system, mainly in the form of economic and military aid from Western Europe, the United States, and Japan.

The economy, which has a narrow productive base, had a large trade deficit in the 1980s and was heavily reliant on emigrant remittances and foreign aid. The economy grew at healthy rates in the 1970s and 1980s, and inflation was kept to 5 percent a year until the mid-1980s. There was, however, a large fiscal deficit that was mainly financed by foreign grants. The price system was heavily distorted by subsidies and government controls. This impeded the development of manufacturing and exports and reduced the efficiency of the economy

By the mid-1980s, the inflow of remittances and aid declined, largely due to the fall in oil revenues in the Persian Gulf. In the period 1976–1980, workers' remittances and foreign aid made available to the central government equaled about 37 percent of GDP a year on average. In the period 1986–1990, it fell to an annual average of 22 percent.[32] This resulted in a worsening of the balance of payments and of the government budget. The government reacted by increasing its borrowing: in 1985, total public-sector debt equaled 49.1 percent of GDP; and in 1990, it came to 126.5 percent. The foreign debt rose from the equivalent of 133.9 percent of GNP in 1990 to 223.5 percent in 1990.[33] At the same time, the government maintained price controls to counteract inflationary pressures, with the result that distortions and disincentives continued in the domestic economy.

In 1981 and 1982, the current account on the balance of payments deteriorated sharply, because foreign aid was not large enough to cover the trade deficit. The deficit persisted throughout the 1980s due mainly to the fall in transfers of workers and of aid from the governments in the Gulf.

In 1988, there was a large devaluation and an easing of monetary policy, which led to an acceleration of the inflation rate. In 1989, the government again devalued the dinar, unified the exchange rate system, liberalized the foreign exchange system, and introduced a package of measures to reform trade, agriculture, and the public sector. These measures were taken with the agreement of the IMF and the World Bank and constituted the first medium-term structural adjustment and reform program.

As a result of its strong reserves position in the early 1980s, Jordan found it relatively easy to raise funds on international markets. It used these funds to cover current as well as capital spending, and the ratio of foreign debt to GDP and to exports rose sharply. Repayment was bunched in the late 1980s, and accordingly, 20 percent of spending in the 1989 budget was allocated for servicing civilian debt.[34] In 1988, the growth of the external debt burden and the reduction in private capital inflows resulted in financial instability and bank failures. Investment fell, as did GDP: between 1986 and 1990, the average annual rate of growth of GDP fell continuously, from 7 percent to −13.5 percent. By the spring of 1989, the debt burden had become too large for the economy to fund, and IMF assistance was required.

In February 1989, drastic action was announced against moneylenders in Jordan as the dinar fell against foreign currencies. This followed rumors that the Central Bank was running out of reserves. In the same manner, Jordan withdrew a $150 million Euro-loan that it was trying to float because of the poor response it was meeting on international markets.[35] It also called for tight credit policies and ceilings on borrowing by the public sector. In April of that year, there were riots following the announcement of price rises agreed upon between the government and the IMF. At the center of the program was a large cut in the budget deficit. In July, Jordan reached agreement with its creditors in the Paris Club that accounted for 50 percent of its foreign debt. The rescheduling agreement resulted in debt relief worth $587 million over eighteen months. Other debt relief from countries outside the Paris Club was worth an additional $645 million.

Jordan's economy was seriously affected by the Gulf crisis of 1990–1991. Its trade links with Iraq were disrupted, and it therefore lost much of a major export market. Furthermore, it lost transit revenues from the shipment of goods from Aqaba to Iraq. Large numbers of Jordanians and Palestinians returned to Jordan from the Gulf, posing serious problems for the labor market. The country was also threatened with a loss of remittances, but this did not materialize because those who returned home brought funds with them. Many of them invested these funds in housing and in opening businesses, thus helping to stimulate the economy.

After the end of the Gulf War, economic reforms continued and Jordan benefited from economic aid from abroad. Inflation was kept at a moderate pace, although food prices rose as subsidies were cut, which caused social and political unrest. The current account deficit and the budget deficits were kept at manageable levels, but economic growth faltered sharply in 1996 and 1997 (see Figure 5.4 later in this chapter).

Like the other economies examined in this chapter, the process of reform did bring financial stability, but growth rates decelerated and problems of unemployment and poverty remained.

Morocco

Morocco's economic reform program began in the late 1970s, but only after 1983 were tougher measures taken to improve the balance of payments and to restructure the public sector. Since 1983, economic policy has experienced many zigzags and uncertainties. Despite this, there have been solid achievements in reducing inflation and in strengthening the balance of payments and the public-sector deficit. After 1986, the emphasis moved from stabilization to structural adjustment, and Morocco received strong external support. In the 1990s, however, the economy continued to suffer from bad harvests, which reduced overall economic growth and resulted in high unemployment.

In 1973, following the massive increase in international oil prices, the world price of phosphates quintupled. Phosphates were Morocco's major export, and the increase in export revenues that resulted from the price rise more than compensated for the rise in the price of such major imports as oil and wheat. On the basis of the increased export revenues, large increases in public-sector investment were implemented. Subsidies on commodities, many of which were imported, were increased, and in 1975, military spending rose as a result of the conflict in the former Spanish Sahara.[36]

By 1976, the real price of phosphates had fallen back to its 1973 level. This reduced the value of exports and government revenues, but public spending was not reduced accordingly. The external account went into deficit, equal to 16.5 percent of GDP in 1977, as did the state budget, the deficit on which reached 18.1 percent of GDP in 1976. These deficits were financed by large increases in foreign borrowing.

The second oil shock of 1979 came before Morocco had fully adjusted to that of 1973. Although measures were taken to stabilize the economy in 1978 and 1979, they were insufficient. By the end of 1982, foreign debt had risen to the equivalent of 68 percent of GDP, compared with about 18 percent at the end of 1979.[37] In March 1983, there was a foreign exchange crisis: foreign exchange reserves fell from $218 million in January of that year to $36 million at the end of June, and they were not enough to service the external debt and pay for vital imports.[38] Morocco turned to the IMF and the World Bank for assistance and embarked on a structural adjustment program.

Reform Programs Since 1983

There were significant differences between the policies followed by the Moroccan government in the period up to 1982 and those agreed upon with the IMF and the IBRD from 1983 onward. In the period 1976–1977, attempts were made to reduce domestic demand using restrictive monetary policies and increased taxation on imports. In 1978, public investment was reduced, import restrictions tightened, and import taxes increased further.[39] In 1980, the emphasis was more on increasing internal taxes than on import taxes. The anti-export and anti-import bias in economic policy weakened, but pressure for public-sector investment to meet social policy objectives continued. The 1983 budget was, as a result, expansionary, and this brought on the financial crisis of March 1983. The policies followed after 1983 involved reducing import taxes and licensing; the exchange rate depreciated in order to increase exports and reduce imports, and measures were taken to reform the domestic tax system and to restructure the public sector.

The economic policy in the spring of 1983 involved considerable zigzags. In March 1983, strict import controls were introduced, and then they were eased in order to reduce the damage to key sectors of the economy. The government resisted attempts to reduce the investment budget. When it realized that the only way to get IMF support was to reduce it, a revised budget was issued in July, with a 12.5 percent overall expenditure cut and a 27.3 percent reduction in the investment budget, along with promises of further cuts in the FY 1984/85 budget.[40]

In August 1983, details of the subsidy cuts were announced, and these resulted in sharp increases in the prices of a range of basic foodstuffs. In December 1983, electricity prices rose by 20 percent, and the price of other services provided by the state also rose: water, post, and public transport costs rose. Petrol prices, insurance premiums, and tobacco prices were also increased. Butane gas, used for cooking, also rose in price. Although minimum salary rates were increased in August 1983, those did not compensate for the rise in the cost of living. The measures were decided on in conjunction with the IMF and were designed to save between $135 and $160 million a year.[41]

At the end of 1983, King Hassan announced that an "income census" was to be carried out in order to determine who could afford to pay increased prices for basic commodities. The census was taken in December 1983, but it became clear the following month that price rises would affect the whole population and that the burden was not just to fall on the rich. In January 1984, riots thus broke out, and up to 600 people may have been killed in different cities in Morocco.[42] Following the riots, on 22 January, the king announced that the price rises would be cancelled. At the same time, the government accounted that the cancellation would apply to proposed price rises and not to those already implemented.[43] This announcement meant that $187 million would have to be added to the budget estimates for subsidy costs in 1984.[44]

On 21 March 1984, the king announced that as a result of the census, extra assistance would be given to the poorest sections of the population. Prices of basic commodities were to be frozen, and state subsidies for those items would be increased to $377 million, nearly double their 1983 level. In 1982, $203 million was spent on subsidizing basic commodities, and in 1993, $198.7 million. In 1994, they reached an all-time peak, despite the government's intention of reducing them. Along with the freeze on prices on basic commodities, the king announced a jobs creation program.[45]

Calls by the World Bank and others for economic reforms have been traditionally paralleled by domestic calls for political reforms. Both involve decentralization and a weakening of centralized control, which is exercised by corruption. In the context of economic growth, these reforms are possible because socioeconomic stability is not threatened. But in the case of Morocco, its reliance on a narrow range of products (including, of course, agriculture, which was subject to the vagaries of the weather) left it vulnerable to economic disruption. This was despite the diversification and liberalization program that Morocco introduced and persisted with over the last fifteen years, with the strong support of the IMF and the World Bank.

Morocco's privatization program was approved by Parliament in 1989. It proposed that 112 companies be privatized by 1996. The program was launched in 1992, and sales began in 1993, when a diverse group of companies were privatized. In 1994, the pace increased, with twenty-seven companies sold, including the major state holding company, Societe Nationale d'Investissements. In 1995, the original list of firms to be privatized was modified: some companies were withdrawn from the list and others were added, including the national airline and the telecommunications corporation. Between 1989 and 1993, the privatization program yielded 7.4 billion dirhams (DH) (equivalent to U.S.$820 million), of which DH 1.3 billion was raised in 1995.[46]

Despite the zigzags in policy, the Moroccan economy underwent considerable liberalization in the 1980s and early 1990s. In the period 1983–1985, the emphasis of policy was on fiscal contraction through reductions in public-sector investment and huge restraint. This was supported by tight monetary policy, including controls on the volume of credit and an exchange rate policy designed to improve the competitiveness of the economy and increase exports. Inflation averaged 7.5 percent a year in the 1980s, and the real exchange rate fell by 40 percent.[47] This helped to reduce imports and encourage exports. The main aim of the policy in this period was to stabilize the economy, especially the balance of payments.

The development of a consensus around the need for structural reforms was in place by 1986.[48] The reforms became more credible given the support of the IMF and the World Bank and by the leadership provided by the king and his endorsement of key technocrats who developed the policy. In addition, the beneficiaries of the reforms were already important supporters of King Hassan.[49]

The second phase of reforms, which began in 1986, stressed structural change rather than stabilization but did not ignore budgetary changes. Reforms of the tax system were introduced in order to increase its elasticity, improve the distribution of the tax burden, and reduce distortions. Public spending was brought under control, and changes were made in its composition. The exchange rate system was reformed to further reduce the number of distortions in the economy and enhance competitiveness. This involved linking the nominal exchange rate to a currency basket of Morocco's main trading partners. Tariffs largely replaced quantitative restrictions on imports, and tariff rates were reduced. The maximum tariff rate was reduced from 400 percent in 1980 to 60 percent in 1984 and to 35 percent in 1993.[50] There were also changes in the way in which public-sector companies were run. The investment code was modified, and pricing policies were reformed.

These reforms were supported by the IMF and the World Bank. The IMF provided nine arrangements between 1980 and 1993, committing Special Drawing Rights (SDR) 3.04 billion to Morocco under standby and extended arrangements. By the end of March 1993, Morocco had used SDR 1.73 billion. The IMF also provided technical assistance to the Moroccan government.[51] In addition, between 1983 and 1992, Morocco's official creditors in the Paris Club provided debt relief under six reschedulings, with a total value of $6.9 billion. Between 1986 and 1992, foreign commercial banks agreed on three reschedulings worth $6.7 billion. Moreover, between 1980 and 1993, the World Bank committed $5.4 billion to Morocco, of which $4.2 billion was disbursed.

The Economy Since the Reforms

In the period 1980–1983, prior to the reforms, the economy grew by an average annual growth rate of 2.4 percent. In 1984–1987, it grew by 4.1 percent, and in the years 1988–1991, it grew by 5.9 percent. This gradual acceleration suggests that the reforms were successful, but during the period 1992–1995, GDP nevertheless fell by an annual average of 0.3 percent. In 1996, GDP rose by an estimated 12.1 percent, but the following year, it was estimated to have fallen by 2.3 percent as a result of sharp fluctuations in agricultural production.[52]

The period 1980–1997 was therefore one of very unstable growth. According to the IMF, this was due to policy slippage, poor harvests, and the unfavorable development of Morocco's terms of trade.[53] The primary sector (agriculture, livestock, and fishing) provided inputs for different industrial subsectors, and so the fall in agricultural output due to drought affected wider sections of the economy. The scale of fluctuations in primary-sector output due to the weather was massive. In 1981, output fell by 28.6 percent; in 1987, by 23.6 percent; and in 1992, by 36 percent. In good years, such as 1982 and 1986, it rose by 35 percent and 36.7 percent, respectively. In 1982 and 1991, the primary sector accounted for 15.3 percent and 19.9 percent of GDP, respectively; in the drought years of 1981 and 1992, it accounted for 12.9 percent and 14.9 percent of GDP, respectively.

The aim of structural reform policies was to increase allocative efficiency within sectors; in agriculture, this resulted in a move towards a more profitable crop mix. Another effect was that the share of internationally traded goods in the economy rose. Within the traded goods sector, the aim was to reduce the economy's dependence on phosphates so as to make the composition of exports less reliant on volatile international commodity markets. In this respect, there was a significant improvement. Manufacturing output rose by an annual average of 4.1 percent in the 1980s, which was a considerable achievement given that this was the decade of restructuring, and it compared well with other countries undergoing similar processes.[54]

As we shall see for the case of Tunisia, Morocco's share of total investment in GDP fell during the 1980s and early 1990s. In 1976–1980, it was 27.4 percent; in 1980–1983, 25.6 percent; in 1984–1987, 24 percent; in 1988–1992, 23.2 percent; in 1992, 22.4 percent; and in 1996, 20.2 percent.[55] This was due to reductions in public spending that had accounted for the bulk of investment. The aim of the reforms was to encourage private-sector investment, and this was a major success. Noncentral government investment, which was accounted for mainly by that of the private sector, rose from 10.8 percent of GDP on annual average in 1976–1980 to 13.8 percent in 1980–1983, to 15.7 percent in 1984–1987, and to 19.4 percent in 1988–1991. In 1992, it came to 19.2 percent, and in 1996, to 16.9 percent.

According to the IMF, the productivity of investment increased in the 1980s because decisions were made on the basis of prices closer to those dictated by the market than previously. This meant that quality improvements made up for the fall in the volume of investment. The effect of this on growth was not clear, given the very unstable pattern of growth during the 1980s and early 1990s. It is likely that an increase in the productivity of investment benefited growth but was outweighed by other factors, such as adverse weather and the deterioration in the terms of trade.

Structural reforms were also intended to increase the savings rate, particularly from domestic sources, so as to improve the economy's ability to fund investment without incurring balance-of-payments problems. In countries where remittances are a significant and permanent feature, these can be tapped as savings from a "national" rather than a "domestic" source. Gross national savings rose from 16.5 percent of GDP in 1970–1980 to 17.5 percent in 1981–1983 and to 22 percent in 1985–1992. There was, however, no change in the share of domestic savings in GDP, and that of the non-central-government sector was estimated to have declined in the period 1989–1993 as compared with the period 1980–1988. Throughout this period, the government increased its savings, and remittances from abroad enabled the private sector to increase the share of gross national savings in GDP. The evidence of a significant domestic change resulting from the reforms is ambiguous. As in Egypt, the reforms did not attract remittances but did not significantly affect domestic savings.

Areas of unambiguous success were the reduction in inflation and the improvement in the balance of payments and the external debt. In the period 1980–1983, the consumer price index rose by an annual average of 9.7 percent. In 1984–1987, it rose by 7.9 percent, and in 1988–

1992, by 6.6 percent. In 1993–1995, it averaged 5.4 percent, and in 1996–1997, 2.0 percent.[56]

In the foreign sector, there was an improvement in the current account of the balance of payments. In the period 1980–1982, the deficit averaged $1.7 billion a year; in 1983–1985, it averaged $823 million; and in 1986–1988, it fell to $285 million. In 1989–1991, it rose to $465 million; in 1992–1994, it averaged $576 million; and in 1995, it jumped to $1.5 billion.

Although the reforms made it possible to borrow abroad with greater ease and on more favorable terms, they also reduced the amount of government investment that was financed by foreign borrowing. The other main change was the increase in manufacturing exports that occurred as a result of the removal of many distortions in the economy. The reforms attracted remittances, and there was a strong increase in tourism revenues in the 1980s. The diversification of exports and sources of foreign finance helped to insulate the economy from the effects of fluctuating phosphate prices and those of droughts. There was, therefore, an improvement in the current and capital accounts, at least until 1995 (see Figure 5.3).

From the mid-1980s, there was also a fall in the debt service burden. The volume of the debt peaked in 1984 and, as a percentage of GDP, was nearly halved by 1991. In 1985, the debt service ratio reached 70 percent of exports and fell to 40 percent in 1992. This improvement resulted from the debt rescheduling agreements. In 1990, as a result of Morocco's support for the U.S.-led coalition against Iraq, Saudi Arabia cancelled its $2.7 billion debt.

Economic growth was very weak during the period 1990–1996, averaging 2.9 percent a year. Even taking good and bad harvest years together does not change the general picture: in 1993, when the harvest was poor, GPD fell by 1 percent; in 1995, when there was a very bad harvest due to the lack of rain, GDP fell by 7 percent. The years that followed bad harvests saw a recovery: in 1994, GDP rose by 10.4 percent, and in 1996, by 12 percent, partly because of the low base of the previous years. As has been said, 1997 was another bad year, with a 2 percent fall in GDP (see Figure 5.4).

With a population growth rate of 2.1 percent a year, Morocco's average income per capita rose by 0.8 percent. Public-sector wages were frozen between 1993 and 1996; unemployment increased from 15.9 percent in 1993 to an average of 20.4 percent in the period 1994–1996. Urban unemployment increased from 322,000 in 1982 to 803,000

Figure 5.3 The Balance-of-Payments Current Account: Egypt, Jordan, Morocco, and Tunisia, 1980–1997

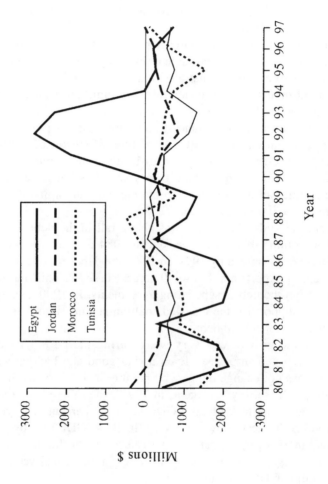

Sources: IMF, *International Financial Statistics Yearbook, 1997;* and IMF, *International Financial Statistics, May 1999.*

Figure 5.4 Growth of GDP: Egypt, Jordan, Morocco, and Tunisia, 1980–1997 (Constant Prices, Annual Increase %)

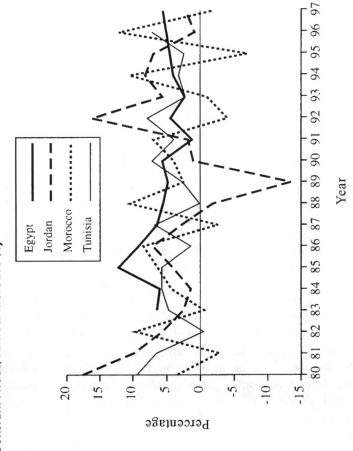

Sources: IMF, *International Financial Statistics Yearbook, 1997 and 1999.*

in 1990–1991, or from 12 percent to 20 percent.[57] In 1996, it reached
28.5 percent, due to the drought that caused major losses in agriculture
in 1993 and 1995 and cumulative effects on the whole economy. The
exodus from rural to urban areas accelerated as a result of the collapse
in rural output. This increased pressures on social services and the
infrastructure, but the number of jobs created outside agriculture was
not large enough to absorb all the new entrants into the labor market.[58]
The gap between rural and urban incomes rose as farm incomes were
affected by drought.[59] Unemployment among the young (fifteen- to
twenty-four-year-olds) was higher than the average rate. In 1994, it
peaked at 39.9 percent, and in 1996, it was 32 percent.

Evaluation

Morocco's various reform measures have had major effects on the
country's domestic and foreign finances. Inflation has been reduced, as
has the budget deficit. The balance of payments has strengthened, and
deficits on the trade account have become sustainable because the capital account is stronger. This, in turn, reflects the improved foreign debt
position. There are grounds for believing that allocative efficiency has
improved—that the economy has become more efficient—as a result of
the removal or reduction of many distortions.

   The real economy—industrial and agricultural production and
GDP—has performed less well. Growth has fluctuated sharply because
of the harvest: in 1995, for example, production in the agriculture, livestock, and fishing sector fell by almost 44 percent. It constituted nearly
15 percent of the economy in that year, and as a result, GDP fell by 7
percent. The socioeconomic effects of the bad harvest have been
described; what needs to be added is that it caused a sharp rise in
imports and a deterioration in the current account. What has changed is
that this did not cause a major financial crisis: the reforms had strengthened the foreign account to the point where the economy could cope
financially. Stable and sustained economic growth, however, remains
elusive.

Tunisia

Tunisia gained its independence in 1956 and then, in common with
other Arab and developing countries, began to establish a public sector

and to create a planning framework and government investment programs. Wages, prices, trade, and credit, as well as foreign exchange, were controlled by the state. At the same time, emphasis was placed on investment in education, health, and social security. In the late 1960s, private-sector investment began to be favored, and support was given to private-sector activity by means of protection against imports. Although the private sector was subject to many controls, between 1962 and 1971, it accounted for 22 percent of fixed investment. This investment was encouraged by the overvaluation of the exchange rate, which made imports of capital equipment cheaper than they would otherwise have been, and by low tariffs on intermediate goods and capital equipment. These factors, together with a well-developed banking system (which, until the early 1980s, was subject to credit and interest rate controls), helped to stimulate economic growth.[60]

The rise in oil prices during the early 1970s increased government revenues and enabled the government to pay higher wages to civil servants and to those working in the public sector. The 1970s were years of fast economic growth, averaging 7.4 percent a year. This growth was broadly based; real value added in the manufacturing sector increased by 11 percent annually. Investment rose from 20 percent of GDP in 1970 to 29 percent in 1980, and during the same period, savings rose from about 17 percent of GDP to nearly 25 percent. The budget deficit was low, averaging 2 percent of GDP in the 1970s, and the balance-of-payments current account deficit was also manageable, at the equivalent of 6 percent of GDP on an annual average basis. This was made possible by successful demand management policies and by a real depreciation of the exchange rate of the Tunisian dinar. Aid from abroad was largely concessional, and so the total debt servicing-to-exports ratio rose modestly from 10 percent in 1970 to only 12 percent in 1980.

In 1981, the international oil price fell, and there was a decline in the estimate of Tunisia's oil reserves. In addition, phosphate production and manufacturing output declined and exports fell. Agricultural output declined because of bad weather and agro-industries suffered as a result. The fall in petroleum and phosphate prices worsened Tunisia's terms of trade. Fiscal policies remained expansive, and monetary policy accommodated the fiscal expansion. The official response to the deterioration in economic conditions was to tighten price controls and restrict imports. This added to the rigidity of the economy and increased distortions. Between 1981 and 1984, domestic demand rose faster than GDP, resulting in pressure on the balance of payments. Tourism revenues and remittances declined, and interest payments on foreign debt rose. The foreign exchange reserves declined. In 1985, the budget deficit was cut and domestic price controls were liberalized, as were imports and investment terms, but the terms of trade continued to deteriorate, as did agricultural production and revenues from tourism.

The 1986 Reforms

In August 1986, the Tunisian government announced that a new economic strategy would be adopted. This was designed to improve the allocation of resources by ending controls on prices, trade, investment, and foreign exchange and by adjusting the exchange rate to a more realistic level via devaluation. More resources would be made available for the private sector by reducing government spending and by improving monetary management. A standby loan arrangement was also negotiated with the IMF, and this was followed by a four-year extended arrangement. In the same year, a loan was negotiated with the World Bank for the agricultural sector. In 1987, an industrial and trade policy adjustment loan was extended, and structural adjustment loans were made available in 1988 and 1991 and a second agricultural adjustment loan, as well as a public enterprise reform loan, in 1989. Tunisia did not seek debt rescheduling and serviced its debt on schedule.[61]

The economic reforms covered fiscal policy, monetary policy, and the banking system; changes in the way that the public sector was run; reforms of the investment code, designed to encourage the private sector; and reforms and rationalization of the foreign trade regime and the foreign currency systems. The details of each of these measures are outlined below, and then their effects on the economy are examined.

The problems of adjustment were first felt in the budget because the fall in oil prices reduced government revenues: in 1982, the petroleum sector contributed 20 percent of government revenues, and in 1986, 12.0 percent.[62] In addition, aid from official Arab sources declined as a share of GNP from 1.9 percent in 1977 to 0.2 percent in 1983.[63] The private sector and the balance of payments were also affected by a fall in remittances from 4.6 percent of GNP in 1982 to 3.2 percent in 1985.[64]

Fiscal policy reforms included the introduction of a value-added tax, a single personal income tax system, and a simplified corporate tax. These changes were designed to improve efficiency, equity, and the elasticity of the system. Tax incentives to the private sector were improved and numerous distortions removed. Measures were introduced to slow the growth of public-sector wages. Steps were also taken to gradually reduce subsidies.

The budgetary system itself was reformed, with all public spending and revenues coming under the budget. During the period 1982–1986, only 76 percent of public revenues and 37 percent of total government expenditures were recorded in the budget.[65] The net effect of these measures was a reduction in the ratio of total government spending and lending to GDP, from 40.7 percent in 1982–1986 to 33.4 percent in 1987–1991. The budget deficit, after allowing for grants received from abroad, fell from an annual average of 5.4 percent of GDP in 1982–1986 to 4.1 percent in 1987–1991.[66] These reductions were much less dramatic than those experienced in Morocco in 1983 or in Egypt in 1991 because the fiscal imbalance in Tunisia before the reforms began was less severe.

Public-sector investment was reduced, with the expectation that private-sector investment would take its place, thus initially maintaining and eventually increasing total capital formation. Efforts were made to increase the efficiency of investment by eliminating potentially unsuccessful projects and concentrating public resources on infrastructure, education, and health.

In the monetary sector, policy was designed to reduce the growth of domestic credit and the money supply and to move financial resources away from the public sector and toward the private sector. Interest rates were increased in 1987 in order to encourage the holding of interest-bearing local currency deposits and to discourage that of cash and foreign currency. Measures were also taken to strengthen the banking system and increase the role of market forces by reducing administrative controls. New financial instruments, including treasury bills, were introduced in order to deepen the capital market by providing an instrument for medium-term financial investments.

Structural reforms were designed to liberalize the economy by ending or reducing government controls and to open the economy toward exports. The measures included decontrolling prices at the production and distribution stages and reducing subsidies. In 1990, the share of agricultural and manufactured goods subject to price controls was 30 percent; in 1994, it was 13 percent.[67] Public-sector enterprises were transferred to nongovernment shareholders through either privatization or liquidating nonviable firms. By early 1993, forty public enterprises had been privatized. Controls in private-sector investments were eased, and the investment code was unified with the effects from 1994.

Foreign trade was liberalized through the lifting of restrictions on imports of raw materials, some finished products, spare parts, and capital goods. From 1985 onward, imports of consumer goods were also liberalized. The tariffs on imports were lowered, and their range was reduced in 1987–1988. In 1990, 74 percent of the economy was protected by quantitative restrictions on imports; in 1995, this had fallen to only 8 percent. The average tariff rate was reduced from 40 percent in 1986 to 33 percent in 1994.[68] Finally, measures were taken to make the dinar convertible. This involved increasing the allowances for invisible transactions carried out by the banks. Study allowances were increased for those going abroad, as were business allowances. In January 1993, it was announced that the dinar would be convertible for current account transactions. The only restriction remaining was on transferring capital abroad.

The Economy Since the Reforms

Tunisia's reform program consisted more of structural adjustment than stabilization. This was because the deficits in the budget and the balance of payments were less serious than in Egypt and Morocco. There was, therefore, less need to stabilize the economy by reducing demand, especially in the public sector. The structural adjustment program was implemented in 1986 with the assistance of loans from the World Bank for different sectors and with support from the IMF. Tunisia has gone further than any other Arab country in liberalizing its economy, both in terms of domestic policies and in terms of opening it to the world economy. Despite this, problems remained in the period under consideration.

Between 1982 and 1986, the economy grew by an annual average rate of 2.8 percent. In the period 1987–1992, growth averaged 5.2 percent. However, if longer periods are compared, then the pattern is reversed. Between 1976 and 1985, the economy grew by 11 percent a year; between 1986 and 1996, growth averaged 4.3 percent a year.[69] The slowdown was due to a number of factors. In 1990–1991 the Gulf crisis affected the level of economic activity throughout the Middle East; in 1992–1993, there was a recession in Western Europe, Tunisia's largest market, and there were three bad harvests in the years 1993–1995 due to drought. Additionally, the investment/GDP ratio declined.

This was due to uncertainties over reforms in the investment code and the elimination of duties on capital imports. Between 1992 and 1997, GDP grew by an annual average rate of 4.2 percent, well in excess of the rate of growth of the population.[70]

On the negative side, total investments, as a share of GDP, were lower after 1986 than before. In 1988, the rate fell to its lowest level, as a share of GDP, since 1960.[71] This was due to the reduction of public investment and the inability of the private sector to fully compensate for it. From 1988 to 1993, there was an increase in investment from 22 percent of GDP to 31 percent. Although these were higher levels than in many Arab states, they were lower than those experienced in the 1960s and 1970s. The capital output ratio, often referred to as the incremental capital output ratio, is the amount of extra investment or capital required to make an extra unit of output. This ratio fell from 10:1 in 1987 to 6:1 in 1992.[72]

The move to greater efficiency takes time and provides hope for sustained growth, but whether this growth will materialize remains an open question. The economy needs to continue to diversify and to develop the agricultural sector so that it is less affected by unfavorable weather conditions. And there is some evidence that this has begun. In 1988–1989, drought resulted in slow growth of GDP (1.8 percent) and relatively fast inflation (7.5 percent). During the 1994–1995 drought, the economy grew at 3.5 percent and inflation peaked at 5.5 percent. In 1996, the economy benefited from good rainfall, and an upturn in the European economy and growth was estimated at 7.1 percent and, for 1997, 5.4 percent.[73]

Positive achievements of the stabilization program included a reduction in inflationary pressures and an improvement in the balance of payments. The volume and burden of external debt also declined. Despite this, the World Bank stated that Tunisia's economic reform program has been progressing too slowly, and it is consequently falling behind such competitors as China and Turkey. Between 1990 and 1994, Tunisian exports per head increased by an annual average of 2.5 percent in real terms, compared to a 5 percent average in the developing world. GDP per capita rose by an average of only 2 percent a year, also less than the average for developing countries. The World Bank urged the government to speed up the liberalization of foreign trade, continue privatization, and increase the flexibility of the labor market.[74]

In 1996, the World Bank agreed to provide $250 million in loans to help Tunisia implement its association agreement with the EU. These loans were designed to help fund employment services and retraining. They were also intended to help private entrepreneurs improve the quality of their products and to help the government cope with the loss of revenue from import duties due to the agreement with the EU. The Bank agreed to provide an additional $250 million in return for a government promise that 122 companies would be privatized.

Tunisia's reform program has been praised as one of the most successful in the Arab world. It has succeeded because the government has lived up to its commitments. It has worked closely with the IMF and the World Bank in implementing very orthodox proposals. The president, Zine al-Abidine Ben Ali, backed decisions taken by Western-trained and oriented technocrats who were given the authority to develop reforms.[75] The significance of presidential support for the reforms was considerable and contrasted with the weaker economic policymaking system in Egypt.[76]

Evaluation

Tunisia's successful implementation of reforms since the mid-1980s has been widely recognized. Although the rate of growth has been slower in many years since the reforms than before, growth has been sustainable in that it has not induced budgetary, balance-of-payments, or foreign debt crises.

Tunisia suffers form a chronic trade deficit, which averaged $1.9 billion a year between 1992 and 1997. It was partly financed by tourism revenues and by the remittances of Tunisian workers abroad. These sources of finance were not large enough to finance the trade deficit. There was also a deficit on the service account, and the volume of transfers did not cover the total of the two deficits. As a result, the current account of the balance of payments was in deficit throughout the period. The size of the deficit depended in large part on unstable sources of foreign revenue; as such, the economy was vulnerable to changes in the international economy.

In the period 1990–1995, the European Union accounted for about 80 percent of Tunisian exports and 70 percent of its imports. Its exports have been heavily concentrated: clothing and textiles account for about 50 percent of exports. Its share of European markets has failed to grow at anything like the rate of its competitors in that market. Furthermore, its position in the EU market for textiles and clothing will deteriorate as the terms of the Multifiber Arrangement (MFA), which gave it privileged access, are abolished.

European countries have invested in Tunisian plants producing textiles and clothing for the European market. These plants do not have free access to the domestic market, which remains protected. As a result, a dual system has developed; one for export and another for the domestic market. Because of the protection offered to producers for the domestic market and the restriction on entry into the domestic market placed on the exports, the technologies, costs, and efficiency levels of these plants have varied.

After three disappointing years, 1993 to 1995 in which GDP rose by an annual average of only 2.6 percent, 1996 and 1997 saw a recovery, with an average annual rate of 6.3 percent. This took place against a background of low inflation, averaging under 4 percent a year, despite rises in administered prices. The balance of payments remained manageable, with imports rising as a result of higher investment, which accounted for 26.1 percent of GDP. Gross savings also rose to 22.7 percent of GDP in 1997, one of the highest rates in the Arab world.[77]

Notes

1. Mattione, *OPEC's Investments,* p. 12, table 2.5.
2. Thomas et al., eds., *Restructuring Economies,* p. 11.
3. Divan and Squire, "Private Assets," p. 69.
4. van den Boogaerde, "Financial Assistance," p. 87.
5. el-Erian and Fennell, "The Economy of the Middle East," pp. 9–11.
6. Henry, *The Mediterranean Debt Crescent,* pp. 38–43.
7. Vickers and Yarrow, *Privatization,* p. 426.
8. Nellis and Kikeri, "The Privatization of Public Enterprises," pp. 78–79.
9. Vickers and Yarrow, *Privatization,* p. 428.
10. Stiglitz, *Whither Socialism?* pp. 171–196.
11. Amin, *Egypt's Economic Predicament,* pp. 16–17.
12. World Bank, *Trends in Developing Countries, 1996,* pp. 152–158.
13. Holt and Roe, "The Political Economy of Reform," p. 204.
14. Richards and Waterbury, *A Political Economy,* 1996, p. 226.
15. Calculated from IMF, *International Financial Statistics Yearbook, 1994.*
16. Richards, "The Political Economy," pp. 1721–1730.
17. World Bank, *Trends in Developing Countries, 1996,* p. 155.
18. Ibid.
19. World Bank, *Trends in Developing Countries, 1995,* p. 158.

20. IMF, *International Financial Statistics, June 1997.*
21. Calculated from IMF, *International Financial Statistics Yearbook, 1997;* and IMF, *International Financial Statistics, August 1998.*
22. World Bank, *Trends in Developing Countries, 1996,* p. 152.
23. *MEED,* 1 March 1996.
24. *MEED,* 8 March 1996.
25. *Middle East Executive Report,* March 1996.
26. EIU, *CR: Egypt, 1996,* no. 4, pp. 39–40.
27. EIU, *CP: Egypt, 1996–97,* p. 15.
28. Calculated from IMF, *International Financial Statistics, June 1998.*
29. Subramanian, "Egypt."
30. *MEED,* 12 April 1998.
31. World Bank, *Peace and the Jordanian Economy,* p. 23.
32. Calculated from Maciejewski and Mansur, eds., *Jordan,* p. 14, table 3.2.
33. Ibid., p. 26, table 4.2; World Bank, *Global Financial Development, 1998.*
34. EIU, *CP: Jordan, 1990–91,* p. 31.
35. *MEED,* 7 February 1989.
36. Horton, *Morocco,* p. 5.
37. Ibid., p. 6.
38. EIU, *CR: Morocco, 1983,* no. 4, p. 9.
39. Horton, *Morocco,* p. 31.
40. EIU, *Quarterly Economic Report (hereafter QER): Morocco, 1983,* no. 4, p. 9.
41. EIU, *QER: Morocco, 1984,* no. 2, pp. 6–8.
42. Ibid., p. 6.
43. Ibid., p. 10.
44. Ibid., p. 17.
45. EIU, *QER: Morocco, 1984,* no. 3, p. 17.
46. EIU, *CP: Morocco, 1996–97,* p. 11.
47. Richards and Waterbury, *A Political Economy,* 1996, p. 237.
48. Nsouli et al., *Resilience and Growth,* p. 8.
49. Richards and Waterbury, *A Political Economy,* 1996, p. 239.
50. Nsouli et al., *Resilience and Growth,* p. 8.
51. Ibid.
52. IMF, *International Financial Statistics, August 1998.*
53. IMF, *World Economic Outlook, May 1998,* pp. 152–153.
54. Richards and Waterbury, *A Political Economy,* 1996, p. 238.
55. IMF, *Morocco,* p. 8.
56. Calculated from IMF, *International Financial Statistics, August 1998.*
57. Richards and Waterbury, *A Political Economy, 1996,* p. 238.
58. IMF, *IMF Survey,* 13 January 1997.
59. EIU, *CP: Morocco, 1996–97,* pp. 14–16.
60. UN, *World Economic and Social Survey, 1996,* p. 160.
61. Nsouli et al., *Path to Convertibility,* p. 2.
62. Ibid., p. 6, table 1.

63. van den Boogaerde, "Financial Assistance," pp. 41 and 89.

64. Ibid., p. 84.

65. Nsouli et al., *Path to Convertibility*, p. 5.

66. Ibid., p. 6, table 1.

67. World Bank, *Trends in Developing Countries, 1996*, p. 506.

68. Ibid.

69. IMF, *International Financial Statistics Yearbook, 1997;* and IMF, *International Financial Statistics, August 1998*.

70. Calculated from IMF, *International Financial Statistics, June 1998*.

71. UN, *World Economic and Social Survey, 1996*, p. 163.

72. Ibid.

73. IMF, *International Financial Statistics, August 1998*.

74. EIU, *CP: Tunisia, 1996*, p. 15.

75. Richards and Waterbury, *A Political Economy*, 1996, p. 233.

76. Rivlin, "Soft and Hard States."

77. IMF, *World Economic Outlook, October 1996*, quoting Press Notice 98/45, Internet version dated 26 June 1998.

CHAPTER 6

Syria's Hesitant Road to Reform

This chapter looks at the reforms that have been enacted in Syria since the late 1980s. These reforms were drawn up and implemented without the involvement of the IMF or the World Bank or other international bodies. The reforms have been extremely hesitant and have been sacrificed to political needs; the economy has suffered as a result.

Between 1990 and 1994, the Syrian economy grew at a healthy rate, but there was little structural change. The balance of payments benefited from inflows of foreign aid and remittances, and it attracted expatriate Syrian capital. Oil revenues were also high, and the economy enjoyed the benefits of having one of the strongest agricultural sectors in the Arab world. Syria, however, has been one of the slowest countries in the Middle East in tackling the problem of rapid population growth. Accordingly, the annual increase in the labor supply was rapid, and when the rate of economic growth decelerated in the second half of the 1990s, one of the results was a rise in unemployment.

The Economy in the 1970s and 1980s

In the 1970s, Syria's gross domestic product increased by an annual average of 10 percent in real terms.[1] Agricultural production rose by 8.6 percent a year on average, while industrial production increased by 9 percent, and that of services by about 11 percent.[2] Although the 1970s were years of growth, the economy did not experience structural change. This meant that while in 1970, agriculture accounted for 20 percent of GDP, industry 25 percent, and services 48 percent, in 1980

135

and in 1990, the shares were virtually unchanged. The increase in the share of industry was due to the development of the oil sector rather than to the industrialization of the economy; the share of manufacturing in the economy hardly changed.

In the early 1970s, the Syrian economy experienced nationalization, protection against imports, large-scale investment by the state, the expansion of the public sector, restrictions on the private sector, subsidization of many goods and services, a multiple exchange rate system, and tight controls over the movement of capital in and out of the country. The banking system was totally controlled by the government, and capital was allocated on the basis of politicobureaucratic decisions. Following severe economic difficulties in the mid-1980s, a move toward economic liberalization occurred in the late 1980s and the early 1990s.

Economic policy in the 1970s focused on import substitution, which meant that domestic production was favored and protected by taxes and quantitative restrictions on imports. Emphasis was placed on increasing industrial employment and expanding the role of the public sector, while at the same time, private-sector activity was permitted within strict limits. The broad aim was to transform the country within the ideological framework of Arab socialism, from an agriculturally based economy to an industrial one. Industry was to be the leading sector; it would embody new technology, which would increase productivity, output, and living standards.

Syria benefited from foreign aid from both the USSR and the Arab Gulf states, some of which was used to fund public-sector investments. Private remittances also increased as Syrians joined other Arab emigrants to work in the Gulf after the 1973–1974 rise in oil prices. As a result of the decline in Gulf oil revenues in the mid-1980s and disputes between Syria and the GCC states over Syria's support for Iran in the Iran-Iraq War, capital inflows declined. The fall in the oil revenues of Gulf states also reduced the demand for Syrian labor there, and remittances consequently declined. These factors, accompanied by bad harvests due to drought in 1982–1984, led to a near-zero economic growth rate between 1982 and 1985. This deterioration, in turn, led to a series of changes in economic policies, at first in the direction of austerity and later toward liberalization.

Given the country's backward technological state, turnkey projects were imported; whole factories were bought from foreign firms, and they supplied personnel to set them up. They therefore required very limited Syrian inputs and labor in the early stages. Syria lacked the skilled labor to operate many of these factories, and the heavily politicized and centralized management systems employed failed to make optimal use of the investments after they were completed. Many investments were made, but the results, in terms of output, were disappointing. After the October 1973 war, financial aid from Arab Gulf states increased. These funds were used to purchase industrial equipment in order to set up new factories.[3] The projects were not absorbed into the economy, and when technical problems arose, Syria was dependent on foreign labor to put things right.

Most economic activity was carried out within the framework of a series of five-year plans that were all inspired by the Soviet Union's experience and that were used in other Arab countries that had adopted models of Arab socialism. The main aim of the plans was to generate fast economic growth through public-sector investment. The emphasis of the plans varied, with a larger share of funds being allocated to industry in the 1970s and 1980s than in the 1960s. The share of services in total investment doubled from about 20 percent in the first plan (1961–1965) to 41 percent in the sixth plan (1986–1990). The share of agriculture declined from 40 percent of investment in the first plan to 19 percent in the sixth plan, but it received a greater emphasis in the seventh plan (1991–1995).[4]

Another important aspect of these plans was the breakdown of investment between the public and the private sector. In the 1970s and 1980s, the public sector was dominant: its share in total planned investment rose from 63 percent in the first plan (1961–1965) to 81 percent in the fourth plan (1976–1981). However, the actual amount invested in the public sector was always much lower than planned; in the first plan, it came to 32 percent, half the planned level. In the subsequent five plans, it varied from a peak of almost 70 percent in 1971–1975 to a low of 55 percent in 1986–1990. This was due to the failure of the government to obtain finances for projects in the plan and its inability to undertake all that it hoped to because of administrative failings. On the other hand, the private sector exceeded its share in every plan, suggesting that a more decentralized approach would have been more successful.

The 1980s were much more problematic for the Syrian economy than the 1970s. Between 1980 and 1990, the economy grew by an annual average of only 2.4 percent. Syria's military involvement in Lebanon deepened, and its support for Iran in the war against Iraq resulted in its isolation within the Arab world. This was another factor explaining the

decline in capital inflows from the Arab world. It was against the background of slow economic growth and balance-of-payments difficulties
that Syria began to reform its economy in the late 1980s. This was not
done on the basis of a comprehensive program, but rather as a series of
ad hoc attempts to cope with increasing internal pressures.[5]

Economic Developments in the 1990s

Some of the problems that affected the Syrian economy in the 1970s
and 1980s continued into the early 1990s. These included rapid population growth; reliance on rental incomes, such as workers' remittances
and foreign aid; a very small manufacturing sector; formidable bureaucracy and politicization of the public sector; high defense spending and
a large military establishment; economic isolation; and water and electricity shortages. The government subsidized prices through a complex
budgetary system and administered other controls, with distorting
effects throughout the economy.

The period 1990–1994 was one of fast economic growth, with GDP
increasing by an annual average of 7.5 percent. In the period 1995–
1996, it was 6.5 percent, and in 1997–1999, it was estimated at –2.9
percent (see Figure 6.1). The deceleration was due to a number of factors. The manufacturing sector suffered from increased competition
from imports that resulted from the liberalization of foreign trade. The
adoption of more stringent financial policies by the government
squeezed demand and thus helped to slow the rate of growth. Crude oil
production and refining output declined in 1996. The very sharp fall in
imports, together with the weak export performance in 1997, also suggests that the economy experienced a slowdown from 1996. A liquidity
crisis in the second quarter of 1994 that developed when a number of
pyramid financial schemes in the informal capital market collapsed
caused financial losses and reduced confidence in the economy.[6] These
trends were reinforced by a drought that had severe effects on agricultural production in 1999.[7]

Like many other Arab countries, Syria has traditionally depended
on a number of external sources of income. These have included aid
from Arab states (in the form of loans and grants) and remittances from
workers abroad. In recent years, oil exports revenues have also played
an important role in economic growth, and these are, at least in part, a
function of internationally determined prices and demand. Changes in

Figure 6.1 Growth of GDP: Syria, 1990—1999 (% per Annum)ᵃ

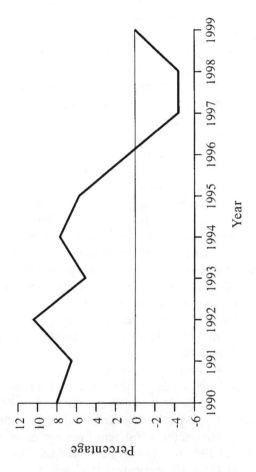

Sources: IMF, *International Financial Statistics, December 1998;* EIU, *CR: Syria, 1999,* no. 3; U.S. Department of State, *Country Commercial Guide, appendix B.*
Note: a. Figures for 1998 and 1999 are estimates.

aid and remittance flows, as well as in oil revenues, have had significant effects on the economy, but their levels have been largely outside the control of the government. Since 1994, there has also been a significant inflow of capital from Syrian residents abroad who have been investing in new projects under Investment Law No. 10 of 1991.

The increased resources available to the economy from abroad have been used to increase investment. In 1990, investment equaled 13 percent of GDP; in 1995, it was 16 percent. This rise says nothing in itself about the sustainability of the investment rate or the efficiency of its use. An indication that the increased rate was not sustainable is the fact that the excess of imports over exports rose from the equivalent of 0.4 percent of GDP in 1990 to 7.1 percent in 1995. This meant that investment and consumption, or domestic demand, were increasingly reliant on imports. Given the weaknesses of Syria's balance of payments, this would not be sustainable in the long run.

Although economic reforms have not been comprehensive, there have been some changes in recent years. These have had ideological significance in that the regime now wants the private sector to play a major role, especially in investment. Private capital has been invested in sectors of the economy that were previously closed to it. In 1994, private investment was permitted in heavy industry, cranes, turbines, generators, iron and steel, cement, and flour milling. In the same year, subsidies on electricity and fuel oil were reduced, and the government announced that public-sector firms should begin to operate on a commercial basis with much less interference from the state. In 1996, a private concern was permitted to build an electricity-generating plant and a sugar refinery. Interest was also expressed by the private sector in investing in a petroleum refinery.

In 1985, the private sector accounted for 34 percent of total gross fixed investment and the public sector accounted for 66 percent. In 1990, the figures were 55 percent and 45 percent, and in 1995, 56 percent and 44 percent, respectively. This reflected two trends. The first was a reduction in public-sector investment from a peak of 13.3 billion Syrian pounds (£S) in 1985 to a low of just under £S 5 billion in 1990 and £S 8.6 billion in 1995, all in constant 1995 prices. It also reflected an increase in the volume of private-sector investment, from £S 6.8 billion in 1985 to £S 6.7 billion in 1990 and £S 11.0 billion in 1995, also measured in 1995 prices.[8] This shift in the pattern of investment was, perhaps, the most important achievement of the liberalization program.

The efficiency of investment may have improved as market forces and the private sector played a greater role in the economy and as investment decisions were made more on an economic than on a politicobureaucratic basis. There are, however, no accurate measures of the efficiency of investment. Large investments were made in the transport sector, with a huge increase in the number of minibuses imported. This was a response to shortages that had been experienced and led to economic improvements, but investment needed to be concentrated in industrial productive capacity to have a sustained effect on the economy. The failure to invest more in sectors where the payoff was in the medium or long term reflected the private sector's lack of willingness to take risks.

In the period 1986–1989, there was a near–40 percent decline in the volume of investment. In 1990, a recovery began, but by 1995, the level of investment was still 2 percent lower than in 1985.[9] Since 1990, investment (mainly in the private sector) has increased, but domestic savings have not. In 1990, savings and investment were in balance: domestic savings equaled 16.9 percent of GDP, while investment came to 16.5 percent. By 1994, savings were 16.2 percent of GDP, while investments equaled 30.3 percent and were increasingly funded out of the external deficit. The gap between domestic savings and investment rose from 0.4 percent of GDP in 1990 to 14.2 percent in 1994, which meant that the economy had become reliant on foreign funding to maintain its rate of growth. Both the public and private sectors imported capital to fund investment projects. One of the objectives of economic policy was to encourage the repatriation of Syrian funds, and this occurred after the introduction of Law No. 10 in 1991. The open question was whether the sources of funds would be available in the future. The weakness of the economy was the low level of domestic private savings, which was related to the lack of development of the banking sector and the low level of average incomes. The share of investment in GDP fell from 29.3 percent in 1995 to 25.2 percent in 1996.[10]

Structural change takes time, and it is therefore necessary to measure development over a period of five to ten years. Figures from the United Nations on the structure of Syria's GDP are available for the period up to 1994. Table 6.1 shows that between 1980 and 1994, agriculture's share in the economy declined by 4.1 percent; the mining and quarrying sector's share tripled as a result of the expansion of the oil sector. Although manufacturing increased in absolute terms, it was very significant that its share in the economy declined. In 1998, it accounted for only 7 percent of GDP, less than in 1985.[11] The government services

Table 6.1   GDP by Kind of Activity: Syria, 1980–1994
            (% in 1985 Prices)

	1980	1985	1990	1994
Agriculture, hunting,				
forestry, and fishing	25.1	21.2	20.0	21.0
Mining and quarrying	7.2	7.1	23.2	20.3
Manufacturing	6.3	7.7	5.5	5.8
Electricity, gas, and water	0.1	0.2	0.8	0.9
Construction	5.8	6.8	2.5	2.5
Wholesale and retail trade,				
restaurants, and hotels	22.7	22.2	17.9	19.7
Transport storage and				
communication	8.3	9.8	10.5	11.7
Finance, insurance, real estate,				
and business services	6.7	5.0	4.4	4.6
Other services	2.5	2.7	1.7	4.7
Government services	15.3	17.3	13.5	8.8
GDP	100.0	100.0	100.0	100.0

Source: UN, *National Accounts Statistics, 1993 and 1994,* pt. 2.

sector expanded rapidly between 1980 and 1985, and then its share fell in the late 1980s and 1990s.

There were also changes in the external sector. The value of Syrian exports fell from $4.2 billion in 1990 to $2.9 billion in 1998. Exports to Russia, other former members of the USSR, and formerly communist countries of Eastern Europe declined from a value of $1.4 billion in 1990 to $100 million in 1998. The European Union took an increased share of Syrian exports: 42 percent in 1990 and 50 percent in 1998, but the value of exports nevertheless fell by 8 percent.[12]

Population Growth

The rapid growth of Syria's population is the most serious problem facing the country. In 1960, Syria had a population of 4.6 million; in 1996, it was 14.6 million.[13] There are signs that the rate of growth is slowing, but it remains fast and poses formidable problems in terms of providing basic services and employment (see Table 6.2).

In 1996, the deputy prime minister for economic affairs stated that the annual population growth rate had reached 3.5 percent, which added

**Table 6.2   Population: Syria, 1987–1997
(in Millions)**

1987	10.97
1988	11.34
1989	11.72
1990	12.12
1991	12.53
1992	12.96
1993	13.39
1994	13.84
1995	14.32
1996	14.62
1997	14.95

Source: UN, *Demographic Yearbook, 1997.*

450,000 people a year,[14] and in the same year, President Hafez al-Assad referred to Syria's population as between 15 and 16 million.[15]

Syria was one of the last countries in the Arab world to experience an end to demographic explosion.[16] Population growth rates in most of the Arab states of North Africa, including Egypt, stabilized and began to decline in the period 1985–1990. This slowdown was due to lower birthrates. As explained earlier, it takes eighteen to twenty-five years to see the effect of such decreases in the labor market, for not until then is there a reduction of the number of new workers looking for employment each year. But there has been a revolution in the demand for education and other services, which, in terms of demands on the state budget, has offset the decline in population growth.[17] In 1960, Syria and Tunisia had populations of similar size, 4.6 million and 4.1 million, respectively. By 1996, Syria's population had increased more than threefold, to 14.6 million, while Tunisia, which has gone further than any other country in the Arab world toward population transition, experienced a rise of 117 percent, to 9.1 million.

The crude birthrate in Syria remained roughly constant between 1960 and 1987. Over the five subsequent years, it declined by 11 percent. Death rates fell dramatically, by two-thirds between 1960 and 1992, with much of the improvement occurring after 1975. The combination of a slow fall in the birthrate and a rapid decline in the death rate (at least until 1987) constituted an increase in the natural rate of growth in the population. This rose by 28 percent between 1960 and 1975. The rate peaked at 4 percent a year in 1987, an exceptionally high rate of increase by international standards, and declined to 3.6 percent in 1992. This remained one of the highest rates of increase in the world.

Syria's population policy has hovered between two poles. The first was designed to increase the population in what was felt to be an under-populated country: more people would strengthen the nation politically and economically. But since the 1970s, there has been greater emphasis on providing women with access to education and work rather than encouraging them to have more children. Although more women were being educated at higher levels and the female participation rate in the labor force rose, this did not reduce fertility rates. By the 1980s, though, with the economy in crisis, there was a decline in fertility.[18]

In 1999, the United Nations published estimates of possible future trends for the Syrian population. Under a medium-variant forecast, in the year 2000, the population would reach 16.1 million; in 2005, 18.2 million; and in 2010, 20.3 million.[19] The World Bank has estimated that Syria's population will stabilize by the year 2035. By that time, it will have reached 66 million. A stable population is defined as one in which age and sex-specific mortality rates have not changed for a "long" time and fertility rates have remained at replacement levels.[20] The UN's fore-casts have been criticized for being too pessimistic, but two prominent demographers who have provided alternative and more optimistic esti-mates suggest that the population will reach 26.4 million in the year 2025.[21]

These forecasts indicate that, even with an active population policy, demographic growth will remain a major problem in Syria. It will rein-force the trend toward urbanization and will put pressure on the food and water supplies, as well as on government spending. It will result in a relatively high rate of increase in the labor force for many years, with serious consequences for employment and for socioeconomic stability. This is the reason why Syria cannot afford to stand still economically. If the economy fails to grow, then unemployment will increase and per capita incomes will fall.

The Labor Force

Closely related to the issue of population growth is the increase in the Syrian labor force, a function of the combination of population rates and the rate of actual participation in the workforce. There has been an increased recognition of the seriousness of this problem in recent years. At the beginning of 1997, a report was published in the Syrian press that stated that the labor force would rise from 4.225 million in 1994 to 7.29 million in 2011. This was based on a forecasted population of 21 million in 2011 and an increase in the share of women in the workforce, from 16 percent in 1995 to 25 percent in 2011.[22] The cost of providing employment for an additional 3 million people by the year 2011 has been put by a Syrian source at $60 billion.[23]

Natural growth is the first factor determining how fast the labor force will grow. The potential number of those seeking first-time employment equals the number of twenty- to twenty-four-year-olds in the population (the age of entry into the job market rises as educational opportunities expand), which depends on the number of people born each year. In 1985, there were 751,000 in this age group; in 1990, 886,000; and in 1994, just over 1 million.[24] Syria is expected to experience an increase in the number of potential job entrants until the year 2015; only after then will the benefits of lower birthrates begin to be felt on the job market. Other Arab countries, most notably Tunisia, will experience a decline from as early as the year 2005. If, in 1990, there were 100 new job entrants in each of Syria and Tunisia, then in the year 2005, there will be 200 in Syria and 130 in Tunisia. In the year 2015, there would be over 200 in Syria and under 100 in Tunisia.

This analysis assumes that the female participation rate in the labor force remains stable. Yet it is reasonable to assume that it will rise, as it has in the past: between 1970 and 1992, the female share of the labor force rose from 12 percent to 18 percent. In Tunisia, it rose from 12 percent to 25 percent.[25] According to Phillippe Fargues, in the unlikely event that women catch up with the men's level of economic activity by 2025 (as measured by their participation rate in the labor force), the total demand for employment will rise by 300 percent over its 1990 level. In Tunisia, the increase was forecast at 70 percent. In this scenario, population growth will contribute 125 percent to the growth in demand for jobs in Syria and only 15 percent in Tunisia. The balance will be due to the increase in the female participation rate.[26]

In 1978, unemployment was officially estimated at 90,000, or 1.6 percent of the labor force. In 1991, it came to 236,000, or 2.7 percent.[27] These official figures understate the problem of unemployment, but the fact that the official rate rose is an indication that the problem is becoming more serious. There is also the problem of underemployment—that is, workers in the public sector and elsewhere who produce little and are a burden on the organizations that employ them and the economy as a whole.

The Manufacturing Sector

There are a number of features of the manufacturing sector in Syria that were significant in the late twentieth century. First was the very small share of the sector in the economy. In 1992, manufacturing accounted for just under 6 percent of GDP, a very low share even by Middle Eastern standards. For comparison, in Turkey, its share was 23 percent; in Jordan, 15 percent; in Egypt, 12 percent; in Morocco, 19 percent; and in Tunisia, 17 percent.

The second feature consisted of the sharp fluctuations that occurred in manufacturing output. In the 1980s, and especially between 1986 and 1989, the economy as a whole was subject to severe fluctuations, but changes in manufacturing output were even more severe. During the period 1970–1980, MVA rose by an annual average of 5.9 percent. In the 1980s, it rose by only 0.7 percent, and in the period 1990–1993, by 6.7 percent; but that was not enough to increase its share of the total.

The third feature was the low ratio of value added to gross output. As explained earlier, value added is a measure of the relationship between output and inputs; it measures the original contribution of the sector in question, the net of the value of inputs. In 1993, value added equaled 13.4 percent of gross output in manufacturing. The average for the period 1983–1992 was 15.5 percent. Value added in 1992 was only 5.5 percent above its level ten years earlier. The low level of value added reflected the state of development in Syria. In South Korea, by way of contrast, there was an increase in the share of value added in gross manufacturing output from 24.6 percent in 1983 to 26.4 percent in 1992.[28]

Another important feature of the manufacturing sector was the degree of public ownership. No figures are available on the sectoral level, but they can be reasonably approximated on the basis of trends in the economy as a whole. The private share accounted for a growing proportion of manufacturing activity in the late 1980s and early 1990s. The low share of manufacturing in GNP can be explained by the low investment priority that it received in the 1980s, the inefficiency of the investment process, the inability of the economy to absorb turnkey projects, and the failure to allocate credit to the manufacturing sector. In the early 1990s, the state allocated more for investment in manufacturing, and the private sector was being encouraged to invest as well. These two factors made the increase in output possible.

Oil

Oil has been the leading sector in the Syrian economy since 1990. In 1992, the level of oil production was more than three times its 1982 level. In 1986, oil revenues were $336 million; in 1995, they rose to $2.4 billion (see Table 6.3). In 1995, oil accounted for about 20 percent of GDP and 60 percent of exports.[29] As is shown in "The Fiscal Balance" section below, it also accounted for a substantial part of government revenues. Oil, more than any other factor, permitted the economy to grow and gave the government unprecedented room for maneuver.

More than a dozen foreign oil companies have explored for oil in Syria since the late 1980s. They were encouraged by Shell's discovery on the Euphrates River in Dayr al-Zur in eastern Syria. The other

Table 6.3   Oil Production and Revenues: Syria, 1986–1998

	Production (in Thousands b/d)	Export Revenues (in Millions $)
1986	200	336
1987	288	449
1988	312	407
1989	350	1,907
1990	408	1,903
1991	473	1,836
1992	542	2,157
1993	588	1,939
1994	598	1,983
1995	610	2,352
1996	600	2,541
1997	563	2,177
1998	553	1,342

Sources: Arab Petroleum Research Center, *Arab Oil and Gas Directory,* Paris 1999; and calculated from EIU, *CP: Syria, 1996–96* and *1996–97,* and EIU, *CR: Syria, 1998,* no. 4, and *1999,* no. 3.

companies failed to discover oil outside Dayr al-Zur, and their exploration contracts expired. In some cases, other companies took over the
areas being explored.[30] Between 1987 and 1990, remittances of profits
by foreign oil companies from Syria annually averaged $624 million. In
the period 1991–1994, this increased to an average of almost $1.2 bil-
lion (see income debit figures in Table 6.7).

On 1 January 1997, Syria had estimated proven oil reserves of 2.5
billion barrels, which at the rate at which it was used in 1996, would
last for 11.3 years.[31] At present, about half of Syria's oil production is
exported.[32] The future volume of exports will depend on domestic consumption levels. A growing economy will consume more oil, assuming
no change in the relative price of oil inside Syria. A stagnant economy
would result in little growth or a decline in consumption. Under the first
scenario, oil export revenues would fall both because of decreasing production and increasing domestic demand; under the second, they would
fall because of declining production.

Gas

Proven reserves in 1991 were estimated at 225 billion cubic meters, of
which associated gas, produced as a by-product of oil, accounted for 97
billion m³.[33] In 1996, reserves were estimated at about 200 billion m³.[34]
At the current rate of use, these reserves will last for about fifty years.
Syria's gas reserves are, by Middle East standards, relatively small, and
this means that its export potential is very limited. Given plans to
increase domestic use of gas in generating electricity, there is unlikely
to be a surplus for export. The expansion of gas production in Syria has
been even more dramatic than that of oil. In 1984, production was estimated at less than 10 million cubic feet per day—about 100 million
ft³/d in 1986 and about 500 million ft³/d in 1995. Gas accounted for 3.2
percent of domestic energy needs in 1990, and it was forecast that it
would meet 30 percent of these needs by the year 2000.

The government wants to use gas in power stations and in industrial
plants in order to increase the availability of oil for export. But the
process of conversion has been slow. Consumption (both for electric
power generation and other uses) has risen very sharply from about 100
million ft³/d in 1992 to about 500 million ft³/d in 1995. It was forecast
to reach about 700 million ft³/d in the year 2000.[35]

Electricity

In September 1993, in response to massive electricity shortages that had resulted in continuous blackouts, President Assad stated that "every citizen has the right to a steady supply of electricity."[36] Contracts were awarded for eight 125-megawatt (MW) gas-fired plants, to be financed by Kuwait. This measure, together with large increases in government expenditure in the electricity system, was a response to years of prolonged power cuts. The relatively fast economic growth of the early 1990s exacerbated the shortages and brought the system to near collapse.[37] In 1993, 11.7 billion kilowatt-hours (kWh) of electricity were generated. In 1994, this increased by nearly 20 percent, to 14 billion kWh, and in 1995, by a further 16 percent, to 16.2 billion kWh. This was the result of the government's investment program and the availability of foreign finance. By way of contrast, Israel, with a population of 5.8 million, had a generating capacity of 7,736 MW in 1996 and production of 32.5 billion kWh.[38]

Two power station projects were completed in the 1980s, adding only 600 MW to the nation's generating capacity. In the early 1990s, a Russian-built plant went into operation after a decade of construction, and this added only 400 MW. Installed capacity in 1994 was 4.157 million kilowatts (kW); 0.9 million was provided by hydroelectric sources and 3.257 million by thermal power stations. An additional 2,000 MW were required by the year 2000 to cope with a forecasted growth of demand of 7 percent a year. The projected cost of the expansion program was about $1 billion in 1995 prices.[39] A 1,000-MW plant at Aleppo (costing $400 million and being financed by Saudi Arabia), a new 300-MW plant near Damascus, and the expansion of the Tishreen power station on the Euphrates are all being planned. Japan has also agreed to lend Syria the equivalent of $585 million to build a new 600-MW power station at al-Zara. In 1986, Japan lent Syria the equivalent of $175 million to expand the Banias power plant, and in 1991, it lent the equivalent of $383 million for the construction of the 600-MW Jandar power station.[40]

In early 1994, AEG of Germany was awarded a contract to build five electricity substations, but the European Investment Bank has blocked funding for the contract because of arrears on debts owed by Syria to EU states.[41]

Agriculture

Agriculture accounts for a larger share of employment in Syria than in the rest of the Arab world. As has already been mentioned, Syria has one of the strongest agricultural sectors in the Arab world. In 1992, the food gap, or difference between food imports and exports, was $187.6 million, or $14 per capita.[42] This compared favorably with a food gap in the United Nations Economic and Social Commission on West Asia (UNESCWA) area as a whole (Lebanon, Syria, Yemen, Bahrain, Kuwait, Oman, Qatar, South Arabia, Egypt, Jordan, UAE, Iraq) of $10.6 billion, or $82 per capita. According to UNESCWA, Syrian agriculture progressed because of increased investment, reforms of agricultural pricing, and other policies.[43]

In 1993, Syria had a cultivated area of 5.7 million hectares, mainly rain fed. Agriculture accounted for 30 percent of employment and 60 percent of nonoil exports.[44] Industries closely related to agriculture—textiles, leather, tobacco, and food processing—accounted for 25 percent of output in the economy and about 50 percent of manufacturing employment. Agricultural production rose by 30 percent in the decade 1986–1996; but on a per capita basis, it fell by 4 percent. Given the increase in the population of nearly 40 percent, this was a considerable achievement (see Table 6.4).

Table 6.4 Agricultural Production: Syria, 1988–1998 (in thousands of tons) (1989–1991=100)

	Production			Production Per Capita		
	Agriculture	Cereals	Food	Agriculture	Cereals	Food
1988	126.3	198.7	130.1	134.8	214.0	139.1
1989	87.3	45.3	86.7	90.3	47.1	89.6
1990	105.0	122.4	106.8	105.1	123.4	106.9
1991	107.7	132.3	106.6	104.7	129.5	103.6
1992	126.9	181.9	125.0	119.9	173.0	118.1
1993	114.8	219.5	116.2	105.6	203.3	106.9
1994	121.8	221.3	124.9	109.1	199.7	111.9
1995	132.5	244.0	135.4	115.7	214.7	118.3
1996	148.0	238.9	150.7	125.9	204.7	128.2
1997	136.9	174.1	131.5	113.6	145.4	109.0
1998	156.6	219.2	154.2	126.7	178.5	124.7

Source: FAO, "Production," *Yearbook, 1998,* vol. 52.

A major emphasis was placed on the production of cereals for domestic use, and this resulted in a 40 percent increase in the area planted with cereals between 1979–1981 and 1995, a 26 percent rise in yields, and a 90 percent jump in production. Production of cotton lint rose by 55 percent over the same period.[45] Imports of cereals fell from $382 million in 1990 to $192 million in 1994. In 1992, Syria achieved self-sufficiency in wheat, with a harvest of 3 million tons; in 1996, wheat production reached 4.2 million tons. Wheat is grown in the private sector, but the state-run General Establishment for Cereal Processing and Trade is responsible for marketing. About 60 percent of wheat produced is durum (which is better suited to the manufacture of pasta than bread), and this, together with the lack of milling capacity, means that wheat imports are necessary. The large increase in wheat production has not been accompanied by an expansion of storage facilities. The country suffers a chronic shortage of storage silos; much grain is stored in the open, with large consequent losses. Heavy investments are being made in both milling and in storage.

The total cropped area in 1990 equaled 4.8 million hectares, and this has changed little since then.[46] Less than 20 percent of the cultivated area is irrigated, the rest being rain fed. Efforts to increase irrigation depend on the volume of water in the Euphrates River, but this has been affected by Turkey's use of its water and poor canal structures for distributing water in Syria. Between 70 and 75 percent of the cropped area is taken up with wheat, the main staple crop, and barley, the main feed grain. Cotton is the main export crop and accounts for 20–25 percent of agricultural exports.

In the recent past, government policy was aimed at reducing reliance on imports and increasing exports. It did this through trade, production, and pricing policies. It set procurement prices for major crops and controls on interest rates, agricultural input prices, and energy and transport prices. The government also favored one crop over another by changing input and the procurement of state purchasing agencies. Bread, rice, sugar, and tea prices were controlled by the government, whereas fruit and vegetable production and prices were market determined. Agricultural exporters are now allowed to retain all of their earnings.[47]

Large investments have been made in irrigation. In 1983, 580,000 hectares were irrigated; in 1993, an estimated 906,000 hectares.[48] In fact, irrigation has accounted for up to 75 percent of the state budget for agriculture. The objective was much higher production: the 15 percent of cultivated land that was irrigated produced 50 percent of the total agricultural output. The other incentive was that production on rain-fed land (85 percent of the total) fluctuated greatly each year. A total of 1.25 million hectares could potentially be irrigated from surface water. In 1992, the total area irrigated with surface water and groundwater was 900,000 hectares. In 1991, farmers also irrigated 451,000 hectares from wells. Cotton, sugar beet, tobacco, and sesame crops were produced only on irrigated land. More fruit and vegetable production was on irrigated land. The value of exports of fruit and vegetables rose from $165 million in 1990 to $236 million in 1994.[49]

Although Syria has achieved major increases in agricultural output, serious problems remain in that sector. The pressure of population has, along with other factors, resulted in the use of land, water, and forests beyond their natural limit, and the result has been environmental degradation. This has meant deforestation, desertification, overcultivation, soil damage and erosion, overpumping of groundwater, and pollution. All these factors threaten the long-term sustainability of the agricultural effort. The trade-off has been higher current output at the risk of threats to future output.[50]

Water

In 1993, agriculture accounted for 85 percent of water use in Syria. The industrial demand for water rose by almost 900 percent in the 1980s, and the rapid growth of population was also a competing source of demand.[51] Syria's water supply is derived from rainfall, from rivers crossing its borders, and from groundwater that is pumped to the ground and is used mainly to irrigate crops. It should be noted that figures for Syrian water resources are poor and that there are large differences between those used by, for example, the World Bank and those by the FAO.

According to the World Bank, renewable water resources per capita fell from 1,196 cubic meters per capita in 1960 to 439 in 1990 and will fall to 161 by the year 2025.[52] Public irrigation projects have been large in scale, the main example being the Euphrates River Project. This river is the main source of Syria's irrigation water, and development plans aim to add 650,000 hectares of irrigated land. Salinity, waterlogging, and reduced river flows have hampered this. Salinity and waterlogging date back to the 1960s.

Private projects operate on a very small scale. Individual farmers have been encouraged to drill wells. They have received subsidized credits to buy subsidized fuel to operate imported pumps bought with an overvalued currency. With urban demand for fruit and vegetables increasing, the incentives to drill have been strong. This has helped to increase the irrigated area and expand agricultural production, but at a cost. Overpumping of aquifers for irrigation has caused saltwater to be absorbed in the coastal plains. The irrigation system itself is inefficient: 40 percent of water is lost.[53] And Syria faces acute and immediate shortages of water for domestic use in its large cities.[54]

The flow of water into Syrian territory from the Euphrates River at the Turkish border was estimated at 26.3 billion cubic meters in 1997. Turkey has agreed to supply 15.75 billion m³ to Syria, while the rest is to be kept by Turkey, using the dams constructed under its South East Anatolian Development Project, known by its Turkish acronym, GAP.[55] Syria has agreed to share the water of the Euphrates crossing its border with Iraq on a 58/42 percent (Iraq/Syria) basis. As a result, it supplies Iraq with 9 billion m³ annually. In the early 1990s the internally derived surface flow added 0.5 billion m³, and 12 billion m³ was lost in outflow to other countries and the sea. Consequently, 5.5 billion m³ of surface water was available for use in Syria. A total of 1.5 billion m³ of groundwater was drilled, giving a total supply of 7.0 billion m³. Rainfall also equaled 7.0 billion m³, of which 6.0 billion was available for agriculture.

Syria, then, is a country with a significant water deficit. It has a "significant water constraint" and limited ability to mobilize investment to improve the water management system. In the future, it will have to generate foreign exchange in nonagricultural sectors in order to pay for food imports and thus reduce pressure on water resources.[56]

The Fiscal Balance

Of all the official statistics available on Syria, those on the budget should be treated with the greatest caution. This is because they do not cover all forms of spending that the government carries out: the largest gap is in military imports. In addition, changes in exchange rates make comparisons between years problematic and different exchange rates are sometimes used within each budget. For example, in the 1994 budget, foreign loans were apparently entered at an exchange rate of U.S.$1.00=£S 43, while local revenues were entered at a rate of

U.S.$1.00 = £S 23.[57] Another important feature of the budget is that significant areas of spending are conditional on the receipt of concessionary loans or grants from abroad: the budget contains revenue items titled "exceptional financing." If these are not received, then the projects in question are delayed or scrapped.

Table 6.5 shows that Syria's fiscal performance improved between 1986 and 1989. In 1989, there was, once again, a deficit, but between 1990 and 1992, there was a surplus that increased each year. The surplus virtually disappeared in 1993, and in 1994, there was a large deficit. When foreign grants are excluded, then the deficits were even larger. In 1995, the deficit was reduced by nearly 50 percent as a result of a 17 percent increase in revenues, mainly from taxes, and only a 7 percent rise in spending.

In terms of the revenue account, several points are notable. First, the share of tax revenue was very low. This reflects the government's unwillingness, and possibly its inability, to impose direct burdens on the population. Revenues from the public sector, which included many ostensibly productive companies, fell as a share of total revenues from 39 percent in 1986 to 20 percent in 1990 and to just under 15 percent in 1995. Despite this, the government had numerous expenditure commitments and, as a result, relied on borrowing abroad as well as at home.

The budget excludes much of the spending on subsidies through the government's Price Stabilization Fund (PSF). These subsidies are paid on a range of basic commodities, the most important being that on wheat. The PSF receives transfers from the state budget and earns some revenues from sales of subsidized commodities. These cover only about one-third of expenditures, and the balance, or deficit, is funded by borrowing from the Central Bank of Syria. Between 1990 and 1994, the deficit on the PSF averaged the equivalent of 3.4 percent of GDP. In 1992, the deficit peaked at about 4.4 percent, and in 1996, it was estimated to have fallen to 2.1 percent as a result of reduced subsidy levels and higher consumer prices. These deficits should be added to the budget deficit (and to any other extrabudgetary accounts that could be identified) in order to calculate the overall fiscal deficit.

The decline in foreign receipts is partly reflected in budgetary figures. In 1994, nominal expenditures in the consolidated state budget were to increase by 17 percent; in 1995, by 12.3 percent; and in 1996, by 15.7 percent. On the basis of an estimated annual inflation rate averaging 20 percent in the period 1993–1995, it seems that public-spending declined in real terms and that the state ceased to be the leading sector

Table 6.5 The Budget: Syria, 1986–1996
(in Millions £S, Actual Amounts)

	1986	1987	1988	1989	1990	1991	1992	1993	1994	1995	1996
Total revenues and grants	26,189	32,088	44,337	51,800	59,402	80,960	92,038	95,483	113,156	131,898	154,019
Revenues	24,128	28,276	38,181	48,344	58,639	70,965	85,788	92,619	111,892	131,002	152,231
Taxes	12,791	19,028	26,689	35,782	44,796	156,361	72,082	72,244	88,416	106,367	108,061
Grants	2,061	3,812	6,156	3,426	763	9,995	6,250	2,864	1,264	896	1,788
Total spending	34,456	35,443	42,018	53,067	58,481	76,776	85,765	95,368	132,016	141,957	155,596
Defense spending	14,440	14,327	14,612	16,654	18,429	32,483	33,412	29,948	37,270	40,500	40,746
Balance (excluding grants)	–10,328	–7,167	–3,837	2,159	258	–5,811	–23	2,749	–20,090	10,955	–1,577
Balance	–8,267	–3,355	2,319	–1,267	921	4,184	6,273	115	–18,860	–10,059	–3,265

Source: IMF, *Government Financial Statistics Yearbook, 1998*.

in the economy. A large increase in public sector investment was budgeted in 1994, but judging by its past record, the government could not achieve its target increase of 15.7 percent in 1996. As a result of the pressure of demand against a background of fairly inelastic supply, inflation accelerated from about 12 percent in 1993 to about 20 percent annually in 1994 and to an estimated 22 percent in 1995. This meant that, on the basis of the budget plan, the real level of government spending fell in the three years 1994, 1995, and 1996.

The reliance on oil revenues and the limited contribution of taxation to the budget reflect the weakness of the state vis-à-vis the rest of society. Although the Syrian state has not been afraid to use force against its own citizens as well as against foreigners, it is nevertheless a "soft state," illustrated by its very limited ability to mobilize resources and push forward development programs effectively. Nazih Ayubi has noted the paradox that Arab states that are, in his terminology, often "fierce," are also "soft," or ineffective in development terms.[58] Third, grants from abroad have played a decreasing role since the early 1990s, and this resulted in a fall in the budget surplus followed by the reemergence of a deficit in 1994. Fourth, subsidies, especially on foodstuffs, continue to be significant, although their share in GDP has declined. Finally, the government continues to borrow at home and abroad in order to finance the budget deficit.

Table 6.6 gives a breakdown of budget proposals between 1992 and 1997. A comparison between Tables 6.7 and 6.8 shows that there was a big shortfall in revenue in 1993, mainly because foreign loans were not obtained as planned. This resulted in lower spending on all items except the military, where spending rose above the planned amount. The same pattern prevailed in 1994 and 1995.

The Defense Burden

Over the course of the 1990s, the spending on the military, as measured by the defense budget, failed to increase in line with inflation. As a result, the real volume of defense spending fell, as did its share of GDP. In 1990 prices, defense spending in 1986 was $3,675 million, and in 1994, it was estimated at $2,302 million. The share of defense in GDP fell from 11.2 percent in 1986 to 7.0 percent in 1994.[59] The fall was due to the failure to increase the budget in line with inflation and the depreciation of the exchange rate. According to Table 6.5, defense spending

**Table 6.6   The Budget Proposals: Syria, 1992–1997
(in Millions £S)**

	1992	1993	1994	1995	1996	1997
Total revenues	93,042	123,018	144,162	162,040	188,050	211,125
Taxes	29,408	29,489	40,456	48,903	57,371	67,296
"Various revenues"	25,285	25,285	39,755	44,720	31,805	23,818
Concessional loans	13,904	9,000	0	0	0	0
Foreign loans	5,607	22,868	24,530	24,282	22,396	22,184
Domestic loans	0	11,026	12,742	12,039	8,441	8,071
Total spending	93,042	123,018	144,162	162,040	188,050	211,125
National security	27,173	27,888	36,549	39,987	41,741	43,860
Justice	14,955	18,101	21,246	24,300	27,982	28,965
Education	4,589	8,839	10,567	12,936	14,647	15,471
National debt	8,003	8,905	7,452	9,763	12,978	14,436

Source: MEES, 4 August 1997.

accounted for 42 percent of budget expenditure in 1986, 32 percent in 1990, 39 percent in 1994, and 21 percent in 1997. Arms imports are not included in the defense budget and are funded with foreign aid.

The burden of defense was larger than budgetary figures suggest, not only because arms imports are excluded. Syria conscripts manpower for the armed forces and has large paramilitary and state-security forces. It also has about 35,000 troops in Lebanon. Although military manpower is cheap in that conscripts earn minimal amounts, the military complex has spread into other sectors of the economy, especially construction and trading. This military-industrial complex has to be supplied and appeased when policy is made, and this has economic as well as political costs.

The Balance of Payments

Between 1985 and 1990, there was a major improvement in the balance of payments, with the current account moving from a deficit of $1.0 billion a year (average for 1983–1985) to a surplus of almost $1.8 billion in 1990. This was made possible by an increase in oil export revenues and the inflow of aid from the Gulf states resulting from circumstances surrounding the Gulf War. Between 1990 and 1994, the current account deteriorated, but in 1995, there was an improvement as a result of oil revenues that increased exports and lowered imports due to the downturn in the level of domestic activity. In recent years, there has also been an increase in remittances of Syrians abroad recorded in the balance of payments (included in the "Income: credit" entry in Table 6.7). The gradual liberalization of the exchange rate system encouraged Syrians to remit funds home.

Between 1990 and 1992, private-sector exports rose from $650 million to $1.8 billion as a program to repay debt to the Russian Federation in kind was implemented. This was suspended in 1992, and since then, Syrian firms have been trying to reorientate their exports to Western Europe and to other regions.

Between 1990 and 1994, exports measures in dollars declined by 20 percent, mainly because of the loss of traditional markets in Eastern Europe and the former USSR, while imports rose by 123 percent. This was due to the liberalization of imports, which allowed the private sector much greater freedom to bring goods into the country.

The services account improved from a deficit of $18 million in 1990 to a surplus of $358 million in 1994. This was largely due to an increase in revenues from tourism. Net income flows were –$786 million in 1990 and –$359 million in 1994. The balance on goods, services, and income moved from a surplus of $1,674 million in 1990 to a deficit of $359 million in 1994.

The net level of transfers changed little in the period 1988–1995, but the composition of these transfers was transformed. In 1988, transfers received by the government (grants from foreign governments and from official bilateral and multinational bodies) totaled $537 million; in 1995, they came to only $12 million. The volume of workers' remittances increased by 53 percent between 1988 and 1992, to $550 million and then fell to $400 million in 1995. According to the IMF, just over $1 billion of other current transfers entered Syria in 1994–1995.[60] The Fund does not provide a definition of these funds, but it is reasonable to assume that they were funds invested in Syria by expatriates taking advantage of the Investment Law No. 10 regulations and/or other remittances.

The other main change in the balance of payments in the 1990s was the increase in so-called other capital received by the government. In 1989, the government received concessionary loans of $590 million. This sum rose continuously to reach nearly $1.6 billion in 1993. The total for the period 1989–1993 was $5.2 billion.[61] Most of these loans

Table 6.7 The Balance of Payments: Syria, 1990–1997
(in Millions $)

	1990	1991	1992	1993	1994	1995	1966	1997	1998
Exports of goods, (FOB)[a]	4,156	3,438	3,253	3,203	3,329	3,858	4,178	4,057	3,113
Imports of goods, (FOB)[a]	2,062	-2,354	-3,512	-3,476	-4,604	-4,001	-4,516	-3,603	-3,307
Balance on goods	2,094	1,084	159	-273	-1,275	-143	-338	454	-172
Services:									
Credits	874	1,065	1,281	1,595	1,863	1,979	1,833	1,604	1,795
Debits	-892	-1,002	-1,102	-1,442	-1,611	-1,537	-1,555	-1,489	-1,481
Balance on services	-18	63	197	153	358	442	278	115	314
Income									
Credit	430	415	619	432	638	444	534	421	389
Debit	-831	-1,096	-1,214	-1,064	-997	-983	-1,017	-925	-995
Balance on income	-786	-1,031	-1,145	-632	-359	-539	-399	-504	-606
Balance on goods, services, and income	1,674	465	-258	-738	-1,382	-240	-543	-16	-464
Current transfers: net	88	234	313	535	591	607	624	499	523
Current account	1,762	699	55	-203	-791	367	81	483	59

Source: IMF, *International Financial Statistics, December 1999*; and IMF, *International Financial Statistics Yearbook, 1999*.
Note: a. Free on Board.

consisted of concessionary lending by Gulf Arab states and Arab regional and multinational agencies. Between 1981 and 1988, no such loans were received.

External Debt

At the end of 1996, Syria's total external debt equaled $21.2 billion. About $14.6 billion of this was owed to the former USSR. A total of $16.7 billion was long-term debt and $4.7 billion was short-term debt (see Table 6.8). Short-term debt equals arrears on short- and long-term debt minus export credits granted by foreign banks and companies. As arrears in Syria have increased, so has the short-term debt, and as a result, the share of short-term debt in the total has risen. Between 1990 and 1995, total external debt rose by $4.2 billion, or 24 percent; short-term debt increased by $2.6 billion, or 120 percent.

**Table 6.8   Foreign Debt: Syria, 1980–1997
            (in Millions $)**

	Total	Long Term	Short Term
1980	3,552	2,921	631
1990	17,068	14,917	2,151
1991	18,942	16,353	2,589
1992	19,017	15,913	3,104
1993	19,976	16,235	3,741
1994	20,558	16,540	4,018
1995	21,318	16,757	4,562
1996	21,420	16,698	4,722
1997	20,865	16,254	4,611

Source: World Bank, *Global Finance Development, 1999*, vol. 2.

One of Syria's main debtors was the World Bank, and in July 1997, Syria agreed to repay the Bank $526.4 million that was owed. A total of $256.9 million was to be paid in August 1997, and $1.6 million was to be paid each month over a five-year period. This was considered to be a milestone in improving Syria's international creditworthiness.[62]

In 1996, Syria and France agreed on a deal under which France would write off 30 percent of the $370 million owed to it, with the balance to be repaid after a five- to seven-year grace period. Negotiations with Germany have been stalled because of Syria's refusal to accept German demands that it repay debt owed to the former German Democratic Republic. Syria also contests Russia's claim for repayment of debts owed to the former USSR.

Conclusion

The future for the Syrian economy depends on economic reforms. A reduction in the defense burden would also be beneficial, although it is unlikely in the foreseeable future. The country can expect a reduction in oil revenues as the twenty-first century gets under way, as well as increasingly serious problems as a result of fast population and labor force growth rates. Other rental incomes, foreign aid, and workers' remittances have uncertain prospects in that they are largely related to economic developments in the Gulf and are not expected to improve in the near future.

The government has not been short on advice about what to do. In April 1997, the United Nations Industrial Development Organization (UNIDO) presented a report in Damascus on the prospects for Syrian industry. UNIDO stated that the development of private-sector investment banks, the creation of a stock exchange, and other financial measures would enable Syria to generate the employment needed to cope with the increase in the labor force in the coming years. It would also attract up to $8 billion in investment, thus strengthening the balance of payments as well as bringing foreign technology and expertise to the country.[63] This advice, like much else, has not been taken, or at least has not been acted on in order to generate a critical mass of reforms.

The pace of economic reforms has been influenced by changes in the volume of rental incomes. The combination of a decline in foreign aid, falling remittances from Syrians in the Gulf, and bad harvests led to a serious economic crisis in the early 1980s. In 1985, the government's initial reaction to the crisis was to take steps designed to reduce imports; the exchange rate was reduced, and private-sector firms were encouraged to finance imports with funds held abroad. Since then, reforms have been introduced but never at a pace or on a scale that would create confidence among private investors, as has taken place in Egypt lately.[64]

Reform of Syria's highly centralized economy in recent years has come virtually to a halt, partly because the balance of payments has

been healthy and has not exerted pressure for change. Since the introduction of the 1991 Investment Law No. 10, there has been limited
progress toward a more liberal economic system. There have been calls
for a loosening of restrictions on foreign exchange transactions, but as
of the time of this writing, these have not been agreed to. Considering
Syria's large public sector, transfers to the public and private sectors, a
lack of bank lending, and no capital market, the budget has run a sizeable deficit that has been financed in part by printing money. This has
been inflationary, and since economic growth rates have declined, the
country is now suffering from inflation of about 20 percent a year and
rising unemployment. Since the introduction of Law No. 10, Syria has
managed to persuade only one multinational company to invest in the
manufacturing sector: Nestlé of Switzerland took a 60 percent stake in a
foodstuffs plant that will cost a total of $20 million.[65]

In 1995, a prominent Syrian economist summarized his country's
recent economic development in the following terms. The fall in capital
inflows in the early 1980s revealed imbalances in the economy and
rigidities in its structure and showed how reliant it was on the rest of the
world. The government responded with reforms focused on the
exchange rate, foreign trade, and price controls. It began to encourage
exports rather than discourage imports and favored a larger role for the
private sector. As in Egypt during the early years of its economic opening in the 1970s, the foreign trade sector in Syria benefited from the
reforms more than the domestic economy did. In 1987, the private sector accounted for 46 percent of nonoil exports, and in 1994, 78 percent.
Its share in nonoil imports rose from 26.6 percent in 1987 to 63.2 percent in 1994.[66]

These measures helped to boost the growth rate, but the real source
of growth was oil, which took the place of capital imports. The foreign
currency earned from oil exports was invested in the infrastructure and
in public-sector industry. Agriculture was liberalized, and farmers were
offered prices that provided greater incentives to produce. As in China,
these reforms were introduced within the tight constraints of the existing political and economic infrastructure; but, unlike China, Syria has
not reduced the ruling party's involvement in the economy, nor has it
established significant contacts with international firms and multilateral
organizations.[67]

Syria faces two looming economic problems. The first is that oil
revenues are expected to decline in the medium term, with no other
potential source of foreign exchange that could replace it on a stable

and sustainable basis. The second, even more serious problem is that of population growth, which forces the economy to run in order to stand still. Without increasing oil revenues, the economy is likely to cease growing; as such, per capita incomes will fall. This will leave the government with only one option: economic reform.

The problems faced by Syria's economy are in large part those of management. If it moved toward a more market-oriented system, then the gains in terms of productivity would be considerable. Reforms in agriculture have resulted in an export surplus of fruit and vegetables, and this would apply to other sectors if the right steps were taken. The government is not short of ideas on how to reform the economy; the question is whether it actually wants reforms that would strengthen the private sector at the expense of the state and the party. And the answer, at the time of writing, is "no." Reforms have taken place when rental incomes are low; when rental incomes are high, the government has avoided making changes that unsettle some of the key groups that support it. These include the Alawite minority, the peasantry, the Baath Party, government bureaucracies, and the army and security forces. Syria has yet to experience a combination of reforms and high rental income. The irony is that reforms designed, inter alia, to make the economy more self-sufficient would attract both Syrian and foreign capital, which would bring vitally needed technology and know-how.

Syria does have a number of economic advantages. It has sizeable gas reserves and oil that is expected to yield significant export revenues into at least the second decade of the twenty-first century, at current rates of extraction.[68] It also has one of the strongest agricultural sectors in the Arab world. On a more hypothetical level, the potential exists to obtain economic rents in exchange for political changes; some of the benefits of a peace treaty with Israel would be aid and investment from the West. Tourism has a large potential, given the wealth of Syria's archaeological sites. Even more significant would be the gains from domestic reforms.

Notes

1. World Bank, *World Development Report, 1994*, p. 165.
2. Ibid.
3. Perthes, *Political Economy*.
4. EIU, *CP: Syria, 1995–96*, pp. 14–16.
5. Melhem, "Syria," pp. 2–7.

6. U.S. Department of State, *Country Commercial Guide 1996.*

7. EIU, *CR: Syria, 1999,* no. 3, pp. 21–23.

8. Calculated from Syrian Arab Republic, Central Bureau of Statistics, *Statistical Abstract, 1994,* pp. 514–515, and *1995,* p. 526.

9. Ibid., *1994,* pp. 514–515, and *1995,* p. 526.

10. IMF, *International Financial Statistics, November 1997.*

11. UNESCWA, *Survey of Economic and Social Developments, 1998–99,* p. 36.

12. IMF, *Directions of Trade Statistics Yearbook, 1999;* and IMF, *Directions of Trade, September 1999.*

13. UN, *Demographic Yearbook, 1984* and *1997.*

14. al-Wasat, 24–30 June, quoted in Foreign Broadcast Information Service (hereafter FBIS), 28 June 1996.

15. Radio Damascus, 17 February, quoted in FBIS, 20 February 1996.

16. Fargues, "Demographic Explosion or Social Upheaval?" pp. 156–157.

17. Ibid., p. 159.

18. Courbage, "Evolution démographique," pp. 725–750. Phillippe Fargues comes to similar conclusions about Egypt in an important paper, "State Policies and the Birth Rate in Egypt," pp. 115–138. Taken together, these works suggest that the effects of government policies on demographic trends in the Middle East need to be reexamined.

19. UN, *World Population Prospects.*

20. World Bank, *World Development Report, 1994,* pp. 211–213 and 241–242.

21. Courbage, "Fin de 'l'explosion,'" pp. 180–191.

22. *Ha'aretz,* 28 February 1997.

23. Ibid.

24. UN, *Demographic Yearbook, 1986, 1991,* and *1995.*

25. World Bank, *World Development Report, 1994,* p. 219.

26. Fargues, "Demographic Explosion or Social Upheaval?" p. 162.

27. Syrian Arab Republic, Central Bureau of Statistics, *Statistical Abstract, 1991.*

28. UN, *National Accounts, 1992,* pp. 1140–1141, and *1993,* p. 1294.

29. EIU, *CP: Syria, 1997–98,* p. 23.

30. *Arab Oil and Gas,* 1 October 1995.

31. British Petroleum, *BP Statistical Review.*

32. EIU, *CP: Syria, 1997–98,* p. 23.

33. Ibid., *1995–96,* p. 32.

34. U.S. Department of Energy, Energy Information Agency Web page, accessed 19 June 1997.

35. *MEED,* 19 September 1995.

36. Quoted in *The Middle East and North Africa, 1995,* p. 854.

37. EIU, *CP: Syria, 1995–96,* p. 26.

38. Israel, Central Bureau of Statistics, *Statistical Abstract, 1997.*

39. *MEED,* 11 August 1995.

40. *Arab Oil and Gas,* 1 October 1995.

41. *MEED,* 3 March 1994.

42. UNESCWA, *Agriculture and Development in West Asia*, p. 18.

43. UNESCWA, *Survey of Economic and Social Developments, 1994*, pp. 86–87.

44. UNESCWA, *Survey of Economic and Social Developments, 1993*, p. 100.

45. FAO, *Quarterly Bulletin of Statistics*, p. 110.

46. FAO, *State of Food and Agriculture, 1993*, p. 189.

47. Ibid., p. 163.

48. FAO, "Production," *Yearbook*, p. 15.

49. FAO, "Trade," *Yearbook*, p. 331.

50. UNESCWA and FAO, *Resource Conservation*, 1996.

51. FAO, *State of Food and Agriculture, 1993*, p. 174.

52. World Bank, *A Strategy for Managing Water*, table A-4.

53. Sadik and Barghouti, "Water Problems," p. 20.

54. Bakour and Kolars, "The Arab Mashrek," p. 133.

55. Allan, "Overall Perspectives," p. 72.

56. Allan, "Economic and Political Adjustments," pp. 376–380.

57. *MEES*, 23 May 1994.

58. Ayubi, *Overstating the Arab State*, pp. 447–458.

59. Stockholm International Peace Research Institute, *Handbook*, p. 202, table 6.B.3.

60. IMF, *Balance of Payments Yearbook, 1996*, p. 463.

61. IMF, *Balance of Payments Yearbook, 1994*, pp. 483–486.

62. *MEED*, 29 August 1997.

63. EIU, *CP: Syria, 1997*, p. 18.

64. Rivlin, "Structural Adjustment," pp. 169–196.

65. *MEED*, 16 May 1997.

66. Calculated from Sukkar, "Syria," p. 8, and from the Syrian Arab Republic, Central Bureau of Statistics, *Statistical Abstract, 1994*, pp. 256–257.

67. Sukkar, "Syria," pp. 4–5 and 61.

68. EIU, *CP: Syria, 1996–97*, p. 23.

CHAPTER 7

The International Environment: Economic Relations with the European Union

Globalization has become a dominant theme in development economics. World trade has been growing faster than the world economy for more than twenty years, and the links between countries have therefore become a major factor in determining their economic performance and thus an increasingly important part of their economic policy.

Globalization has been reinforced in recent years as a result of a number of factors. Information and communications technology has developed rapidly: quality has improved and costs have fallen. International trade, especially in developing countries, has been liberalized (some Arab examples were analyzed in Chapter 5). Foreign investment has increased, mainly by multinational firms based in developed countries starting plants in developing economies. At the same time, foreign aid (government to government and through multilateral agencies) has declined in absolute terms and as a share of total international capital flows. Capital markets have become more international as a result of the liberalization of regulations and improved telecommunications. Finally, more countries have joined international trade bodies such as the World Trade Organization or regional trading bodies (see below), partly because of the collapse of communism in Eastern Europe and because of economic pressures.

Staying out of this increasingly global economy is increasingly dangerous.[1] But staying in requires ever-harder adjustments, as was shown in Chapter 5. In the 1980s and 1990s, world trade grew more slowly than in the 1960s and 1970s, when the East Asian states grew so rapidly. Although trade growth accelerated in the period 1994–1996, the crisis in East and Southeast Asia reduced growth rates in 1997–1998.[2]

In addition, between the 1960s and the 1980s, developed countries introduced an increasing number of nontariff barriers on imports from developing countries. This also made it harder for states developing after those in East Asia to benefit from international trade as the former had done. The Uruguay Round agreements of GATT, signed in 1994, and other measures will help to reduce nontariff barriers, but not overnight.

The IMF and the World Bank have recommended economic reforms of the kind examined in Chapter 5 to help countries take advantage of the international opportunities available. The closest trading bloc for most Arab states was the European Union, and this chapter examines the links among these two areas. For purposes of comparison, it also looks at the links between Israel and Turkey and the EU. It also examines attempts at regional economic integration in the Maghreb (Algeria, Morocco, and Tunisia) and in the eastern Mediterranean (Egypt, Israel, Jordan, and Palestine). Emphasis is placed on trade relations, the movement of labor, and developments in private- and public-sector capital flows. These regional developments are placed in the context of changes in the international trading system. Conclusions are drawn about the relationship with the EU and the modest effect that it is expected to have on the economies in the Mediterranean region.

The Barcelona Declaration

In November 1995, the fifteen members of the EU and eleven Mediterranean countries (Algeria, Cyprus, Egypt, Israel, Jordan, Lebanon, Malta, Morocco, Syria, Tunisia, and Turkey), plus the Palestinian Authority, signed a declaration in Barcelona, Spain. The Barcelona Declaration stated that a multinational framework for relations between the two groups of countries would be created to include a political and security partnership, an economic and financial partnership, and another in social and human affairs. The two groups were very unequal economically. In 1997, the fifteen members of the EU had a combined GDP of $8,130 billion, nineteen times that of the Mediterranean group ($428 billion). The EU population was 374 million; that of the Mediterranean group, 225 million. Average GDP per capita in the EU was about $21,750, compared with the average level of $1,900 in the Mediterranean group, or $1,500 if Israel was excluded.

The Barcelona Declaration aimed to complete a Euro-

Mediterranean free trade area by the year 2010. This would permit reciprocal free trade in manufactured goods and preferential and reciprocal access for agricultural products between the EU and the Mediterranean countries, as well as free trade among the latter. Together with states that were part of the former Yugoslavia, this free trade area would, if created, constitute the largest such area in the world, with close to forty countries and a population of up to 800 million.[3]

There were two broad motives for the EU's Mediterranean initiative. The first was political: the EU wanted to contribute to the Middle East peace process, which it saw as led by the United States. In so doing, it aimed to maintain or improve its political and economic status in the region. It also feared the threat of instability from the region; the impact of Islamic fundamentalism in Algeria and in other parts of the Middle East and, in that context, the presence of 7 million Muslims in Europe, gave rise to anxiety about social and political stability in EU member states. The potential pressure for increased emigration from North Africa, if socioeconomic conditions deteriorated there, was a related worry and was, perhaps, the single most important reason for the development of the EU's Mediterranean policy in the 1990s.[4]

Like the United States in its relations with Mexico, the EU saw partial economic integration with its poorer southern neighbors as a way of reducing the pressure for migration. Emphasis is placed on the word "partial": none of the free trade arrangements negotiated between developed and developing countries permit free movement of labor, as the EU does between it own members. In order to reduce incentives for migration, policies were therefore designed to encourage movements of goods, services, and capital, in part to reduce geographic disparities in income levels.[5] Furthermore, the EU initiative did not offer any significant improvement in access to its markets for the Mediterranean producers of agricultural products, textiles, and clothing. These were the products in which many Mediterranean countries had a comparative advantage. Without increased access to EU markets, the benefits for the North African states in particular, but also to Egypt and Palestine, would be limited. Mediterranean exports of textiles to the EU have been affected by international trade liberalization that has given cheap Southeast Asian producers greater access.

The EU also wanted to secure its position as the major supplier of industrial goods to its southern neighbors. In 1990, EU exports to the Mediterranean group were worth $44 billion and in 1998, they came to $71 billion (see Table 7.1). Growth was limited by the fall of oil

**Table 7.1   EU-Mediterranean Trade, 1990–1998
(in Billions $)**

	1990	1995	1996	1997	1998
EU Exports to:					
Algeria	6,498	6,083	5,647	4,900	5,840
Egypt	5,487	6,461	7,216	7,600	8,170
Israel	6,933	12,814	12,258	13,400	12,080
Jordan	1,036	1,347	1,492	1,300	1,250
Lebanon	988	3,243	3,390	3,500	3,160
Libya	3,437	2,993	3,124	3,100	2,910
Morocco	4,597	6,057	5,885	5,900	6,630
Syria	1,114	1,815	1,796	1,500	1,730
Tunisia	3,877	5,445	5,342	5,800	6,300
Turkey	10,363	17,441	22,217	24,200	23,340
Total	44,330	63,699	68,367	71,200	71,410
Total to Arab states	27,036	33,444	33,872	33,600	35,990
EU Imports from:					
Algeria	9,126	7,801	8,496	9,400	7,580
Egypt	3,075	4,443	4,620	3,200	2,560
Israel	4,884	6,206	6,096	7,500	7,980
Jordan	111	162	196	200	190
Lebanon	128	142	156	200	180
Libya	10,242	7,578	8,856	8,800	6,350
Morocco	3,912	5,234	5,429	5,300	5,720
Tunisia	2,926	4,443	4,620	4,700	4,980
Syria	1,624	2,282	2,468	2,300	1,690
Turkey	8,172	12,029	12,593	13,300	15,890
Total	44,200	50,320	53,530	54,900	53,120
Total from Arab states	31,144	30,635	33,605	34,100	29,250
EU exports minus EU imports	130	13,379	14,837	16,300	18,290

Sources: IMF, *Directions of Trade Statistics Yearbook, 1997; Directions of Trade, December 1999.*

revenues in Algeria and Libya and by recession in many countries of the Mediterranean group; but despite that, the demand for EU products in other countries grew strongly, and in 1997, the EU accounted for about 60 percent of imports in Mediterranean countries.[6] The Mediterranean was therefore a market worth investing in, both politically and economically.

EU interest in the Mediterranean was part of a pattern of increasing regionalism in international trade, the best example of which, apart from the EU itself, was the North American Free Trade Agreement (NAFTA), which included the United States, Canada, and Mexico and was signed in 1993. The United States agreed to the Mexican initiative for the creation of a free trade area because it understood the long-term advantages of close economic links with a large, neighboring, developing country. In the short and medium term, cheap Mexican labor would encourage U.S. industrial investment in Mexico, and this would affect investment and employment in the United States. In the longer term, the development of the Mexican economy and the consequent rise in incomes there would provide a larger potential market for U.S. exports, as well as a continuous source of profit from the investments made there. Faster economic growth in Mexico would reduce the pressure to emigrate to the United States.

The Mexican-U.S. agreement on the creation of NAFTA was a cause for concern among other countries in Central and South America and in the Caribbean. They feared that their exports would be frozen out of North American markets once Mexican goods gained preferential access. As a result, twenty-six countries from the Americas signed then President George Bush's Enterprise for the Americas Initiative, aimed at moving toward a free trade area with the United States. In and around Europe, the creation of a single market in the EU prompted the European Free Trade Area countries (i.e., Iceland, Liechtenstein, Norway, and Switzerland), Cyprus, the Maghreb states, Turkey, and the Central and East European countries (CEECs) to seek membership or closer association with the EU.[7]

In recent years, developing countries have been the fastest-growing markets in the world, and only by offering them preferential access to its markets will the EU (and other developed countries) secure access to them. The benefits for industrialized countries of closer links with developing countries are demonstrated by the fact that 20 percent of industrialized countries' exports went to developing countries in the late 1980s; in 1995, this had risen to 25 percent and was expected to exceed 33 percent by the year 2000.[8]

The EU wanted to secure advantages in the Mediterranean, but it was much more cautious in its approach than the United States was toward Mexico. There were a number of reasons for this. First, the EU is itself a group of nations engaged in a complex and prolonged process of economic integration. Second, since the end of communism in Eastern Europe and the former USSR, the EU has given priority to relations with CEECs.[9] This has been reflected in aid levels to the CEECs that exceeded those to the Mediterranean countries until 1999. In the period 1991–1994, EU aid to CEECs was more than twice that granted to the Mediterranean countries.[10]

Largely because of the economic reforms that the CEECs have enacted, but also because of the nature of agreements signed with the EU, trade with the CEECs has grown much more rapidly than that with the Mediterranean countries. In 1992, EU exports to Poland, Hungary, the Czech Republic, Slovakia, Bulgaria, the Baltic States (i.e., Estonia, Latvia, Lithuania), Albania, and Slovenia equaled $31 billion. In 1997, they came to $83 billion, an increase of 116 percent. EU exports to the Mediterranean group rose more slowly, by 46 percent, from $48 billion to $71 billion.[11] The CEECs and other countries, mainly in Asia, are also becoming formidable competitors for some of the Mediterranean countries on EU markets (see section titled Trade and Development as well as Conclusion below, in this chapter).

The EU, particularly its largest member, Germany, has also been concerned about the implications of social, political, and economic instability in Eastern Europe. The EU's ability to absorb immigrants has declined as a result of a serious recession that has contributed to increased structural unemployment. In 1995, 10.7 percent of the EU's labor force was unemployed. Unemployment in Spain was 23.7 percent; in Italy, 11.4 percent; in France, 12.1 percent; and in Germany, 7.8 percent. These levels of unemployment will fall, according to the EU, only after some years of relatively robust economic growth.[12]

In 1993, there were 1.1 million immigrants from Eastern Europe and the former Soviet Union living in the EU, compared with 4.3 million from the Mediterranean. The possibility of increased emigration from Albania, Bulgaria, Czechoslovakia, the Czech and Slovak Republics, Hungary, Poland, and Romania was made more real by unemployment, which rose from 1.7 million in 1990 to 6.3 million in 1993.[13] The potential number of ethnic Germans and others in the former USSR who might, in certain circumstances, try to move west was considerable.

Legal immigration into the EU has increased: net immigration from all countries rose from an annual average of 140,000 in 1980–1984 to 290,000 in 1985–1988 and 800,000 in 1989–1990.[14] Pressure to migrate to Western Europe, and especially to the EU (then named the European Community [EC]), increased in both Eastern Europe, as a result of political and economic changes, and in the Mediterranean region, for reasons that will be examined below.

In 1974, there were 1.4 million North African residents in the EU and a similar number of Turks.[15] The total number of Turks, Moroccans, Algerians, and Tunisians living in the EU rose from 3.48 million in 1985 to 4.3 million in 1992, an increase of almost 24 percent.[16] In 1992, there were 2.35 million Turks, 1.08 million Moroccans, 640,000 Algerians, and 250,000 Tunisians in the EU. These were defined by citizenship; there were others who had acquired EU member states' citizenship and yet others who had entered the EU illegally. The two latter groups are not included in the figures given here.[17] There were also Egyptians, Jordanians, Lebanese, Libyans, and Syrians living in the EU: in 1993, the EU reported that there were 50,000 Egyptians living in Greece.[18]

In the period 1978–1988, 141,000 people migrated from the Mediterranean region to the southern member countries of the EU.[19]

These migrants moved to the EU and to other countries in Western and northern Europe in order to improve their economic position. There was, to put it simply, more work at higher wages than in their countries of origin. This was a function of economic weakness in the Mediterranean countries (with the exception of Israel) and the relative prosperity of the EU and Western and northern Europe in general. The demand for immigrant labor in the EU has, however, declined in recent years due to high levels of structural unemployment.

In 1989, the EU had 8 million foreign residents, 25 percent of whom were immigrants from Eastern Europe and states of the former Soviet Union. In the 1990s, southern members of the EU, which traditionally exported labor, attracted relatively large and partly illegal immigrations, mainly from North Africa.[20] Emigration has eased problems of unemployment in Mediterranean countries; it has also brought in foreign currency. Emigrants send funds home; these remittances constitute a significant part of Mediterranean countries' foreign earnings.

Although the capacity of the EU to absorb more Mediterranean workers has declined, the factors pushing people to leave Mediterranean countries have not abated. Between 1990 and 2010, the population of working-age citizens in the countries of the southern shore of the Mediterranean is expected to increase by an average of 5 million a year.[21] If the domestic use of labor remains unchanged, then 40 million new workers will get jobs at home and 6.5 million will emigrate, or 365,000 a year on average.[22]

The much faster rate of population growth in the Mediterranean than in the southern member states of the EU (and even more so in the northern member states of the EU) has created what has been called a "conflictual situation" between the two groups of countries, which is expected to worsen in coming years. In 1995, the World Bank stated that European demand for immigrant labor would continue to decline as a result of high levels of structural unemployment and immigration from the CEECs.[23] Since then, there has been some improvement in the EU economy. The United Nations has suggested that in the long term, during the period up to 2050, the European population will decline and age. As a result, the ratio of those of working age to those above it will deteriorate seriously. Immigration may be a solution to the shortage of labor.[24]

There are, however, grounds for hope. The Maghreb countries have experienced a demographic transition, and as a result, their rates of population have declined.[25] Emigration to Europe was one of the causes; during the oil boom of the 1970s and early 1980s, emigrants from Egypt, Syria, and other Maghreb countries went mainly to the Gulf. The Gulf countries, having experienced a massive and sudden increase in oil wealth, imported labor, partly because their own populations were so small. They therefore encouraged larger families, something that had its effect on immigrants from poorer Arab countries. The immigrant, whose stay in the oil-rich Gulf was usually short, returned home to have a larger family than he might have done without the funds earned in the Gulf and the example of large families there. The Maghreb emigrants to Europe settled into a different society, with much lower average family sizes. In the 1960s, Moroccan migrants in Europe had large families (6.5 children, on average, as at home). By 1990, the average number of children in the Moroccan migrant family in Europe was 3.5. This transition had its effect at home, partly by example and partly through other socioeconomic processes that are beyond the scope of this discussion.[26]

Virtually all emigrants from Algeria, Morocco, Tunisia, and Turkey live in Europe, the vast majority in EU member states. This, or course, is closely related to the issue of workers' remittances, which changed between 1987 and 1993. After fluctuations from 1987 to 1990, there was a decrease in the real value of these remittances. In 1990, for instance, the total value of workers' remittances to Morocco, Tunisia, and Turkey was $5.9 billion, and in 1995, $5.3 billion, a fall of 11 percent in nominal terms and a fall of about 20 percent in real terms.[27]

The EU's Mediterranean policy was shaped by internal pressures and compromises involving both the northern states, led by Germany, the main sensitivity of which was Eastern Europe, and the southern states, such as Spain, France, and Italy, which were more sensitive to developments in the Mediterranean. The southern EU states have more immigrants from the Maghreb than the northern EU states. In 1992, France and Italy had 1,536 million immigrants from the Maghreb out of a total non-European population of 2,285 million (67 percent). Germany had 134,000 from the three North African states out of a total non-European population of 5,343 million (2.5 percent). There were, however, 1,918 million Turks in Germany (36 percent of the total non-European population), giving that country considerable interests in the wider Mediterranean region.[28]

The southern EU states, although more exposed to emigration from North Africa, are also more exposed to competition from the Mediterranean. Part of the comparative advantage of the Mediterranean countries is in agriculture, and this is where the southern European countries have significant comparative advantages. They have, therefore, tried to protect themselves from competition from Mediterranean agricultural production in the trade agreements that have been signed. The share of agriculture in total gross value added in 1992 was over 3 percent in each of Italy, France, and Spain. In Portugal it was 6.3 percent, and in Greece, 17 percent. This compares with 1.2 percent in Germany and 1.5 percent in the UK.[29] The protection of agriculture is relatively more important for the southern EU states, and the common agricultural policy of the European Union provides support and ensures protection. As a result, the southern European states face a dilemma: they want to ensure stability in the Mediterranean region, but they are unwilling to expose themselves to competition from states in that region.

Another consideration in EU policymaking is the fact that Mediterranean countries (mainly Libya and Algeria) are major suppliers of its fuel (see Table 7.3 later in this chapter). In 1992, they supplied 24 percent of the EU's total energy needs, 32 percent of its natural gas, and 27 percent of its oil.[30] Stability in the Mediterranean would also help to secure these energy supplies, both by reducing the chance of military intervention in the eastern Mediterranean against tankers and by reducing the threat of boycotts by suppliers, as occurred in 1973.

The International Trade System and EU Trade Policy

In order to understand how the trading relationship between the EU and the Mediterranean states has developed, it is necessary to look at the international context. The current international trading system is based on the 1947 GATT, the most important provision of which was the most-favored-nation (MFN) clause. This was incorporated in Article I of GATT and stated that "any advantage, favor, privilege or immunity" granted by one country (i.e., a contracting party to GATT) to another must be extended "immediately and unconditionally to the like product originating in or destined for the territories of all other contracting parties."[31] The extension of the bilateral benefits negotiated among countries was the basis for moving toward freer international trade and away from tariffs and other trade restrictions that had done so much damage to the international economy before World War II.

Yet there were exceptions to the MFN rule in GATT. One of the most important was contained in Article XXIV, which allowed formation of free trade areas or customs unions.[32] The European Economic Community (EEC) was formed in 1957 under this article.[33] Its members were permitted to discriminate in favor of one another and against other GATT members that were not part of the EEC. The EEC created a customs union among six countries through the abolition of tariffs within the community and the establishment of a common external tariff. Discrimination, through this external tariff, against imports from outside the EEC did not reduce extraregional trade.[34]

The creation of the EEC contributed to rapid economic growth and thus to an increase in imports from outside the community. In this way, trade creation effects outweighed trade distortion effects, and the world economy benefited from the creation of a discriminatory trade organization.[35] The Treaty of Rome obliged EEC members to treat their former colonies as they treated one another. The former colonies were required to treat their imports from the EC and from one another as they treated imports from their former colonizers.[36] Accordingly, Algeria, Morocco, and Tunisia were given special status, as will be seen. The EEC helped developing countries, including those in the Mediterranean, by granting them preferential access to its tariff levels on imports and also by reducing or ending nontariff trade barriers.[37] By the 1990s, most developing countries had some form of preferential access to EC/EU markets. Seventy African, Caribbean, and Pacific countries linked to the EU through the Lomé Convention have the most extensive benefits. The Mediterranean countries also have benefits.

Another exception to MFN treatment is contained in Article XIX of GATT, which allowed countries to react to injury to domestic producers caused by imports. Eventually, the Multifiber Arrangement was developed on the basis of this article, which greatly restricted trade in textiles, affecting Mediterranean exports to the EU. The Uruguay Round of GATT, signed in Marrakech, Morocco, in April 1994, contained clauses that would lead to the abolition of the MFA and open EU markets to a wider range of goods from Southeast Asia and Latin America. Under the terms of the Uruguay Round agreements, much greater emphasis was placed on trade in services and in intellectual property. International trade in these items has grown faster than that in goods during recent years, and they will come under the General Agreement on Trade in Services and the Trade Related Intellectual Property Agreements, designed to liberalize trade in services and in intellectual property.

On 1 January 1995, GATT was succeeded by the World Trade Organization. Apart from the EU, the only other members of the WTO in the Mediterranean region were Egypt, Israel, Morocco, Tunisia, and Turkey. Countries that were not members of the WTO were under no obligation to offer MFN terms to their trading partners.

The Development of the EU: Mediterranean Economic Relations, 1957–1996

The Treaty of Rome, signed in 1957, set up the European Community. At that time, Algeria was part of France, and the latter insisted that independent countries in the French Franc Zone (which included Morocco and Tunisia) should have special relations with the EC. In 1959, Turkey applied for membership, and in 1963, an association agreement with the EC was signed, containing clauses that foresaw the customs union. This was implemented on 1 January 1996.

In the early 1960s, Israel was granted a nonpreferential trade agreement. This meant that the EC granted MFN tariff rates on specific industrial imports from Israel, without requiring Israel to do the same on industrial goods that it bought from the EC. Relations with Morocco and Tunisia and the newly independent Algeria remained unformulated. In 1969, association agreements were signed with Morocco and Tunisia, valid for five years, giving Morocco and Tunisia free access to EC markets for almost all industrial exports and privileged access for some agricultural goods.[38]

In 1970, a preferential trade agreement was signed with Israel: the EC would now allow specific Israeli industrial imports with tariffs at below MFN rates. The agreement with Israel was balanced by an offer to favorably consider signing preferential trade agreements with Mediterranean Arab countries. In 1972, the European Commission of the EC put forward plans for a global Mediterranean policy. This followed a series of problems resulting from the ad hoc way in which EC-Mediterranean relations had developed; from the planned entry of Denmark, Ireland, and the United Kingdom into the EC in 1973; and from changes in the international trading system. The EC Commission proposed that a free trade area be created: tariffs on manufactured goods would be phased out by 1977, and the EC would grant concessions covering at least 80 percent of each Mediterranean country's agricultural exports. The Mediterranean countries would reciprocate, with timing depending on their levels of development. There would also be cooperation over capital and labor flows. Within this framework, negotiations with the Maghreb and with Israel began.

In 1975, a free trade agreement with Israel was signed, which involved the abolition, over time, of tariffs on industrial goods traded between the two sides. In 1976, cooperation agreements with the Maghreb countries were concluded. These offered free access to EC markets for manufactured goods produced in the Maghreb; there were also provisions for agricultural exports, financial aid, and improved social security for Maghreb workers in the EC.[39] In 1977, cooperation agreements were signed with Egypt, Jordan, Syria, and Lebanon. Thus the EC had, in the five years after 1972, signed an array of agreements of different kinds with Mediterranean countries, all containing provisions for freer access to EC markets for industrial goods and some concessions for agriculture.

Algeria

In March 1997, talks began on Algeria's accession to the EU-Mediterranean partnership initiative. The EU offered financial support for Algeria's economic reform program, but its human rights record and policies proved a stumbling block in the negotiations. Algeria estimated that the implementation of a free trade zone between it and the EU would result in the loss of revenues from taxes on imports worth $1.2 billion, double the amount that it could expect to receive in EU assistance under the partnership initiative.[40]

Morocco and Tunisia

In July 1995, Tunisia signed an association agreement with the EU. In January 1996, Morocco also signed an association agreement. These agreements aimed to boost trade and contained measures in the areas of investment, competition, and regulation policy designed to create a Mediterranean market. They also rekindled interest in the Arab Maghreb Union (AMU; i.e., Algeria, Libya, Mauritania, Morocco, and Tunisia). Morocco and Tunisia have since been negotiating ways of increasing trade (see below).

The association agreements will not offer much in terms of increased access for Moroccan and Tunisian industrial products on EU markets. This is because sensitive items will remain controlled and non-sensitive items have almost quota-free access.[41] The main benefits will be in freedom of services and capital movement, with effects on direct foreign investment.[42] The adoption by Mediterranean countries of EU policies and regulations, designed, among other things, to encourage direct foreign investment, will promote exports, increase competition in domestic markets, and raise the level of efficiency in the economy.[43] Morocco and Tunisia will receive more aid and technical assistance from the EU and its member states as a result of the association agreements and the Barcelona Declaration. In exchange, Morocco and Tunisia will reduce barriers on imports over a period of twelve years.

Moroccan and Tunisian exports are highly concentrated in agricultural and labor-intensive items, which the EU considers sensitive because they compete with relatively weak EU industries, which are in need of protection. The EU has negotiated voluntary export restraint agreements with these two countries. Although some of the quotas agreed upon for textile and clothing exports to the EU have been exceeded without EU objections, the prospects for increasing these exports are not good. This is, in part, due to increasing competition from so-called outward processing exports from CEECs and, more generally, to the availability of low-cost products from other new suppliers.

Under the recently signed agreements, exports of sensitive items to the EU remain subject to restrictions. Economic liberalization has increased the share of sensitive items in total exports from 5.8 percent of Moroccan exports in 1970 to 7.0 percent in 1992 and from 3.6 percent of Tunisian exports in 1970 to 6.5 percent in 1992.[44] These countries are therefore very reliant on the export of a limited number of products: they have high export concentration ratios.

Another aspect of the association agreements and moves toward closer EU-Mediterranean links is the loss of customs duties on imports into the poorer partners. A total of 28 percent of Tunisian government revenues come from taxes on trade. A total of 68 percent of Tunisian imports come from the EU, generating 58 percent of trade tax revenue. Much of this is accounted for by consumer goods, and the potential loss of revenue as a result of the agreements is considerable.[45]

Egypt

During 1995, negotiations began between the EU and the government of Egypt, with a view to signing European-Mediterranean agreements. Egypt is also discussing the formation of a free trade area with the EU. Egypt, which has one of the lowest export ratios in the Middle East, is seeking to increase its sales abroad and sees an agreement with the EU as a means to that end. Its exports are dominated by agricultural products, but the EU has offered a free trade agreement for industrial goods, in which it has the competitive advantage, with quotas for agricultural goods. In 1997, Egypt hoped to receive a 750,00-ton quota for exports of potatoes to the EU; the latter offered 220,000 tons. A similar imbalance applied to oranges, rice, and cut flowers, and these gaps prevented an agreement from being reached at the Malta meeting of EU and Mediterranean foreign ministers.[46] Egypt is the largest recipient of aid from the EU in the Mediterranean.

Jordan

Jordan's is a highly protected economy, but since 1989, the country's external trade regime has been liberalized. The maximum tariff rate was reduced to 50 percent, and the average nominal tariff rates were reduced from 34.4 percent to 25 percent in 1992. The degree of tariff differentiation was also reduced.[47]

Jordan is not a member of the WTO and has no preferential trade agreements. Trade with Arab countries involves bilateral barter arrangements, and the MFN agreement with Israel contains benefits for Jordanian goods exported to Israel.

In October 1995, Jordan and the EU began discussions on an association agreement, with the aim of creating an industrial free zone. The EU has offered economic, technical, and financial support and is keen to support a free trade zone between Jordan and its neighbors, especially Egypt, Israel, and the Palestinian territories.[48] In April 1997, after six rounds of negotiations, Jordan and the EU signed an association agreement that envisages the creation of a free trade area between the sides over a twelve-year period. The agreement came into effect on 1 January 1999 and included provisions for free trade in agricultural and industrial goods. Initially, some Jordanian agricultural exports will be allowed into the EU without restrictions, others with quotas, and yet others with customs duties. Jordan will reduce its duties on imports of industrial goods from the EU, with capital goods gaining duty-free status in 1999 and other goods benefiting from phased duty reductions over a five-year period. Jordan was also granted a grace period of seven years in which to review and rewrite its intellectual property rights laws so as to make them acceptable internationally. European officials conceded that this may hurt the pharmaceutical and chemical sectors, which play a major role in the Jordanian economy. An agreement was also reached to tackle the problem of third-country nationals traveling illegally from Jordan to the EU.

Spain opposed a clause in the agreement that stated that the variety and quantity of tomato paste that Jordan could export to the EU could be revised by the two sides. It feared that this might create a precedent among Mediterranean countries that have partnership agreements with the EU and that this would damage its interests. In order to secure an agreement, Jordan agreed to omit the clause.

Under the 1997 agreement, standards and rules-of-origin restrictions imposed by the EU meant that total Jordanian exports remained very low. Jordan will benefit from cumulative rules of origin, which will allow it to add inputs imported from Europe to its products with the products still being considered as originating in Jordan.[49]

Lebanon

Talks with Lebanon on a partnership agreement also began in 1995. The stumbling blocks in the way of an agreement have been the EU's demand that Lebanon end import duties within eight years and its reluctance to allow imports of Lebanese agricultural goods without quotas.[50] The EU also wants Lebanon to provide more secure residency rights for Palestinians living there, given that many have experienced difficulties returning after visits to EU countries.[51]

Palestine

In February 1997, an interim association agreement was signed between the EU and the Palestine Liberation Organization on behalf of the Palestinian Authority. In the agreement, the EU allowed duty-free import of Palestinian industrial goods, while agricultural exports were permitted within quotas. EU industrial goods can be imported without duty by virtue of the Israel-EU trade agreements. As the Israeli government and the Palestinian Authority have created a customs union, all goods available on the Israeli market are, at least in theory, available in Palestinian territories. This access has been granted far more quickly than under the partnership agreements between the EU and other Mediterranean states (including Israel), which all specified a transition over a period of years to duty free access for EU goods.[52]

The EU has been a major aid donor to the Palestinians, committing 289 million in Eurocurrency (ECU) (U.S.$381 million) directly between 1987 and 1995. In 1994, total EU aid (including that of its member states) came to ECU 340 million (U.S.$450 million).[53]

Trade Relations in the Mediterranean

There have been numerous attempts at integration in the Arab world that included countries in the Mediterranean region. Developments in two subregions are worth examining in this context. The first is the Arab Maghreb Union. The second is the relations among Israel, Palestine, Jordan, Egypt, and Turkey.

The Maghreb

In February 1989, the leaders of Algeria, Libya, Morocco, Mauritania, and Tunisia signed the treaty setting up the AMU in Marrakech, Morocco. In 1990, representatives of the EC and the AMU met in Brussels following proposals by Algeria to create a free trade area to be followed by a customs union.

AMU members have not yet established a free trade area, although there are bilateral projects in operation and under discussion. A number of these involve the EU, such as a gas pipeline from Algeria to Italy, which passes through Tunisian territory, and gas pipelines from Algeria to Spain and Portugal, which pass through Morocco. Intra-AMU trade in 1992 equaled $2 billion, less than 4 percent of total AMU external trade. This compares with trade among members of the Association of Southeast Asian Nations[54] that equaled 20 percent of its total external trade.[55] In 1992, intra-EU trade equaled 58 percent of total EU external trade.[56]

In terms of general characteristics of the region, the AMU accounts for 40 percent of the Arab world's land area and, in 1997, had a population of 73 million, or about 17 percent of the total Arab population. It had 2 million expatriate workers in Europe. European tourism, mainly from France and Germany, was its largest source of foreign currency.

The barriers to closer economic integration in the AMU are numerous. There are political barriers: Libya has been subject to a range of international sanctions since 1991; Algeria has been in a state of near civil war for years. There are also what might be called "structural barriers": the countries in the region have a preference for European goods, and given this cultural bias, it is often hard to sell and/or export locally made goods. Much of the production in the region is competitive rather than complementary, which limits trade at the stage of development prevailing in the region. There are, however, differences in emphasis. Algeria and Libya are energy rich. Morocco is relatively more developed in agriculture, manufacturing, and tourism. Morocco and Mauritania have mining sectors. These variations offer opportunities for specialization and trade. The AMU countries nevertheless suffer from rapid population growth, high unemployment, illiteracy, desertification, water shortages, and environmental degradation—all of which inhibit these opportunities.

Despite the fact that the overall level of development in the AMU is much lower than in Europe, there are considerable variations in income levels within the region. GDP per capita in Mauritania is 10 percent of that in Libya. The levels of integration into the international economy are also varied: Morocco and Tunisia are members of the WTO, they have completed IMF-backed structural adjustment programs, and they have partly convertible currencies, relatively dynamic private sectors, and growing nonpetroleum exports. In contrast, Algeria and Libya are less open to international trade, have smaller and much less dynamic private sectors, and low levels of nonpetroleum exports.[57]

There is significant informal trade in the region based on bartering, smuggling, and other unregistered transactions. Morocco and Tunisia have liberalized their import regions, and Tunisia has liberalized its import regimes; hence, trade between them has increased steadily since the mid-1980s. And as mentioned earlier, the conclusion of an association agreement between the EU and Morocco and Tunisia has reawakened interest in the AMU.[58]

The EU has encouraged Mediterranean countries to integrate by removing restrictions on trade, investment, and capital flows. In order to further this integration, the EU has been prepared to allow elements of regional cumulation with regard to rules of origin. In order to qualify for entry into the EU, goods must meet its origin rules. This is to ensure that at least a share of value added (processing or manufacturing) takes place in the country exporting to the EU. Regional cumulation means that countries in the region are treated as one and that exports to the EU of finished goods meet the rules of origin if the imported component originates in the region. The EU applies regional cumulation to the Maghreb states.[59] It has also indicated a willingness to consider cumulation on an ad hoc basis for products produced by joint ventures between countries in the eastern Mediterranean.

Egypt and Israel

In 1980, Egypt and Israel signed a trade agreement allowing MFN treatment of trade between them. The agreement went into effect in 1981. Each country would charge the tariff rate applicable to a commodity under its customs schedule. Under GATT, of which both countries are members, these tariffs were the same as those charged by each party on imports from third countries with which each had an MFN agreement. Trade relations have developed very slowly because of political friction between the two countries. The 1980 agreement included a clause calling for annual meetings of a bilateral committee on trade. This met once in 1982 and then again in 1993.

Israel buys a large share of oil from Egypt, but apart from this, trade between the two countries has been limited. In 1992, according to the IMF, Egyptian exports to Israel equaled $290 million, including oil. The same source gives 1993 exports as $15 million, presumably excluding oil.[60] The Lebanon War, which began in 1982, resulted in a deterioration of relations between the two countries and a fall in trade. Since 1990, with an improvement in the political climate, there has been an increase, although part of the rise in Egyptian exports to Israel is accounted for by sales to Palestine.

Jordan and Israel

In October 1995, following the signing of a peace treaty a year earlier, Israel and Jordan reached an agreement on trade and economic cooperation. The two countries agreed to negotiate the creation of a free trade area and to end discriminatory trade barriers. They agreed on MFN treatment of trade between them. The agreement contained a protocol on tariff reductions. Israel granted Jordan tariff cuts of 100 percent, 50 percent, and 20 percent for three lists of commodities. Jordan granted Israel cuts of 10 percent on a list of commodities and a further 5 percent cut after three years on the same items. The protocol would last for three years, and during that period, the parties agreed to negotiate on expanding the scope of mutual duty reductions and improving market access.[61]

Palestine and Israel

In May 1994, Israel and the PLO signed an agreement in Cairo that contained economic clauses. These envisaged the creation of a customs union between Israel and the Palestinian territories. Goods would move freely between Israel and Palestine, with the exception of a quota on imports on a number of foodstuffs that would be abolished by 1998. A common external tariff would apply on imports from abroad at the level prevailing in Israel. Exceptions were made for limited quantities of certain goods that could be imported into Palestine from Jordan, Egypt, and other Arab and Islamic countries. These would be subject to reduced tariffs. As a result of tension between the Israeli government and the Palestinian Authority, trade was disrupted but not discontinued.

Summary: Hub-and-Spoke Trade Relations

Given the state of political relations in the Mediterranean and the Middle East, the creation of real free trade areas is unlikely, despite moves in that direction. As a result, a hub-and-spoke set of relations between the EU (hub) and the Mediterranean (spoke) will prevail, and this will discourage investment in the latter. The failure to develop free trade agreements between the Mediterranean countries (the exception is the Israeli-Turkish agreement) means that preference is given by the Mediterranean states to imports from the EU. In this way, the hub benefits at the expense of the spoke, and insofar as the latter consists mainly

of poorer countries, the diversion of income is more significant.[62] One
way in which the EU could encourage investment would be to go ahead
with a liberal diagonal cumulation system.

Trade and Development

The importance of trade with the EU for the Arab Mediterranean countries is shown in Table 7.2, which reveals that in 1998, in four of the
eight countries listed, more than 50 percent of imports came from the
EU. In six of them, the EU accounted for more than 50 percent of their
exports. Among the main goods traded were oil and gas. In fact, almost
all Algerian and Libyan exports to the EU consisted of oil and gas.
Between 40 and 60 percent of Syrian exports were oil and gas, and
about 60 percent of Egypt's exports was oil. In 1988, excluding oil and
gas, Mediterranean exports came to about $12 billion. In 1994, nonoil
Mediterranean exports came to about $22.2 billion, an increase of 85
percent. The main increases in nonoil exports were from Turkey, Israel,
Tunisia, and Morocco.

The EU sharply increased its share of Libyan exports over the same
period. This was largely due to the reduction in purchases of Libyan oil
by Far Eastern countries following the implementation of sanctions
against Libya. The UN excluded EU countries—most significantly,
Italy and Germany—from its sanctions regime.

**Table 7.2 EU Share in Arab Mediterranean Countries' Foreign Trade,
1990 and 1998**

	Exports to EU (%)		Imports from EU (%)	
	1990	1998	1990	1998
Algeria	62.6	69.3	79.0	76.7
Egypt	43.6	52.2	39.4	36.9
Jordan	10.4	10.6	39.7	31.9
Lebanon	25.9	25.1	39.1	44.8
Libya	60.8	90.1	60.9	59.1
Morocco	50.0	80.5	60.9	64.5
Syria	44.8	57.8	41.8	44.0
Tunisia	71.9	86.3	76.8	70.6

Sources: IMF, *Direction of Trade Statistics Yearbook, 1997;* and IMF, *Directions
of Trade, December 1999.*

Table 7.3 examines the composition of EU-Mediterranean trade. In 1997, agriculture accounted for 8.8 percent of EU exports to the Mediterranean and 11.1 percent of Mediterranean exports to the EU. The EU strictly limits imports of agricultural goods, including those of Mediterranean Arab countries.[63] Manufacturing accounted for 81 percent of EU exports and 48 percent of Mediterranean exports. Out of this, textiles and clothing took 8 percent of EU exports and 11 percent of Mediterranean exports, but in value terms, they were almost equal throughout the period. In 1990, fuels accounted of 40 percent of Mediterranean exports; in 1998, they took only 21 percent. The Mediterranean Arab countries had comparative advantages in textiles and clothing and fresh fruit and vegetables. These were precisely the areas in which the EU imposed limits on its imports. The other area of comparative advantage was in oil and gas (exported by Libya and Algeria). The value of exports of these products to the EU was affected by the fall in oil prices during the period 1990–1998. Combining all these factors explains the dismal performance of exports to the EU, which fell by 13 percent over that time span.

Table 7.3 The Composition of EU-Mediterranean[a] Trade, 1990–1997 (in Billions $)[b]

	1990	1991	1992	1993	1997
EU exports to Mediterranean countries:					
Agriculture	6.6	5.4	5.6	6.3	6.5
Manufacturing	46.2	45.0	45.0	50.2	61.3
Textiles and clothing	4.8	4.8	4.4	5.0	5.9
Other	5.2	6.1	4.7	5.5	5.9
Total	58.0	56.5	55.3	62.0	73.7
Mediterranean exports to EU:					
Agriculture	5.2	5.6	4.8	4.3	5.2
Manufacturing	20.9	23.0	21.0	21.7	26.8
Textiles and clothing	10.3	10.6	10.4	10.4	11.5
Fuels	21.5	21.3	19.6	16.2	9.9
Other	6.2	3.8	4.2	2.8	4.8
Total	53.8	53.7	49.6	45.0	46.7

Sources: EU, *The EU and World Trade: EU Trade Development for the Year 1993, 1994;* and EU, *World Trade 1997 Comparison EU, US, Japan.*

Notes: a. In addition to the countries analyzed in this chapter, "Mediterranean" here includes Albania, Ceuta and Melila, Cyprus, Gibraltar, Israel, Malta, Turkey, and Yugoslavia.

b. Original source statistics in ECU; dollar conversions calculated by author.

The increase in EU membership in 1995 did not have a major effect on trade with the Mediterranean countries: Austria, Finland, and Sweden accounted for about 8 percent of EU exports and imports in 1995.

The Uruguay Round of talks for GATT codified tariff reductions for exports of developing countries to developed country markets and prevented the use of nontariff barriers by the latter. The agreement meant that countries in the developing world that did not have preferential trade agreements with the EU found it easier to export there. The relative position of countries that have preferential trade agreements will therefore deteriorate.

This process has already started. EU imports from non–Middle East Asian countries rose by 92 percent from 1989 to 1994; those from South and Central America increased by 115 percent.[64] Furthermore, since 1989, the EU has signed preferential trade agreements with East European countries, and its imports from them have expanded rapidly: imports from Bulgaria, the Czech and Slovak Republics, Czechoslovakia, Poland, and Romania rose from $12.8 billion in 1989 to $27.8 billion in 1994, a rise of 117 percent.[65] Between 1989 and 1994, exports from the Mediterranean countries to the EU rose by only 31 percent. Markets have become increasingly global, and countries that carried out reforms in the 1980s, such as Morocco and Tunisia, are finding themselves under increasing pressure. Their production costs are too high compared with those of the new competitors: China, Indonesia, and Thailand, among others. They have, therefore, had to devalue their currencies and take other measures to reduce costs so as to maintain export levels and avoid running into the kind of balance-of-payments crises that affected them in the 1980s. The effect of these measures has been a restriction on demand and economic growth. The experience of Egypt suggests that the medicine can be very bitter, and that of Tunisia and Morocco suggests that many doses are needed.

During the 1980s, the signs of an increasing divide between faster- and slower-growing economies in the Mediterranean became more apparent. Algeria, Libya, Syria, and Jordan suffered from direct or indirect reliance on oil income. When the price of oil collapsed in the mid-1980s, GDP and exports in Algeria and Libya were badly affected. Syria and Jordan experienced falls in remittances and foreign aid that resulted in severe economic difficulties. The total foreign debt of Algeria, Syria, and Jordan rose from $24.7 billion in 1980 to $23.2 billion in 1985 and to $50.8 billion in 1990. There were corresponding increases in their foreign debt-to-GNP and foreign debt-to-export ratios.[66] In contrast, Turkey and Tunisia—and, to a lesser extent, Morocco—reformed their economies. Turkey industrialized, increasing the share of its manufacturing sector from 20.9 percent of GDP in 1980 to 25.5 percent in 1989. In Tunisia, the share of manufacturing in GNP increased from 12.8 percent in 1980 to 16.4 percent in 1989. In Tunisia, and especially in Turkey, the range of industrialized goods that were exported increased greatly.[67]

Israel is an industrialized economy with a per capita income level higher than that of some of the poorer EU countries. Since 1990, it has been one of the fastest-growing economies in the world as a result of the combined effects of large-scale immigration, the Middle East peace process, and inflows of capital from abroad. Turkey is also industrialized, but its per capita income level is close to the Mediterranean average. In recent years, it has suffered from high inflation and rapid population growth. Jordan, Morocco, and Tunisia all carried out structural adjustment programs in the 1980s and are experiencing some of the benefits, but, as indicated at the end of this chapter, Moroccan and Tunisian exports are facing increased competition from outside the region.

Egypt carried out radical financial reforms in 1990 and 1991, and as a result, its budget deficit and balance-of-payments positions have strengthened. Limited economic reforms, in terms of privatization and trade liberalization, have been introduced, and the economy began to grow at a healthy rate from 1995 onward. But Syria, Libya, and Algeria remain very closed economies, despite reforms in Algeria and Syria in the late 1980s and 1990s. Political as well as economic factors stand in the way of their closer integration into an EU-Mediterranean free trade area. Lebanon is, par excellence, the laissez-faire economy of the region. Its economic future will remain unclear until a political settlement between Israel and Syria is achieved. The Palestinian economy is being developed with public- and private-sector initiatives, but close personal contacts with the political leadership are needed for many economic transactions. Palestine's economic future will be determined by the way in which it manages its economy, by its political and security relationship with Israel (and, to a lesser extent, that with Jordan), and, of course, by whether or not it attains full independence and becomes a state.

Those Mediterranean countries whose exports mainly went to the EU in particular suffered from the fact that the EU economy grew more slowly than that of other developed and developing areas. Between

1980 and 1990, the EU economy grew by an annual average rate of 2.3 percent, compared to a world average of 2.9 percent.[68] In the period 1991–1997, the EU's average annual growth rate was 1.6 percent, compared with a world average of 2.2 percent.[69] Since the late 1980s, the Mediterranean countries have also had to contend with a loss in their relative advantage in EU markets, as the latter granted improved access to other countries, such as those in Eastern Europe.

Between 1980 and 1990, the terms of trade of Arab oil exporters declined by 40 percent. Those for diversified exporters in the Arab world also fell. The exports of the Arab countries were very highly concentrated in a narrow range of products. Eight of the ten countries in the Mediterranean group are Arab states, and even the most industrialized of them, Tunisia, suffered from this problem in the 1980s and early 1990s.

Given all these factors, the trade and general economic performance of the eight Mediterranean Arab states has been problematic. The EU-Mediterranean agreements will not significantly change this picture. These countries will benefit from more aid from the EU.[70] Food imports from the EU will become more expensive as the latter reduces agricultural subsidies, in accordance with the Uruguay Round negotiations.[71] In 1993, Algeria, Morocco, and Tunisia had net food imports of $2.44 billion, equal to 9 percent of their total imports. Egypt, Jordan, Lebanon, and Syria had a food deficit of $3.65 billion, equal to 46 percent of their exports.[72] The phasing out of the MFA will further reduce the relatively privileged access that some Mediterranean states have had in EU markets. Much will depend on the internal economic policies that they follow. Israel and Turkey have made more radical steps toward economic liberalization and will reap the benefits. As the EU has warned, the income gap between them and their neighbors will grow if the latter do not follow suit.[73]

Foreign Investment

The conclusion of a number of studies with quite different orientations was that the Mediterranean countries (with the exception of Israel and Turkey) were falling behind many other developing countries in the economic race.[74] This applied to the Arab world as a whole. One area in which this relative decline was particularly marked was foreign investment, which can be an important variable in the development process.

This is especially true in countries that have been unable to raise the skill levels of workers and management to a point where they can absorb foreign technology without the need for foreign investment. The models for this self-sufficient pattern of development, where foreign investment was discouraged, were Japan and South Korea.[75]

Although the volume of foreign investment in Morocco and Tunisia has risen, it remains modest. As much as 90 percent of the foreign investment in Tunisia in 1992–1993 went into the petroleum sector.[76] Foreign investment in the region was affected by political uncertainty, bureaucratic obstruction, corruption, low skill and education levels, inadequate infrastructure, and a lack of cooperation among neighboring countries.[77] Foreign direct investment in Morocco rose from $85 million in 1988 to $601 million in 1994. That in Tunisia rose from $61 million in 1988 to $371 million in 1992 and then fell to $194 million in 1994. Most of these flows appear to have come from Europe. In 1992, 58 percent of foreign direct investment in Morocco came from the EU.[78]

Foreign investment may be as important, or even more important, than trade in assisting development in the Mediterranean region. This assertion is based on the experience of Spain, whose membership in the EC led to an increase in foreign direct investment. Although much of it went into the service sector rather than into industry, it helped to modernize and expand the economy by bringing in new capital, both financial and physical, and introducing new technology and management. It also helped to provide markets in that the firms that invested abroad often wanted to take advantage of cheap labor in order to produce goods more cheaply for markets that they already had. Spain, like other southern states that joined the EU, benefited from subsidies made available by the European Commission in Brussels, which helped it to modernize its infrastructure.

The Mediterranean countries have suffered because they have not received the same level of subsidy and are therefore less able to compete for foreign investment. The agreements with the EU have also discouraged investment in the Mediterranean countries because of the cumulation rules. If the countries in the Mediterranean (or at least those that recognize one another diplomatically) could construct joint ventures and market their products in the EU under unitary cumulation rules, then they would have greater incentives to produce. The countries of the region would also have greater incentives to cooperate.

The volume of subsidies granted to southern EU members has been a major factor enabling them to attract foreign investment, from within and outside the EU. This has made them relatively attractive compared to the Mediterranean countries outside the EU, many of which have had to cut back on assistance to industry as a result of stabilization and structural adjustment programs. The framework for liberalizing capital movements and trade in services among the EU, Morocco, and Tunisia is to be an association council, which has not yet, at the time of writing, come into existence.

The Role of the EU

The Mediterranean countries were offered duty-free access to EU markets for industrial products in the agreements signed in the 1970s. The agreements signed in the 1990s moved those countries toward the creation of free trade areas with the EU, with consequent losses of tariff revenues on imports from the EU. The loss of tariff revenues was equivalent to a gain made by the EU exporter, and the Mediterranean countries were left with a preferential trade system under which imports from countries outside the EU, with which free trade agreements have not been concluded, became relatively more expensive. Israel's removal of quotas and gradual reduction of tariffs on imports from countries with which it does not have a free trade agreement is an attempt to prevent, or at least limit, this kind of distortion. Other countries in the Mediterranean lack this freedom of maneuver because their income levels are lower.

Discriminating against non-EU imports may result in little trade distortion where they constitute a small share of total imports, but high levels of protection may result in greater distortion. The EU may displace intraregional trade in the Mediterranean if the latter group of states does not conclude free trade agreements among themselves. This would particularly hit Turkey's industrial exports and restrict potential Israeli exports to other countries in the Mediterranean and the Middle East, as well as affecting exports of other states in the region.[79]

Given these potential losses, it would seem that unilateral trade liberalization would be preferred over regional trading links. There are a number of reasons why Mediterranean countries have favored regional trading links. Regional agreements are often stronger mechanisms than multinational agreements for locking in economic reforms. They also offer a framework for harmonizing business and trade regulations with the trading partner. Regional agreements further ensure market access by reducing or banning trade restrictions between the parties. Regional agreements are often accompanied by aid flows: this is a major part of the emerging EU-Mediterranean relationship. Regional agreements can be used to begin processes of general trade liberalization. Finally, and often most importantly, there may be political factors or incentives that bring groups of countries together.[80] As a result of the political and economic factors analyzed above, the EU offered privileged status to the Mediterranean countries: it took the initiative to negotiate with them on agreements or responded positively to their suggestions.

What could the EU do to strengthen trading relationships within the Middle East, or at least among those states that have trade agreements with it? The EU permitted "bilateral cumulation," which meant that its Mediterranean partners can include in their products inputs (including some manufactured inputs) from the EU. These products could then be exported to the EU duty free. If there are inputs, including manufactured inputs in the products of EU partners, for them to be allowed into the EU duty free or without quotas, they had to meet stringent rules-of-origin regulations. The regulations regarding textiles and clothing were particularly severe. In 1994, the EU's Commission proposed that "diagonal cumulation" be permitted. This would enable countries with trade agreements with the EU to buy inputs from one another and use them in goods being exported to the EU without having to prove that they underwent "sufficient transformation." The Commission is proposing that this be applied only to "nonoriginating materials" rather than full processing. With regard to countries in the European Economic Area, which includes the EU and a number of countries in Eastern Europe, it proposed "full cumulation," which means that goods can be processed anywhere in the European Economic Area. Full cumulation was permitted between the Magreb countries in the cooperation agreements that they signed with the EC in 1976.[81] This means that there are built-in anomalies and disincentives in the current set of trade agreements. One of the most serious is the fact that the EU does not in practice recognize the Palestinian-Israeli economic agreement. This means that, strictly speaking, goods jointly produced in Palestine and Israel cannot gain duty-free access to the EU. Yet this is a vital area of cooperation that needs to be encouraged in order to strengthen the peace process.

The contrast between the EU and the United States in this regard is significant. The United States has given Israeli and Palestinian producers the option of fully cumulating the costs or values of materials and processing operations so as to achieve originating status under the U.S.-Israel free trade agreement and the U.S.-Palestinian trade arrangement. Goods can be shipped from Israel or Palestine to the United States without violating the direct transport clauses of the agreements. Under the agreements with the EU, Israel and Palestine are treated as separate countries in determining origin.[82] This goes against the Israel-Palestinian customs union agreement and against the spirit of the EU's declarations that it favors the creation of an EU-Mediterranean free trade area.

In contrast with the Mediterranean states, the Visegrad group—Czechoslovakia, Hungary, and Poland—set up the Central European Free Trade Area after completing bilateral agreements with the EU. Had they not done this, firms would have had incentives to invest in the EU so as to get duty-free access to the East European markets, but they would have been discouraged from investing in any of the Visegrad states.[83]

Conclusion

Economic relations between the Arab countries of the Mediterranean and the EU are complex. They have been negotiated bilaterally between each Arab state and the EU. It is conspicuous that, despite the EU's initiative in bringing about the Barcelona Declaration, it did not envisage any change in this. The EU has offered free trade in industrial products (with some exclusions) and quota-controlled imports of agricultural goods, and at the same time it is intensifying the process of economic and financial integration among its members and has declared its intention of expanding its membership eastward in Europe.

The main hope for better Arab access to European markets therefore lies in such multilateral agreements as the Uruguay Round of GATT, which will result in changes in the EU's policy of subsidizing agriculture and excluding imports and the end of the MFA. These measures will mean "worse before better" in that subsidizes on EU foodstuffs exports will decline. Third countries with low labor costs, such as China and India, will gain better access to EU textile and clothing markets at the expense of Arab states that had preferential access. Added to these effects will be losses of tax revenues from the reduction of tariffs on imports.

The opportunities for Arab states arising from globalization will therefore be accompanied by serious adjustment difficulties. Given their resource base and the need for most of them to import food and investment goods, they will have no alternative but to be involved in the international trading system.

Notes

1. Handousa, ed., *Economic Transition*, p. 4.
2. Safadi, "Global Challenges and Opportunities," p. 23; and author's estimates.
3. EU, "Strengthening the Mediterranean Policy," p. 14.
4. Ayubi, ed., *Distant Neighbors*, p. 5.
5. Halevi and Kleiman, "Regional vs. Non-Regional Integration," p. 9.
6. Calculated from IMF, *Directions of Trade Statistics Yearbook, 1997.*
7. UN, *World Economic and Social Survey, 1994*, p. 76.
8. Riordan et al., *World Economy*, p. 76.
9. EU, "Strengthening the Mediterranean Policy," p. 8.
10. Ibid.
11. IMF, *Directions of Trade Statistics Yearbook, 1998.*
12. EU, *European Economy*, pp. 19–20.
13. Ibid.
14. Ibid.
15. de Azevedo, ed., "Migration and Development Cooperation," pp. 25 and 32–33.
16. EU, *Demographic Situation, 1994*, pp. 72–73.
17. EU, *Eurostat Yearbook, 1995*, p. 66.
18. Ibid., pp. 72–73.
19. Quoted in Ayubi, ed., *Distant Neighbors*, p. 221.
20. Riordan et al., *World Economy*, pp. 16–17.
21. Bruni and Venturini, "Pressure to Migrate," p. 394.
22. Ibid., p. 344.
23. Riordan et al., *World Economy*, p. 5.
24. UN, *Replacement Migration, 2000.*
25. Fargues, "Demographic Explosion or Social Upheaval?" pp. 156–179.
26. Ibid.; and Courbage, "Demographic Change in the Arab World," pp. 19–22.
27. IMF, *Balance of Payments Yearbook, 1997.*
28. *International Herald Tribune*, 19 June 1995.
29. EU, *Basic Statistics of the European Union, 1995*, p. 45.
30. EU, "Strengthening the Mediterranean Policy," p. 25.
31. GATT, "The General Agreement on Tariffs and Trade," p. 486.
32. A *customs union* is defined as a trading area with a common external tariff. The level of the tariff may vary by commodity but not by country. A *free trade area* is also one in which trade is unrestricted, but each member state imposes its own external tariffs vis-à-vis third countries.

33. The EEC was founded by Belgium, France, Italy, Luxembourg, the Netherlands, and West Germany. In July 1967, it became the European Community. In 1973, the UK, Ireland, and Denmark joined. In 1981, Greece joined, followed in 1986 by Portugal and Spain. On 1 November 1993, the EC became the European Union, and on 1 January 1995, Austria, Finland, and Sweden became members.

34. Anderson and Nordheim, "Is World Trade Becoming More Regionalized?" pp. 91–109.

35. Shiells, "Regional Trading Blocs," pp. 30–32.

36. EU, *Trade Relations,* p. 6.

37. Ibid., p. 7.

38. EU, *Countries of the Greater Arab Maghreb,* p. 13.

39. Pomfret, *Mediterranean Policy,* p. 23.

40. EIU, *CR: Algeria, 1997,* no. 2.

41. Hoekman, *The WTO, the EU, and the Arab World,* p. 23.

42. Daveri and Faini, "Trade and Integration," p. 4.

43. Hoekman, *The WTO, the EU, and the Arab World,* p. 8.

44. Daveri and Faini, "Trade and Integration," table 3.

45. Hoekman and Djanker, "Catching Up with Eastern Europe?" p. 17.

46. EIU, *CR: Egypt, 1997,* no. 2.

47. Lawrence, *Towards Free Trade,* p. 12.

48. EU, *Europe in Israel,* p. 3.

49. *Daily Report,* FBIS-WEU 97–106, 16 April 1997.

50. EIU, *CR: Lebanon, 1997,* no. 3.

51. Ibid., no. 1.

52. Laanatza, "Impact of the EU-Mediterranean Association Agreements."

53. EU, *The European Union and the Palestinians,* pp. 3 and 10.

54. ASEAN members include Brunei, Indonesia, Malaysia, the Philippines, Singapore, and Thailand.

55. Finaish and Bell, "The Arab Maghreb Union," p. 12.

56. Calculated from IMF, *Directions of Trade Statistics Yearbook, 1995,* p. 73.

57. Finaish and Bell, "The Arab Maghreb Union," pp. 14–23.

58. Daveri and Faini, "Trade and Integration," p. 1.

59. EU, *Trade Relations,* p. 12.

60. IMF, *Directions of Trade Statistics Yearbook, 1995,* p. 187.

61. Government of Israel, Agreement on Trade and Economic Cooperation Between the Government of the State of Israel and the Government of the Hashemite Kingdom of Jordan, 1995.

62. Wonnacott, "Trade and Investment," pp. 237–252.

63. DeRosa, *Agricultural Trade and Rural Development,* p. 19.

64. Calculated from IMF, *Directions of Trade Statistics Yearbook, 1995,* pp. 75 and 77.

65. Ibid., p. 75.

66. Calculated from World Bank, *Word Debt Tables, 1991–92.*

67. EU, *European Economy,* pp. 91–96.

68. Calculated from UNCTAD, *UNCTAD Trade and Development Report, 1995,* p. 4.

69. UN, *World Economic and Social Survey, 1998,* p. 125.

70. Kelly and Fritz-Krockow, "Trade Policies," pp. 52–85.

71. Riordan et al., *World Economy,* p. 46.

72. Ibid., p. 35.

73. EU, "Strengthening the Mediterranean Policy."

74. World Bank, *Claiming the Future;* and Strange et al., "Direct Investment in North Africa," pp. 225–252.

75. Singh, "How Did East Asia Grow So Fast?" pp. 21–22; and Vernon, "Technological Development," p. 29.

76. Zallio, "Morocco and Tunisia," p. 62.

77. Strange, "Direct Investment in North Africa," pp. 225–252.

78. Daveri and Faini, "Trade and Integration," p. 3.

79. Lawrence, "Preferential Trading Arrangements," p. 29.

80. Hoekman and Djankcr, "Catching Up with Eastern Europe?" pp. 9–13.

81. Tovias, "Economic Impact," pp. 113–128.

82. STIMENA, *Regional Economic Development.*

83. Hoekman and Djankov, "Towards a Free Trade Agreement," pp. 129–155.

CHAPTER 8

Conclusion

The Arab states all benefited from the increases in oil wealth that occurred after 1973. The Gulf Cooperation Council states and Libya (as well as Iraq and Algeria) received a direct income boost; those states with much less oil or none sent workers to the oil states and received remittances and economic aid. They also borrowed abroad. Then, in the early 1980s, oil income declined, and the poorer states in the region were forced to adjust because they had not built an economic base that would yield sufficient income to pay the interest on foreign loans.

Following the failures of industrialization strategies based on import substitution and massive state intervention, many Arab states moved toward more free market policies: structural adjustment followed stabilization programs. They also had to correct biases against agriculture that restricted or reduced food production while rapid population growth continued.

Stabilization policies led to financial improvements: budget deficits were reduced, inflation was brought under control, foreign debt burden was rescheduled and reduced, and the balance of payments was improved. Stabilization was followed by structural reforms designed to lay the basis for faster economic growth. Tunisia, which was the first to reform its economy, experienced steady growth. It has often been cited as a model for economic development in the Arab world because its per capita income levels are among the highest outside the GCC. It has been consistent in implementing economic reforms, although, like elsewhere, privatization has been limited. Since 1995, Egypt has experienced relatively fast growth after years of near stagnation. This change took place against a background of low budget deficits, declining inflation rates, a healthy balance of payments, a large increase in foreign exchange reserves, and an improved foreign debt position. Egypt has attracted foreign investors, and its progress is, perhaps, the most important example of the success of stabilization and structural adjustment.

At the time of writing, however, it is not clear how far the strong growth of recent years can be sustained. Jordan made a rapid recovery from the effects of the Gulf crisis of 1990–1991, but its growth rate in 1996 and 1997 was officially overestimated and, in fact, growth slowed sharply. Other indicators associated with stabilization—inflation, the budget deficit, and the balance of payments—remain healthy, but unemployment and poverty threaten stability. Morocco also experienced a major improvement in the financial indicators, but steady growth remained elusive as the economy is subject to large fluctuations in agricultural production determined by the volume of rainfall.

The International Monetary Fund has acknowledged that stabilization and structural reform lead, at least initially, to a slowdown in growth.[1] This partly reflects the fact that growth in the Arab world before the reforms was the result of unhealthy trends that often boosted demand and thus output in unsustainable ways. The question, therefore, has to be asked: How long can the slow-growth phase last before it creates more problems than it solves?

As a result of the slowdown in growth, the rise in unemployment, and the reductions in subsidies, stabilization in the region increased the need for social safety nets but at the same time reduced the funds available for them.[2] Hence, governments came under pressure to do more with less. This required expertise and competent administration, as well as a lack of corruption, if programs were to be successful. The quality of government administration became a crucial variable in maintaining social stability and in making changes in economic policy.

Major factors causing the rise in poverty included increasing unemployment and the decline in the provision of public services. Unemployment in Algeria, for example, doubled between 1988 and 1993 as a result of high population growth and a declining demand for labor.[3] Reduced government spending, which was a central part of economic reform programs, involved lower subsidies on goods and services and higher taxes, which mainly affect the poor. In Egypt, under the structural adjustment program, government spending on basic social services fell from 6.7 percent of total spending in 1991 to 4.2 percent in 1993, but as social pressures and terrorist acts by Islamic fundamentalists increased, it rose to 6.7 percent in 1994.[4]

Performance indices for secondary education, which showed improvements in the late 1970s, have exhibited a slowdown in some Arab states since the mid-1980s. High education levels comprise one of the factors that explain East Asian growth. In the Arab world, economic restructuring has involved the introduction of fees in public education systems. This, together with inflation, resulted in a decline in access to primary education, especially for girls, particularly in Egypt and Morocco. Attainments in the Egyptian educational system have apparently declined as a result of educational reforms as well as financial pressures.[5] This is a worrying factor, because the ability of the population as a whole to benefit from growth and to contribute to it depends on its skills. This is precisely the area in which the World Bank backs public spending.

Real wages adjusted for skill levels in the Middle East are relatively high compared with other parts of the world, although there are some exceptions. As a result, in the absence of rapid growth, moves from the production of untraded goods and services to those of traded goods and services are not powerful enough to achieve full employment at adequate real wage levels.[6] This suggests that conventional stabilization and structural adjustment programs will not produce the right results. In economist's jargon, the economy may get stuck at an equilibrium with high unemployment. Economies need growth in order to readjust, but stabilization programs prevent this. The task of policymakers is therefore to design policies that will bring about adjustment without reducing demand in the economy.

The international economic environment in which Arab economies are liberalizing remains tough. Many developed countries continue to use nontrade barriers against developing countries, and those in the Mediterranean are losing the preferential access that they had in their main market: the European Union. They are not members of any substantial regional trading body, which is a disadvantage in a trading world that has become increasingly regionalized. Yet they have no alternative but to integrate into the world economy. The GCC states, Libya, Algeria, and Iraq all need to sell oil, petroleum products, and gas abroad. The Arab world as a whole needs to import food as well as other goods and services.

Demographic conditions are improving in that birthrates are declining, as is population growth. Despite this, the labor force is still growing relatively rapidly, which means that employment has to be created if social and political stability are not to be threatened. Can this be done amid current growth rates? Can growth rates be accelerated? The Egyptian experience suggests that it may be possible if the government remains committed to reform. The Tunisian experience indicates a need for caution: growth rates have been steady rather than accelerating—between 1992 and 1996, they fluctuated from a low of 2.2 percent to a high of 7.8 percent.

There has been a change in the economic advice that the Arab states have received in recent years. They are no longer being told to simply cut public spending; educational and infrastructure spending are now considered to be beneficial. The question then arises of how to finance them when taxes should be cut. How did the change in theories of growth and policy affect policymakers? This was not necessarily the main cause of the policy changes, but in the 1980s, debt and related problems moved the center of influence toward Washington, D.C. The IMF, the World Bank, and the U.S. government favored stabilization and liberalization and placed much less emphasis on social safety nets or infrastructure investment than they now do. Policies changed because of domestic political factors and dissatisfaction with past performance and in response to international pressures. The recommendations of international agencies also changed because of dissatisfaction with performance of policies they had recommended and changes in the economy theory underpinning them. It may now be possible for governments to intervene in microeconomic terms: pushing forward one industry or investing in education, but only within a strict macroeconomic framework that avoids large budget deficits and criticism from the IMF and the World Bank.

Developments in the World Trade Organization have also militated against government intervention. The subsidies given to firms within one economy are increasingly being considered as unfair trade practices by other countries. As more Arab states join the WTO, they will become increasingly subject to pressures and restrictions on domestic competition and other policies.[7]

Agreements signed by Mediterranean countries with the EU will prevent them from using industrial policy in the way in which the East Asian Tigers did. For example, the association agreement between Jordan and the EU states that "any public aid which distorts or threatens to distort competition by favoring certain undertakings or the production of certain goods [is] incompatible with the proper functioning of the Agreement."[8] This means that when this clause comes into operation, the freedom to intervene will be drastically reduced.

The new growth theory takes account of trends in East Asian economic policymaking. Rapid growth in Japan, South Korea, and Taiwan was based on, among other things, two sets of factors. First, they got what have been called the "basics" right. Among the most important of these basics were relative equality in the distribution of income, falling population growth rates, and large investment in basic education. Literacy rates were high in the 1960s and rose thereafter. Second, they chose a set of policies that, in terms of conventional economic theory, was heterodox if not unorthodox. These policies included close cooperation between the public sector and the private sector. This made possible selective interventions to favor certain industries, which were effective because governments were able to enforce performance criteria on companies. Protection against imports was used in the early stages of industrial development, and only then was export promotion introduced. This was also done to protect the balance of payments. Reliance on foreign investment was limited, but an openness to foreign technology was critical. Fiscal and monetary stability were maintained. As the economies matured, the government's role in promoting industry declined.

Insofar as the success of the East Asian economies in the period 1960–1995 was an inspiration for other developing countries and a source of controversy among analysts and international economic organizations, so the recent crisis in that region will also have an impact on economic thinking and policy. The crisis of 1997–1998 also had lessons for other regions.

The lessons for the Arab states are not straightforward. Getting the basics right is a huge task that involves reducing population growth. Although much has been achieved, especially in North Africa, much remains to be done. With regard to investment in the infrastructure and in education, the new international conventional wisdom favors this, but questions remain as to how to finance it. This is an area where foreign aid could speed up the process of getting the basics right and reduce the deflationary effect of balancing the budget. The use of selective intervention was explicitly backed in the World Bank's *World Development Report* of 1997, but it cautioned that administrative capability and political will are needed if interventions are to be more successful than those of the past. These are related to the pattern of development and the country's culture.

Encouragement of foreign investment was more necessary in the Middle East in the 1990s than it was in East Asia in the 1960s and

1970s for two reasons. The first is that encouraging foreign investment helps to reassure local capital, which, in much of the Middle East, faced nationalization and political hostility during the 1960s. There was no socialist phase in Japan, Korea, or Taiwan, and private capital in those countries was not alienated by the regime, as it was in parts of the Middle East. Second, international opinion and structures have moved strongly in favor of globalization in recent years, and international trade agreements have locked countries into a world of mobile capital. Those that do not join the WTO and/or regional trading blocs will find themselves locked out.

Public- and private-sector cooperation is now possible in Middle East countries that have abandoned socialism, but even in Morocco, which never formally experienced it, the state has been unwilling to privatize.[9] This is due to the role of sectoral pressure groups and also the government's fear of the consequences of privatization for employment. A decline in the role of the state in economic development in Arab countries will, according to the new growth theory, be a function of the level of development. This suggests that only when the Arab states reach the level of development that South Korea and Taiwan reached by the 1980s will they be able to do more about laissez-faire policies.

Where does this leave the Arab states? They have been liberalizing their economies in accordance with IMF and World Bank advice and have run into two problems: slow growth and high unemployment. They have also found that the international economic environment is less encouraging than it used to be. The world economy is growing more slowly, and markets have become increasingly competitive. This situation is in sharp contrast to the international economic environment that existed when the East Asian states were industrializing in the 1960s. The world economy was growing more rapidly then, and there were fewer protective barriers restricting, or even blocking, their exports to developed countries.

Social funds have been set up to tackle unemployment and poverty in Egypt, Jordan, and elsewhere, but the success of this measure has been limited. The governments of these countries have been told to spend less and are now being told to spend better. They have been told that such international trade agreements as the Uruguay Round and their bilateral agreements with the EU will not yield major gains in the foreseeable future, and so they must engage in domestic reforms and regional cooperation in order to secure growth. The question is whether the path they should follow is clear and whether they have the means and the will to follow it.

The diversified economies that chose reform faced opposition from urban groups, which often rioted in protest against the rise in basic commodity prices. These protests caused delays and sometimes limited the scope of reforms, particularly with regard to privatization. They did not, however, prevent the general move toward a more liberalized economy. This suggests that the state had enough power to proceed but that the middle classes were not strong enough to push for a faster pace. The state draws support from workers, peasants, the military, and the middle class (both new and old). Insofar as its main objective is to remain in power, it has acted to overcome the crises of the old system without losing all of the support of those who benefited from it, principally urban workers and bureaucrats. Trying to control these variegated interest groups has been a complex process, and the results in terms of delays, false starts, restarts, and other maneuvers have been the main subject of this book.

Given the size of their oil reserves, the policy options available to Saudi Arabia, Kuwait, and the United Arab Emirates are sui generis. The other states in the GCC will face some of the problems that confront the poorer Arab states today. The oil reserves of Bahrain, Oman, and Qatar will be exhausted within twenty years, and these countries need to plan for the post-oil era. Qatar has huge gas reserves that will supply income for many years but that require much larger investments than oil does. This means maintaining a savings rate high enough to fund investment for the future and ensuring that the investments made are efficient.

All the GCC states face an additional problem: employment—the most sensitive one of all. Its solution requires the development of the private sector, which would result in the spreading of economic power within each country. Although the rulers of GCC states understand the dangers of having large sections of the indigenous population reliant on public-sector employment, given the volatility of state (oil) revenues, they benefit from the allegiance that this creates. This is one reason why privatization has to be limited.

The related issue of bringing public-sector deficits under control depends on spending cuts and/or the introduction of charges for public services. These, in turn, depend on the extent to which the regimes feel that they can "tax" the population without being forced to grant representation. Although oil revenues fluctuate, the huge oil and gas reserves in the region provide most of the GCC states with the collateral needed to borrow themselves out of short-term crises and thus avoid the worst effects of economic adjustment.

Notes

1. Goldsborough et al., *Reinvigorating Growth,* p. 76.
2. Kanaan, ed., *Social Effects,* p. 95.
3. Bingaradi and Guieciour, "Social Safety Nets," p. 69.
4. Dau and el-Amach, "Social Safety Nets," pp. 103–104.
5. Fergany, "A Comment," pp. 234–235.
6. Page, "Comment," p. 241.
7. Lloyd and Sampson, "Competition and Trade Policy," pp. 681–705; and Hoekman and Kostecki, *Political Economy,* pp. 252–257.
8. Article 53.1 of the Euro-Jordanian Association Agreement, quoted by Laanatza, "Impact of the EU-Mediterranean Association Agreements."
9. Khosrowshani, "Privatization in Morocco."

Appendix:
A Note on Theories
of Economic Growth

The neoclassical approach to economic growth and development has largely been based on the Robert Solow's model.[1] This model has four variables: (1) output, which is itself a function of the second variable, (2) capital, (3) labor, and (4) knowledge, envisioned as the effectiveness of labor. Capital, labor, and knowledge are combined at any point in time to produce output; this is true at the microlevel of the firm and at the macrolevel of the economy as a whole. Output changes over time if input changes; output from given quantities of labor and capital rises when knowledge increases, in the form of technological progress. The model assumes constant returns to scale in capital and labor (or effective labor), which means that doubling the quantity of inputs doubles the quantity of outputs.

The assumption of constant returns to scale means that the model considers the economy to be big enough and developed enough to have exhausted the gains from specialization. In a small economy, there are likely to be further opportunities for specialization, which would mean that a doubling of inputs would more than double the level of outputs, which is increasing returns to scale. The model neglects land and other natural resources as inputs in the productive system. If natural resources were important, then doubling inputs of labor and capital would result in output less than doubling, and as a result, there would be diminishing returns to scale.

The model makes many other simplifying assumptions—there is only one good, the government is absent, fluctuations in employment are ignored, production is the result of combining three inputs only—

and the rates of saving, depreciation, population growth, and technological progress are assumed to be constant.

Output per worker varies over time or between different geographical areas in the Solow model as a result of differences in the amount of capital per worker (e.g., the amount of machinery per worker) and in the effectiveness of labor. The impact of changes in the level of capital per worker on output is limited, and this means that only variations in the effectiveness of labor explain productivity differentials. The main conclusions of the Solow model are twofold. First, as the return to capital (i.e., the rate of profit) is a guide to its contribution to output, and as its share in national income is modest, then variations in physical capital do not account for significant parts of economic growth or the variations in income among countries. The second conclusion is that capital accumulation (i.e., investment) cannot explain growth over time, nor can it explain the differences in levels of output and welfare among countries.

Explaining growth in terms of variations in capital stocks among countries and over time is problematic because the growth or variation in capital is often not large enough to explain the changes in output. It also implies far bigger variations in the rate of return to capital than have occurred historically or geographically. All this suggests that differences in physical capital do not account for the differences in output per worker that have been observed.

This leaves the effectiveness of labor as the main factor explaining growth and variation in output levels, but the Solow model says little about what it is. The level of knowledge, which determines the effectiveness of labor, is itself determined exogenously and is therefore not explained in the model. This is one of the main reasons why economists have become dissatisfied with the neoclassical explanation.

One solution is to explain changes in the state of knowledge. Another is to interpret the effectiveness of labor in terms of the education and skills of the labor force, the strength of property rights, the quality of the infrastructure, cultural attitudes toward work, and related factors. Alternatively, capital can be interpreted in a more sophisticated way: it can be more than merely physical capital, and it can yield positive external gains. If the latter applies, then the private rate of return on capital will not be an accurate reflection of its importance in the productive system. Variations in capital, defined and measured in a more sophisticated way, might after all provide an explanation of economic growth and geographic variations in income levels.

The so-called new growth theory attempts to deal with these problems. One approach of this theory models the development of knowledge so as to explain how labor becomes effective or productive over time. The second approach concentrates on capital, especially by considering human capital. This approach suggests that the share of physical capital in income may not be an accurate guide to its importance to the economy.

It is, however, difficult to believe that the acquisition of knowledge significantly explains economic growth or that differences in knowledge explain geographic variations in income levels. For this explanation to hold, there would have to be very long lags in the diffusion of knowledge, and it would be necessary to assume that poor countries do not have access to knowledge. Although they do not have the same access as richer countries have, the difference is not large enough to explain variations in income as large as those that exist today.

The ability to use technology (which consists of knowledge embodied in physical capital or machinery) appears to be the major problem. The ability to use capital depends on the skill and experience of the worker and his or her manager. This is what is meant by human capital. It is made up of the learning, ability, skills, and knowledge of individual workers, and to this should be added the ability, skills, and knowledge of the management team and even the culture of the firm, if that is where production is taking place. Although the human capital models assume constant returns to scale, they suggest that moderate changes in the resources devoted to physical and human capital accumulation or investment affect the productivity of workers, thus helping to explain historical and geographical differences in productivity levels.

Insofar as workers are rewarded for their skill level and that the latter is part of human capital, it is necessary to raise the estimate of the share of income going to capital. Conventionally, profits have been seen as the return on capital and have gone to its owners. Wages and salaries have been viewed as the return to labor and have gone to those who provided it. The human capital model implies that workers provide labor and human capital that earns a return. In the newer models, this has been added to the return on physical capital. The accumulation of human capital is similar to that of physical capital. Adding human capital to the productive system increases the output effects of changes in the resources devoted to the accumulation of physical capital. This enables the model to explain differences in income levels.

The analysis above assumes diminishing returns to physical and human capital together: when a unit of physical capital and a unit of human capital are added, then less than one extra unit of output is produced. It may be that increasing returns exist, in which case the addition of the inputs results in a more than commensurate increase in output. There are several reasons why increasing returns may apply. The first is that learning can be seen as a product of doing. This means that workers, managers, and firms (or individual farmers) learn while they produce and are able to improve efficiency without further investment, a concept that was modeled by Kenneth Arrow in 1962.[2] Output can therefore increase without an increase in inputs; time plays a key role in this process. The second reason may be the presence of external economies of scale. Firms producing similar products may develop a labor force with skills needed by all of them. Firms producing specialized inputs may also develop in geographic proximity, all of which helps to make production in a given firm more efficient. Finally, there may be internal economies of scale within firms as the scale of production increases. All these factors help to make the growth process endogenous because they are explained within the model rather than being exogenous or unexplained, as in the traditional neoclassical model. The fact that some small economies in different parts of the world have income levels similar to those of the largest and richest economies suggests that increasing returns are not the major explanation of economic growth or differences in income levels.

The human capital model makes growth endogenous. Knowledge used in production is generated in research carried out in firms, research institutes, and universities. In these models, knowledge is considered to be a public good, like defense. It benefits many, if not all, firms, and the spillover benefits that accrue to other firms may allow aggregate investment in knowledge to exhibit increasing returns to scale. This enables economic growth to continue and suggests that government encouragement to knowledge-producing, human capital–intensive sectors will promote growth. The implication for developing countries is that emphasis should be placed on the development of human capital and on the exchange of ideas and knowledge through integration into the world economy.[3]

It should be noted that thirty years before the new growth theory emerged, some important models in the Keynesian tradition, such as Nicholas Kaldor and James Mirrlees's, attempted to explain technological progress and thus make it endogenous.[4] Kaldor, in turn, acknowledged Allyn Young's seminal 1928 contribution to the economics of increasing returns.[5]

Increasing returns are a feature of manufacturing industry that takes the form of differentiation or specialization in production. For this to take place, easy communication is needed. This is a major reason why industry is usually located in urban areas. As a result, growth poles develop, drawing in labor from the countryside. It also helps to explain the differences in incomes between urban and rural areas and among different regions and countries.[6] The distribution of income is a more important issue in Keynesian and post-Keynesian economics than in the neoclassical or orthodox mainstream.

The high-tech revolution of recent years has drastically reduced the costs of international telecommunications and has linked them with computer technology. This made geographical distance much less significant for certain industries, enabling sectors of different economies to link up closely. The software sector in Egypt, for example, may have more significant links with companies in Silicon Valley than it does with other Egyptian sectors. This is a further source of economic inequality, as well as economic growth.

Notes

1. Solow, "A Contribution," pp. 65–94.
2. Arrow, "Economic Implications," pp. 155–173.
3. Meier, *Leading Issues,* pp. 102–103.
4. Kaldor and Mirrlees, "A New Model," pp.174–190.
5. Young, "Increasing Returns," pp. 527–542.
6. Kaldor, Tagetti, and Thirwall, eds., *Further Essays,* p. 71.

Bibliography

Allan, J. A. "Economic and Political Adjustments to Scarce Water in the Middle East." In J. Isaac and H. Shuval, eds., *Water and Peace in the Middle East* (Amsterdam: Elsevier, 1994).

————. "Overall Perspectives on Countries and Regions." In Peter Rogers and Peter Lydon, eds., *Water in the Arab World: Perspectives and Prognosis* (Cambridge, Mass.: Division of Applied Sciences, Harvard University, 1994).

Alonso-Gamo, Patricia, Horvitz Fedelino Annalisa, and Sebastian Paris. "Globalization and Growth Prospects in Arab Countries." Working Paper Series (Washington, D.C.: IMF, 1997).

Amin, Galal. *Egypt's Economic Predicament* (Leiden: E. J. Brill, 1995).

Amsden, Alice H. *Asia's Next Giant: South Korea and Late Industrialization* (New York: Oxford University Press, 1989).

————. "Why Isn't the Whole World Experimenting with the East Asian Model to Develop?: Review of *The East Asian Miracle.*" *World Development,* vol. 22, no. 4 (1994).

Anderson, Kym, and Hege Nordheim. "Is World Trade Becoming More Regionalized?" *Review of International Economics,* vol. 1, no. 2 (1995): 91–109.

Arab Oil and Gas (Paris), 1 October 1995.

Arab Petroleum Research Center. Arab Oil and Gas Directory (1999).

Arrow, Kenneth. "The Economic Implications of Learning by Doing." *Review of Economic Studies,* vol. 29 (1962).

Askari, Hossein. *Saudi Arabia's Economy: Oil and the Search for Economic Development* (Greenwich, Conn.: Tai Press, 1990).

Ayalon, Ami. "Egypt." In Ami Ayalon, ed., *Middle East Contemporary Survey, 1990,* vol. XIV (Boulder, Colo.: Westview Press, 1992).

————, ed. *Middle East Contemporary Survey, 1991,* vol. XV (Boulder, Colo.: Westview Press, 1993).

Ayubi, Nazih. *Overstating the Arab State* (London and New York: I. B. Tauris, 1995).

213

————, ed. *Distant Neighbors: The Political Economy of Relations Between Europe and the Middle East North Africa* (Reading, Mass.: Ithaca Press, 1995).

Bakour, Yahia, and John Kolars. "The Arab Mashrek: Hydrologic History, Problems, and Perspectives." In Peter Rogers and Peter Lydon, eds., *Water in the Arab World: Perspectives and Prognosis* (Cambridge, Mass.: Division of Applied Sciences, Harvard University, 1994).

Bardhan, Pranab. "The Contribution of Endogenous Growth Theory to the Analysis of Development Problems: An Assessment." In Jere Behrman and T. N. Srinivasan, eds., *Handbook of Development Economics,* vol. 111B (Amsterdam: Elsevier, 1995).

Barrell, Ray, and Nigel Pain. "Developments in South Asia and Their Implications for the UK and Europe." *National Institute for Economic Research Review,* no. 163 (January 1998).

Bates, Robert H., and Anne O. Krueger, eds. *Political and Economic Interactions in Economic Policy Reform* (Oxford: Blackwell, 1993).

Behrman, Jere, and T. N. Srinivasan, eds. *Handbook of Development Economics,* vol. 111B (Amsterdam: Elsevier, 1995).

Bingaradi, Faris, and Adda Guieciour. "Social Safety Nets: Experiences of Some Arab Countries." In Taher H. Kanaan, ed., *The Social Effects of Economic Adjustment in Arab Countries* (Washington, D.C.: IMF, 1997).

Brezis, Elise. "Trade, FTA, and Hub and Spokes: Long Run Effects on Growth." Paper presented at conference titled "The Evolving Relationship Between the EU and Its Two Peripheries: Experiences in the Cooperation with the Middle East and Eastern Europe," Caesarea, Israel, 1997.

British Petroleum. *BP Statistical Review of World Energy, 1997* (London: BP).

Brookes, Risa. "Political-Military Relations and the Stability of the Arab Region," Adelphi Paper (New York: Oxford University Press for the International Institute for Strategic Studies, 1988).

Bruni, Michelle, and Alessandra Venturini. "Pressure to Migrate and Prosperity to Emigrate: The Case of the Mediterranean Basin." *International Labour Review,* vol. 134, no. 3 (1995).

Central Bank of Jordan. *Monthly Bulletin of Statistics,* 28 June 1998. Available at: www.cbj.gov.jo/docs/bu_4-e.html.

Chenery, Hollis. *Structural Change and Development Policy* (New York: Oxford University Press for the World Bank, 1979).

Cook, M. A., ed. *Studies in the Economic History of the Middle East* (London: Oxford University Press, 1970).

Courbage, Yussef. "Demographic Change in the Arab World: The Impact of Migration, Education, and Taxes in Egypt and Morocco," *Middle East Report,* September–October 1994.

————. "Evolution démographique et attitudes politiques en Syrie." *Population,* vol. 49, no. 3 (1994): 725–750.

————. "Fin de 'l'explosion' démographique en Mediterranée," *Population,* vol. 50, no. 1 (January–February 1995).

————. "Migration international et transition démographique au Maghreb." *Le Maghreb en suspens: Les Cahiers du C.E.R.I.* (Centre d'Études et de Recherches Internationals), no. 8 (1994).

Dau, Khalifa Ali, and Hussein M. el-Amach. "Social Safety Nets: The Social Development Fund in Egypt." In Taher H. Kanaan, ed., *The Social Effects of Economic Adjustment in Arab Countries* (Washington, D.C.: IMF, 1997).

Daveri, Fransesco, and Ricardo Faini. "Trade and Integration: The European Union Versus the Magreb" (Tel Aviv: Center for Economic Policy Research–Pinchas Sapir Center for Development, 1995).

de Azevedo, Raimondo Cagiano, ed. "Migration and Development Cooperation," Council of Europe Population Studies No. 28 (Strasbourg: Council of Europe, 1994).

Denoeux, Guilan. "The Politics of Morocco's 'Fight Against Corruption.'" *Middle East Policy,* vol. 7, no. 2 (February 2000).

Divan, Ishac, and Lyn Squire. "Private Assets and Public Debts: External Finance in a Peaceful Middle East," *Middle East Journal,* vol. 49, no. 1 (winter 1995).

DeRosa, Dean A. *Agricultural Trade and Rural Development in the Middle East and North Africa* (Washington, D.C.: World Bank, 1997).

EIU (Economist Intelligence Unit). *Country Profile (CP),* various countries, various years.

————. *Country Report (CR),* various countries, various issues and years.

————. *Quarterly Economic Report (QER),* various countries, various dates.

Enav, Peter. "Non-OPEC Oil." Unpublished paper, 1998.

el-Erian, Mohamed A., and Susan Fennell. "The Economy of the Middle East and North Africa in 1997" (Washington, D.C.: IMF, 1997).

EU (European Union). Basic Statistics of the European Union, 32nd ed. (Luxembourg: European Union, 1995).

————. *The Countries of the Greater Arab Maghreb and the European Community* (Brussels: Commission of the European Communities, 1991).

————. *The Demographic Situation in the European Union, 1994 Report* (Luxembourg: European Commission, 1994).

————. *The EU and World Trade: EU Trade Development for the Year 1993* (Luxembourg: European Commission, 1994).

————. *European Economy,* no. 60 (1995).

————. *The European Union and the Palestinians* (Brussels: European Commission, 1995).

————. *Eurostat, Statistics in Focus, External Trade Series, European Union (EUR 12) Trade with the Mediterranean Countries: Results for 1994,* no. 9 (Luxembourg: European Union, 1995).

————. *Eurostat Yearbook, 1995* (Luxembourg: Office of Official Publications of the European Communities, 1995).

————. "Strengthening the Mediterranean Policy of the European Union: Establishing a Euro-Mediterranean Partnership." Bulletin of the European Union, Supplement 2/95 (Brussels: European Union, 1995).

————. *Trade Relations Between the European Union and the Developing Countries* (Brussels: European Commission, March 1995).

————. *World Trade 1997 Comparison EU, US, Japan* (Luxembourg: Office of Official Publications of the European Communities, 1999).

FAO (Food and Agriculture Organization). FAOSTAT database. Available at: http://apps.fao.org.
———. *Quarterly Bulletin of Statistics,* vol. 8, nos. 3–4 (1995).
———. *The State of Food and Agriculture* (Rome: FAO, various years).
———. *Towards a Strategic Framework* (Rome: FAO, 2000).
———. Various entries. In *Yearbook* (Rome: FAO, various volumes and years).
Fargues, Phillippe. "Demographic Explosion or Social Upheaval?" In Ghassan Salame, ed., *Democracy Without Democrats: The Renewal of Politics in the Muslim World* (London: I. B. Tauris, 1994).
———. "From Demographic Explosion to Social Rupture." *Middle East Report,* no. 190 (September–October 1994).
———. "State Policies and the Birth Rate in Egypt: From Socialism to Liberalism." *Population and Development Review,* vol. 23, no. 1 (March 1997): 115–138.
FBIS (Foreign Broadcast Information Service). Various sources and dates.
Fergany, Nader. "A Comment." In Taher H. Kanaan, ed., *The Social Effects of Economic Adjustment in Arab Countries* (Washington, D.C.: IMF, 1997), pp. 234–235.
Finaish, Mohamed, and Eric Bell. "The Arab Maghreb Union." IMF Working Paper (Washington, D.C.: IMF, May 1994).
Galal, Ahmed, and Bernard Hoekman, eds. *Regional Partners in Global Markets: Limits and Possibilities of the Euro-Med Agreements* (London: Centre for Economic Policy Research and Egyptian Center for Economic Studies, 1997).
GATT (General Agreement on Tariffs and Trade). "The General Agreement on Tariffs and Trade." In *The Results of the Uruguay Round of Multinational Trade Negotiations: The Legal Texts* (Geneva: GATT, 1994).
———. *International Trade, 1994* (Geneva: GATT, 1994).
el-Ghonemy, M. Riad. *Affluence and Poverty in the Middle East* (London and New York: Routledge, 1998).
Goldsborough, David, Coorey Sharmini, Louis Dicks-Mireaux, Horvath Balazs, Kochhar Kalpana, Mecagni Mauro, Erik Offerdal, and Zhou Jianping. *Reinvigorating Growth in Developing Countries* (Washington, D.C.: IMF, 1996).
Government of Israel. Agreement on Trade and Economic Cooperation Between the Government of the State of Israel and the Government of the Hashemite Kingdom of Jordan (Jerusalem: Government of Israel, 1995).
Ha'aretz (Tel Aviv).
Halevi, Nadav, and Ephraim Kleiman. "Regional vs. Non-Regional Integration: The Middle East" (Tel Aviv: Centre for Economic Policy Research–Pinchas Sapir Center for Development, 1995).
Handousa, Heba, ed. *Economic Transition in the Middle East: Global Challenges and Adjustment Strategies* (Cairo: American University in Cairo Press, 1997).
Handousa, Heba, and Gillian Potter, eds. *Employment and Structural Adjustment: Egypt in the 1990s* (Geneva: International Labour Office, 1991).
Hansen, Bent. *Egypt and Turkey: The Political Economy of Poverty, Equity, and Growth* (Oxford: Oxford University Press, 1991).

Henry, Clement M. *The Mediterranean Debt Crescent* (Gainesville: University of Florida Press, 1996).

Hirschman, Albert O. *Strategies of Economic Development* (New Haven, Conn.: Yale University Press, 1958).

Hoekman, Bernard. *The WTO, the EU, and the Arab World: Trade Policy Priorities and Pitfalls* (Washington, D.C.: World Bank, 1995).

Hoekman, Bernard, and Simeon Djankov. "Catching Up with Eastern Europe? The European Union's Free Trade Initiative." Centre for Economic Policy Research Discussion Paper No. 100 (London: Centre for Economic Policy Research, 1995).

———. "Towards a Free Trade Agreement with the European Union: Issues and Policy Options for Egypt in Galal." In Ahmed Galal and Bernard Hoekman, eds., *Regional Partners in Global Markets: Limits and Possibilities of the Euro-Med Agreements* (London: Centre for Economic Policy Research and Egyptian Center for Economic Studies, 1997).

Hoekman, Bernard, and Michel Kostecki. *The Political Economy of the World Trading System* (Oxford: Oxford University Press, 1995).

Holt, Robert, and Terry Roe. "The Political Economy of Reform: Egypt in the 1980s." In Robert H. Bates and Anne O. Krueger, eds., *Political and Economic Interactions in Economic Policy Reform* (Oxford: Blackwell, 1993).

Horton, Brendan. *Morocco: Analysis and Reform of Economic Policy.* Analytical Case Study No. 4 (Washington, D.C.: Economic Development Institute of the World Bank, 1990).

IEA (International Energy Agency). *The IEA Natural Gas Security Study* (Paris: OECD, 1995).

———. *Middle East Oil and Gas* (Paris: OECD, 1995).

———. *Monthly Oil Market Report,* January 2000.

———. *North Africa Oil and Gas* (Paris: OECD, 1996).

IMF (International Monetary Fund). *Balance of Payments Yearbook* (Washington, D.C.: IMF, various years).

———. *Directions of Trade* (Washington, D.C.: IMF, various months and years).

———. *Directions of Trade Statistics Yearbook* (Washington, D.C.: IMF, various years).

———. "Financial Assistance from Arab Countries and Arab Regional Institutions." Occasional Paper No. 87 (Washington, D.C.: IMF, 1991).

———. *Government Financial Statistics* (Washington, D.C.: IMF, various years).

———. *Government Financial Statistics Yearbook* (Washington D.C.: IMF, various years).

———. *IMF Survey,* 13 January 1997.

———. *International Financial Statistics* (Washington, D.C.: IMF, various months and years).

———. *International Financial Statistics Yearbook* (Washington, D.C.: IMF, various years).

———. *Morocco: Statistical Appendix.* Staff report (Washington, D.C.: IMF, 1998).

————. *World Economic Outlook* (Washington, D.C.: IMF, various months and years).

International Herald Tribune (Paris).

Israel, Central Bureau of Statistics. *Statistical Abstract of Israel* (Jerusalem: Central Bureau of Statistics, various years).

Issawi, Charles. *An Economic History of the Middle East and North Africa* (London: Methuen, 1982).

Jordan Times (Amman).

Kaldor, N., and J. A. Mirrlees. "A New Model of Economic Growth." *Review of Economic Studies*, vol. 29 (1961–1962).

Kaldor, Nicholas (edited by F. Tagetti and A. P. Thirwall). *Further Essays on Economic Theory and Policy* (London: Duckworth, 1989).

Kanaan, Taher H., ed. *The Social Effects of Economic Adjustment in Arab Countries* (Washington, D.C.: IMF, 1997).

Katouzian, Homa. "Oil and Economic Development in the Middle East." In Georges Sabagh, ed., *The Modern Economic and Social History of the Middle East in Its World Context* (Cambridge: Cambridge Univerity Press, 1989).

Kelly, Margaret, and Bernhard Fritz-Krockow. "Trade Policies in Industrialized Countries and Their Impact on Arab Countries." In Said el-Naggar, ed., *Foreign and Intratrade Policies of the Arab Countries* (Washington, D.C.: IMF, 1992).

Khosrowshani, Cameron. "Privatization in Morocco." *Middle East Journal*, vol. 51, no. 2 (spring 1997).

Kolars, John F., and William A. Mitchell. *The Euphrates River and the Southeast Anatolia Development Project* (Carbondale and Edwardsville: Southern Illinois University Press, 1991).

Krueger, Anne O. *The Political Economy of Policy Reform in Developing Countries* (Cambridge, Mass.: MIT Press, 1993).

Krugman, Paul. *Development, Geography, and Economic Theory* (Cambridge, Mass.: MIT Press, 1995).

Laanatza, Marianne. "The Impact of the EU-Mediterranean Association Agreements on Peace and Stability in the Middle East." Paper presented to a conference at Lund University, Sweden, September 1997.

Larsen, Bjorn. "Environment and Natural Resource Management in the Middle East and North African Regions: Some Selected Issues." Draft paper (Washington, D.C.: World Bank, 1995).

Lawrence, Robert. "Preferential Trading Arrangements: The Traditional and the New." In Ahmed Galal and Bernard Hoekman, eds., *Regional Partners in Global Markets: Limits and Possibilities of the Euro-Med Agreements* (London: Centre for Economic Policy Research and Egyptian Center for Economic Studies, 1997).

————. *Towards Free Trade in the Middle East: The Triad and Beyond* (Cambridge: Harvard University, 1995).

Lewis, W. Arthur. "Economic Development with Unlimited Supplies of Labor." *The Manchester School* (Oxford: Blackwell, May 1954).

Little, Ian, Tibor Scitovsky, and Maurice Scott. *Industry and Trade in Some Developing Countries* (London: Oxford University Press, 1970).

Lloyd, Peter, and Gary Sampson. "Competition and Trade Policy: Identifying the Issues After the Uruguay Round." *World Economy,* vol. 18, no. 5 (September 1995): 681–705.

Maciejewski, Edouard, and Ahsan Mansur, eds. *Jordan: Strategy for Adjustment and Growth* (Washington, D.C.: IMF, 1996).

Mahdary, Hossein. "The Patterns and Problems of Economic Development in Rentier States: The Case of Iran." In M. A. Cook, ed., *Studies in the Economic History of the Middle East* (London: Oxford University Press, 1970).

Mattione, Richard. *OPEC's Investments and the International Financial System* (Washington, D.C.: Brookings Institution, 1985).

Mead, Donald. *Growth and Structural Change in the Egyptian Economy* (Homewood, Ill.: Richard D. Irwin, Inc., 1967).

Meier, Gerald. *Leading Issues in Economic Development* (New York and Oxford: Oxford University Press, 1995).

Melhem, Hisham. "Syria Between Two Transitions." *Middle East Report,* vol. 27, no. 2 (spring 1997).

The Middle East and North Africa, 1995 (London: Europa Publications, 1994).

The Middle East and North Africa, 1997 (London: Europa Publications, 1996).

Middle East Economic Digest (MEED) (London: EMAP Business Communications).

Middle East Economic Survey (MEES) (Nicosia, Cyprus: Middle East Petroleum and Economic Publications).

Middle East Executive Report (Washington, D.C.: Middle East Executive Reports, Ltd., March 1996).

Migdal, Joel S. *Strong Societies and Weak States* (Princeton, N.J.: Princeton University Press, 1988).

Mohamedi, Fareed. "Oil, Gas, and the Future of Arab Gulf Countries." *Middle East Report,* vol. 27, no. 3 (July–September 1997).

el-Naggar, Said, ed. *Foreign and Intratrade Policies of the Arab Countries* (Washington, D.C.: IMF, 1992).

NCB (National Commercial Bank). *NCB Economist* (Jeddah: National Commercial Bank), various editions.

Nellis, John, and Sunita Kikeri. "The Privatization of Public Enterprises." In Said el-Naggar, ed., *Privatization and Structural Adjustment in the Arab Countries* (Washington, D.C.: IMF, 1989).

Nsouli, Saleh M., Eken Sena, Duran Paul, Bell Gerwin, and Yucelik Zuhtu. *The Path to Convertibility and Growth: The Tunisian Experience* (Washington, D.C.: IMF, 1995).

Nsouli, Saleh M., Eken Sena, Enders Klaus, Thai Van-Can, Decressin Jorg, and Cartiglia Filippo. *Resilience and Growth Through Sustained Adjustment: The Moroccan Experience* (Washington, D.C.: IMF, 1995).

OAPEC (Organization of Arab Petroleum Exporting Countries). *Secretary General's Twenty-third Annual Report, 1996* (Safat, Kuwait: OAPEC, 1996).

O'Brien, Patrick. *The Revolution in Egypt's Economic System* (London: Oxford University Press, 1966).

OECD (Organization for Economic Cooperation and Development). *Economic Outlook,* no. 63 (Paris, June 1998).
————. *Survey* (Korea, 1998).
Oil and Gas Journal (Tulsa, Okla.: PennWell Corp., various editions).
OPEC (Organization of Petroleum Exporting Countries). *OPEC Annual Statistical Bulletin* (Vienna: OPEC, various years).
————. *OPEC Statistical Bulletin, 1996* (Vienna: OPEC, 1997).
Owen, Roger. *State, Power, and Politics in the Making of the Modern Middle East* (London: Routledge, 1992).
Page, John. "Comment." In Taher H. Kanaan, ed., *The Social Effects of Economic Adjustment in Arab Countries* (Washington, D.C.: IMF, 1997), p. 241.
————. "Securing the Peace Dividend in the Middle East: External Finance and Domestic Effort." *Middle East Executive Report,* October 1994.
Perthes, Volker. *The Political Economy of Syria* (London: I. B. Tauris, 1995).
Pomfret, Richard. *Mediterranean Policy of the European Community* (New York: St. Martin's Press, 1986).
Radelet, Steven, and Jeffrey D. Sachs. "The East Asian Crisis: Diagnosis, Remedies, Prospects." Brookings Papers on Economic Activity, 1998, No. 1 (Washington, D.C.: Brookings Institution, 1998), pp. 1–90.
Ricardo, David. *Principles of Political Economy and Taxation* (London: Pelican, 1971).
Richards, Alan. "Global Financial Crisis and Economic Reform in the Middle East." *Middle East Policy,* vol. 6, no. 3 (February 1999).
————. "The Political Economy of Dilatory Reform: Egypt in the 1980s." *World Development,* vol. 19, no. 12 (December 1991).
Richards, Alan, and John Waterbury. *A Political Economy of the Middle East* (Boulder, Colo.: Westview Press, 1990).
————. *A Political Economy of the Middle East.* 2nd ed. (Boulder, Colo.: Westview Press, 1996).
Riordan, E. Mick, et al. *The World Economy and Implications for the Middle East and North African Region, 1995–2000* (Washington, D.C.: World Bank, 1995).
Rivlin, Paul. *The Dynamics of Economic Policy Making in Egypt* (New York: Praeger, 1985).
————. "The Economics of Monarchy in the Middle East." Unpublished draft, 1996.
————. "The Middle East and Europe: Problems of Writing a Comparative Economic History." Paper presented at the International Workshop on Economic History, Ben Gurion University of the Negev, Beersheba, Israel, December 1998.
————. "Soft and Hard States: The East Asian Lesson for Middle East Economic Development." In Yishay Yafet, Ehud Harari, and Eyal Ben Ami, eds., *Lessons from East Asia for the Development of the Middle East* (Jerusalem: Harry S Truman Institute for the Advancement of Peace, Hebrew University, 1998).
————. "Structural Adjustment and Economic Growth in Egypt, Morocco, and

Tunisia, 1980–96." In Bruce Maddy Weitzman, ed., *Middle East Contemporary Survey, 1996,* vol. XX (Boulder, Colo.: Westview Press, 1998), pp. 169–196.

Rodrik, Dani. "King Kong Meets Godzilla: The World Bank and the East Asian Miracle." Discussion Paper No. 944 (London: Centre for Economic Policy Research, 1994).

———. "The 'Paradoxes' of the Successful State." *European Economic Review,* no. 41 (1997).

———. "Trade and Industrial Policy Reform." In Jere Behrman and T. N. Srinivasan, eds., *Handbook of,Development Economics,* vol. 111B (Amsterdam: Elsevier, 1995).

Rogers, Peter, and Peter Lydon, eds. *Water in the Arab World: Perspectives and Prognosis* (Cambridge, Mass.: Division of Applied Sciences, Harvard University, 1994).

Rosenstein-Rodan, Paul. "Problems of Industrialization of Eastern and South Eastern Europe." *Economic Journal,* June 1943.

Sabagh, Georges, ed. *The Modern Economic and Social History of the Middle East in Its World Context* (Cambridge: Cambridge Univerity Press, 1989).

Sachs, Jeffrey. "Fixing the IMF Remedy." *Banker,* February 1998, pp. 16–17.

Sadik, Abdul-Karim, and Shawki Barghouti. "The Water Problems of the Arab World: Management of Scarce Resources." In Peter Rogers and Peter Lydon, eds., *Water in the Arab World: Perspectives and Prognosis* (Cambridge, Mass.: Division of Applied Sciences, Harvard University, 1994).

Sadowski, Yahya M. *Political Vegetables?* (Washington, D.C.: Brookings Institution, 1991).

Safadi, Raed. "Global Challenges and Opportunities Facing MENA Countries at the Dawn of the Twenty-first Century." In Heba Handousa, ed., *Economic Transition in the Middle East: Global Challenges and Adjustment Strategies* (Cairo: American University in Cairo Press, 1997).

Salame, Ghassan, ed. *Democracy Without Democrats: The Renewal of Politics in the Muslim World* (London: I. B. Tauris, 1994).

Sassanpour, Cyrus, Joharji Ghazi, Kireyev Alexei, and Petri Martin. "Labor Market Challenges and Policies in the Gulf Cooperation Council Countries." Working Paper (Washington, D.C.: IMF, 1997).

Shiells, Clinton. "Regional Trading Blocs: Trade Creating or Diverting." *Finance and Development,* March 1995.

Singh, Ajit. "How Did East Asia Grow So Fast?: Slow Progress Towards an Analytical Consensus." UNCTAD Working Paper (Geneva: UNCTAD, February 1995).

Solow, Robert M. "A Contribution to the Theory of Economic Growth." *Quarterly Journal of Economics,* no. 70 (February 1969).

Stiglitz, Joseph E. "The Role of Government in Economic Development." In Michael Bruno and Boris Pleskovic, eds., *Annual World Bank Conference on Development Economics* (Washington, D.C.: World Bank, 1996).

———. "Some Lessons from the East Asian Miracle." *World Bank Research Observer,* vol. 11, no. 2 (August 1992).

————. *Whither Socialism?* (Cambridge, Mass.: MIT Press, 1995).

STIMENA (Swiss Trade Initiative Middle East North Africa). *Regional Economic Development—A Contribution to the Middle East Peace Process: Trade Relations Among the Core Parties and with Key Third Parties* (Geneva: STIMENA, 1997).

Stockholm International Peace Research Institute. *Handbook, 1997* (Oxford: Oxford University Press, 1997).

Strange, Susan. "Direct Investment in North Africa: The Investors' Perspective," in Nazih Ayubi, ed., *Distant Neighbours: The Political Economy of Relations Between Europe and the Middle East* (Reading: Ithaca Press, 1995).

Subramanian, Arvid. "Egypt: Poised for Sustained Growth." *Finance and Development,* December 1997.

Sukkar, Nabil. "Syria: Strategic Economic Issues." Draft paper for the Workshop on Strategic Visions for the Middle East and North Africa (Gammarth, Tunisia: The Economic Research Forum for the Arab Countries, Iran, and Turkey; and The World Bank, Middle East and North Africa Division, June 1995).

Susser, Asher. "Jordan." In Ami Ayalon and Bruce Maddy Weitzman, eds., *Middle East Contemporary Survey, 1994,* vol. XVIII (Boulder, Colo.: Westview Press, 1996).

Swearingen, Will D. "Agricultural Reform in North Africa: Economic Necessity and Environmental Dilemmas." In Dirk Vandeville, ed., *North Africa: Development and Reform in a Changing Global Economy* (Basingstoke, England: Macmillan, 1996), pp. 68–71.

Syrian Arab Republic, Central Bureau of Statistics. *Statistical Abstract* (Damascus: Prime Minister's Office, various years).

Thomas, Vinod, Chhibber Ajny, Dailami Mansoor, and Jaime de Melo, eds. *Restructuring Economies in Distress: Policy Reform and the World Bank* (Oxford: Oxford University Press, 1991).

Todaro, Michael P. *Economic Development* (New York and London: Longman, 1994).

Togan, Subidey. "Trade Policy Review of the Republic of Turkey." In Sven Arndt and Chris Miller, eds., *The World Economy: Global Trade Policy 1995* (Oxford: Blackwell, 1995).

Tovias, Alfred. "The Economic Impact of the Euro-Mediterranean Free Trade Area on Mediterranean Non-Member Countries." *Mediterranean Politics,* vol. 2, no. 1 (summer 1997).

————. *Tariff Preferences in Mediterranean Diplomacy* (New York: St. Martin's Press, 1977).

UN (United Nations). *Demographic Yearbook* (New York: UN, various years).

————. *National Accounts Statistics* (New York: UN, various years).

————. *World Economic and Social Survey* (New York: UN, various years).

————. *World Population Prospects: The 1998 Revision* (New York: UN, 1999).

UN Department of Economic and Social Affairs. *Replacement Migration: Is It a Solution to Declining and Ageing Populations* (New York: UN, 2000).

UN Office of the Special Coordinator in the Occupied Territories, *Quarterly Report, April 1997*. Available at: www.arts.mcgill.ca/mepp.unsco.

UNCTAD (United Nations Committee on Trade and Development). *Handbook of International Trade and Development Statistics, 1993* (New York: UN, 1993).

———. *UNCTAD Commodity Yearbook, 1993* (New York: UN, 1993).

———. *UNCTAD Trade and Development Report, 1995* (New York and Geneva: UN, 1995).

UNDP (United Nations Development Program). *Human Development Report, 1999* (New York: UN, 1999).

UNESCO (United Nations Educational, Scientific, and Cultural Organization). *World Education Report* (New York: UN, various years).

UNESCWA (United Nations Economic and Social Commission on West Asia). *Agriculture and Development in West Asia* (Amman: UN, 1994).

———. *Survey of Economic and Social Developments in the ECWA Region* (New York: UN, various years).

UNESCWA and FAO. *Resource Conservation Policies and Strategies for Agriculture: Case of the Syrian Arab Republic* (New York: UN, 1996).

UNIDO (United Nations Industrial Development Organization). *Egypt: An Enabling Environment for Investment* (London: EIU, 1994).

———. *Industrial Development Global Report, 1997* (New York: Oxford University Press, 1997).

U.S. Department of Energy, Energy Information Agency. Web site: www.eia.doe.gov/emeu/cabs/.

U.S. Department of State. *Country Commercial Guide, Syrian Arab Republic* (Damascus: Embassy of the United States of America, various years).

van den Boogaerde, Pierre. "Financial Assistance from Arab Countries and Arab Regional Institutions." Occasional Paper No. 87 (Washington, D.C.: IMF, September 1991).

Van Der Wee, Herman. *Prosperity and Upheaval in the World Economy, 1945–1980* (London: Penguin, 1986).

Vandeville, Dirk, ed. *North Africa: Development and Reform in a Changing Global Economy* (Basingstoke, England: Macmillan, 1996).

Vatikiotis, P. J. *The History of Egypt* (London: Weidenfeld and Nicholson, 1976).

Vernon, Raymond. "Technological Development: The Historical Experience." Economic Development Institute of the World Bank Seminar Paper No. 39 (Washington, D.C.: World Bank, n.d.).

Vickers, John, and George Yarrow. *Privatization: An Economic Analysis* (Cambridge, Mass.: MIT Press, 1988).

Wade, Robert. *Governing the Market: Economic Theory and the Role of Government in East Asian Industrialization* (Princeton, N.J.: Princeton University Press, 1990).

———. "Japan, the World Bank, and the Art of Paradigm Maintenance: *The East Asian Miracle* in Political Perspective." *New Left Review,* no. 217 (May–June 1996).

Waterbury, John. *The Egypt of Nasser and Sadat* (Princeton, N.J.: Princeton University Press, 1983).

Weiss, Dieter, and Ulrich Wurzel. *The Economics and Politics of Transition to an Open Market Economy in Egypt* (Paris: OECD, 1998).

Wonnacott, Ronald. "Trade and Investment in a Hub-and-Spoke System Versus a Free Trade Area." *World Economy,* vol. 19, no. 3 (May 1996).

World Bank. *Claiming the Future: Choosing Prosperity in the Middle East and North Africa* (Washington, D.C.: World Bank, 1995).

———. *The East Asian Miracle* (New York: Oxford University Press, 1993).

———. "The Evolving Role of the World Bank: The East Asian Miracle," World Bank Paper, n.d.

———. *Expanding the Measure of Wealth: Indicators of Environmentally Sustainable Development.* Monograph Series No. 17 (Washington, D.C.: World Bank, 1997).

———. *Global Finance Development* (Washington, D.C.: World Bank, various years).

———. *Peace and the Jordanian Economy* (Washington, D.C.: World Bank, 1994).

———. *A Strategy for Managing Water in the Middle East and North Africa* (Washington, D.C.: World Bank, 1994).

———. *Trends in Developing Countries* (Washington, D.C.: World Bank, various years).

———. *Will Arab Workers Prosper or Be Left Out in the Twenty-first Century?* (Washington, D.C.: World Bank, 1995).

———. *World Debt Tables: External Finance for Developing Countries* (Washington, D.C.: World Bank, various volumes and various years).

———. *World Development Report* (New York: Oxford University Press, various years).

WTO (World Trade Organization). *World Trade Organization Annual Report, 1998* (Geneva: WTO, 1998).

Young, Allyn. "Increasing Returns and Economic Progress." *Economic Journal,* December 1928.

Zallio, Franco. "Morocco and Tunisia: A New Round of Structural Adjustment." *Review of Middle East and Energy Affairs,* no. 30 (1995).

Index

Abu Dhabi, 49, 59–60
Abu Dhabi National Oil Company, 59
African Development Bank, 105
Agency for International Development (AID), 13
Agip-ENI group, 63
Agriculture: arable land shortages, 45, 46; challenges facing, 85–86; in East Asia, 17; in Egypt, 9, 87–89; environment and, 41–42; EU agreements regarding, 175, 180; foreign debt and, 71; in Morocco, 87–90, 115, 117, 119, 121, 124; neglect of, 4, 13; in Saudi Arabia, 86–87; in Syria, 135, 150–152; in Tunisia, 87–88
Aid, economic, 65–66, 68. *See also under individual countries*
Albania, 172
Algeria: Arab Mahgreb Union, 182–183; Arab Socialism, 8; economic stabilization programs, 68; economy of, 189–190; emigrant workers from, 72, 173; EU economic relations, 168, 177, 178, 186–188; food imports, 86; foreign debt, 14, 71; gas, 60–61, 63, 78; industry, 91; literacy, 38; oil, 49, 53, 60–61, 77, 188, 199; popula-

tion growth, 31, 33, 39; poverty, 37, 200; remittances, 78
Aluminum, 93
Amsden, Alice, 18, 25
Aquifers, 46, 87, 153
Arab Labor Organization, 36
Arab Mahgreb Union (AMU), 179, 182–184
Arab Socialism: import substitution and, 8–12, 136; industrial development, 91; Soviet Union as inspiration for, 1, 5, 8, 137; urban workers as focus of, 79–80
Arab Socialist Union (ASU), 12
Arab states: Asian economic crisis and, 26, 28; capital investment in, 68; debt writeoffs, 66, 68; East Asia contrasted with, 21–24; economic aid programs of, 65–67, 69; economic aid to, 65–67, 95; education, 38–40, 43; environmental issues, 41–42; foreign interests in, 81–82; health care spending, 39–41; human development index, 41; labor force growth, 34–35; literacy, 38–39; the middle class in, 80–81; military role in, 79; peace process, 169; population growth in, 31; poverty, 37–38, 204; state role in, 78–79, 82; unemployment,

161, 189. *See also* Import substitution; State planning
Industrial policy, 17–19, 90
Infitah, 12
Inflation, 103–104, 106, 108, 113–114, 120–121
International Bank of Reconstruction and Development (IBRD). *See* World Bank
International capital flows. *See* Capital investments
International Monetary Fund (IMF): Algerian programs, 68; Asian economic crisis, 27; economic reforms, 22, 168; Egyptian programs, 12, 68, 82, 101–103, 105, 110–111; foreign interests in the Arab states, 82; foreign worker remittances, 158; goals of stabilization programs, 99; government's economic role, 202; Jordanian programs, 70, 114; Moroccan programs, 70, 116–119, 183; policy debates, 1; stabilization's effect on growth, 200; Tunisian programs, 70, 126, 128, 130, 183; types of projects, 13
Investments: changes in, 68–70; efficiency of, 127, 140–141; foreign, 190–192, 203–204; new growth theory and, 14–15, 209
Iran, 37, 49, 59
Iran-Iraq war, 66, 73, 92, 136–137
Iraq: Arab Socialism, 8; gas, 60, 62; Gulf War, 52–53; industry, 91–92; Jordanian trade with, 114; labor force growth, 34; literacy, 38; oil, 49, 51–52, 61–62, 77, 199; population growth, 33; poverty, 37; private sector development, 14; water, 153
Irrigation, 151–153
Islamic Alliance, 12
Islamic fundamentalism, 169, 200
Israel: bilateral cumulation, 193–194; Camp David agreement, 102; economic agreements with Palestine,

182, 193; economic reforms, 190; Egyptian trade relations, 184; EU economic relations, 168, 177–178, 186; industry, 189; Jordanian trade relations, 180–181, 185; regional trade groups, 192; Syrian peace treaty, 163; tariffs, 192; Turkish trade relations, 185; U.S. free trade agreement, 194; WTO membership for, 177
Israel-Jordan Peace Treaty (1994), 47
Italy, 63, 105, 175, 182, 186

Japan: aid programs, 16–17; balance of payments, 18; causes of growth, 3, 203–204; debt write-offs, 68, 105; financing of Syrian power plants, 149; gas purchases, 59–60; industrial policy, 18–19; investment by, 27, 191; trade policy, 20
Jordan: balance of payments, 113; debt, 14, 70–71, 113–114, 188–189; economic aid to, 78–79, 113; economic stabilization programs, 68, 70, 95–97, 112–115; economy of, 190, 200; Egyptian trade relations, 181; emigrant workers from, 72–73, 114; EU economic relations, 168, 178, 180–181; EU residents from, 173; foreign worker remittances, 45, 73, 75, 113, 188; import substitution, 8, 95; industry, 91–92; Iraqi trade with, 114; Israeli trade relations, 180–181, 185; manufacturing in, 146; mineral resources, 64, 112; population growth, 33; poverty, 37; public spending, 40–41; tariffs, 180; water resources, 47

Kaldor, Nicholas, 15, 210
Keynesian economics, 5, 15, 210–211
Knowledge, 208–209
Korea, Republic of. *See* South Korea
Krueger, Anne, 81
Kuwait: economic aid programs of, 65–66, 68; financing of Syrian

Nestlé, 162
Netherlands, 105
North Africa, 31–32, 37, 45, 169. *See
also* Arab states; *individual coun-
tries;* Mahgreb
North American Free Trade
Agreement (NAFTA), 171
North Sea, 52
Norway, 52, 171

Oil: Algerian, 49, 53, 60–61, 77, 188,
199; Bahraini, 49, 57, 205;
Egyptian, 53, 61, 102, 184; EU
imports of, 93, 175; in the GCC,
48–59, 77–79, 199; income from,
13, 48–55, 188, 201; Iraqi, 49,
51–52, 61–62, 77, 199; Israeli purchases of, 184; Kuwaiti, 49,
51–53, 57, 62; Libyan, 49, 63–64,
77–78, 188, 199; Moroccan, 125;
Omani, 49, 57–58, 93, 205; prices,
51, 96, 125; Qatari, 52, 58, 93,
205; refining, 90, 92–93; as rental
income, 48–49; Saudi, 49, 51–53,
57–59, 93, 205; shocks, 115;
Syrian, 64, 135–136, 138, 140,
147–148, 157–158, 162; Tunisian,
125; UAE, 49, 52, 59, 62, 205
Oman: employment of nationals in,
77; foreign debt, 71; gas, 59–60;
labor force growth, 34; oil, 49,
57–58, 93, 205; population
growth, 32; poverty, 37
Organization for Economic
Cooperation and Development
(OECD), 6, 93, 96
Organization of Arab Petroleum
Exporting Countries (OAPEC), 57
Organization of Petroleum Exporting
Countries (OPEC), 49, 51–55, 57,
62
Ottoman Empire, 78, 80

Pahlavi, Shah Reza, 7
Palestine: bilateral cumulation,
193–194; economic agreements
with Israel, 182, 193; economic

aid to, 79; economy of, 189;
Egyptian trade with, 184; emigrant
workers from, 75; EU economic
relations, 168, 182; free trade
zones, 181; population growth,
33–34
Palestine Liberation Organization,
182
Paris Club, 68, 105, 108, 110, 114,
118
Park Chung Hee, 22
Perfect information, 16
Petrochemicals. *See* Gas; Oil
Petroleum Development Oman, 57
Phosphates: Jordanian, 64, 112;
Moroccan, 64, 96, 115, 119; price
fluctuations, 65; Tunisian, 125
Physical capital, 45–46, 209–210
Pipelines, 61
Poland, 172, 188, 194
Pollution, 42
Population growth: in Algeria, 31, 33,
39; in the Arab states, 31–34;
decline of, 143, 201; in East Asia,
33; economic growth and, 203; in
Egypt, 33, 87, 89; among emigrant
workers, 174; food consumption
and, 85; in GCC states, 32, 49; in
Syria, 135, 142–144, 163; in
Tunisia, 31, 39, 87, 143
Portugal, 175, 182
Potash, 64–65, 112
Poverty, 37–38, 200, 204
Price controls, 127, 151
Price freezes, 117
Price Stabilization Fund (PSF; Syria),
154
Primary products, 5–6
Private sector: in Egypt, 80; in Iraq,
14; in Lebanon, 80; in Morocco,
80, 125, 204; overregulation of,
91; savings, 9–10; in South Korea,
9, 203–204; in Syria, 14, 80,
140–141
Privatization, 99–101, 109–111,
117–118, 127–128, 199
Produced assets, 45

About the Book

What drives economic policymaking and performance in the Arab states? Paul Rivlin finds that domestic and international pressures have combined in the past decade to simultaneously foster change and limit available policy options.

Rivlin examines the socioeconomic issues that are major concerns for policymakers, the role of rental incomes and interest groups, and the particular problems facing the industrial and agricultural sectors. Assessing data from Egypt, Jordan, Morocco, Tunisia, and Syria, he devotes two chapters to the results of stabilization and structural adjustment policies. His insightful analysis is situated in the context of the sharp debate about IMF and World Bank adjustment policies.

Paul Rivlin is senior research fellow at the Moshe Dayan Center for Middle East and African Studies, Tel Aviv University. He is author of *The Dynamics of Economic Policy Making in Egypt* (1985) and *The Israeli Economy* (1992).